The Collected Works of
William Howard Taft

The Collected Works of
William Howard Taft

David H. Burton, *General Editor*

VOLUME I

FOUR ASPECTS OF CIVIC DUTY

AND

PRESENT DAY PROBLEMS

Edited with Commentary by

David H. Burton and A. E. Campbell

OHIO UNIVERSITY PRESS

ATHENS

Ohio University Press, Athens, Ohio 45701
© 2001 by Ohio University Press
Printed in the United States of America

Ohio University Press books are printed on acid-free paper ⊗™

09 08 07 06 05 04 03 02 01   5 4 3 2 1

Four Aspects of Civic Duty copyright 1906 by Yale University;
published December 1906; New York: Charles Scribner's Sons, 1907.
Present Day Problems published New York: Dodd, Mead & Company, 1908.

Publication of *The Collected Works of William Howard Taft* has been made possible in part
through the generous support of the Louise Taft Semple Foundation of Cincinnati, Ohio,
and the Earhart Foundation of Ann Arbor, Michigan.

Frontispiece: Photograph of William Howard Taft in 1906
courtesy of William Howard Taft National Historic Site

Library of Congress Cataloging-in-Publication Data

Taft, William H. (William Howard), 1857–1930.
    Four aspects of civic duty ; and, Present day problems / edited with commentary
by David H. Burton and A. E. Campbell.
        p. cm.—(The collected works of William Howard Taft ; v. 1)
    Includes bibliographical references.
    ISBN 0-8214-1360-0 (acid-free paper)
    1. Citizenship—United States. 2. United States—Politics and
government—1901–1909. 3. United States—Foreign relations—1901–1909. I.
Burton, David Henry, 1925– . II. Campbell, A. E. (Alexander Elmslie), 1929– . III.
Taft, William H. (William Howard), 1857–1930. Present day problems. IV. Title. VI.
Title: Four aspects of civic duty ; and, Present day problems. VII. Title: Present day
problems. VIII. Series: Taft, William H. (William Howard), 1857–1930. Selections.
2000 ; v. 1.
JK1759.T27 2000
323.6'5'0973—dc21

                                                                00-055807

Dedicated to
the Taft family,
for five generations serving
Ohio and the nation

The Collected Works of William Howard Taft

David H. Burton, General Editor

VOLUME ONE
Four Aspects of Civic Duty and *Present Day Problems*
Edited with commentary by David H. Burton and A. E. Campbell

VOLUME TWO
Political Issues and Outlooks
Edited with commentary by David H. Burton

VOLUME THREE
Presidential Addresses and State Papers
Edited with commentary by David H. Burton

VOLUME FOUR
Presidential Messages to Congress
Edited with commentary by David H. Burton

VOLUME FIVE
Popular Government and *The Anti-Trust Act and the Supreme Court*
Edited with commentary by David Potash and Donald F. Anderson

VOLUME SIX
The President and His Powers and *The United States and Peace*
Edited with commentary by Wilson Carey McWilliams and Frank X. Gerrity

VOLUME SEVEN
Taft Papers the League of Nations
Edited with commentary by Frank X. Gerrity

VOLUME EIGHT
"Liberty under Law" and Selected Supreme Court Opinions
Edited with commentary by Francis Graham Lee
Cumulative Index

Contents

PRESENT DAY PROBLEMS

A Collection of Addresses Delivered on Various Occasions

Foreword

William Howard Taft was a special grandfather for me. He died when I was only eight but I had spent summers with him at his vacation home at Murray Bay, Canada, a beautiful community high over the northwest side of the Saint Lawrence River. There we played "sardines in cans," searching for the person hiding somewhere in that very big cottage, which slept twenty-six, without more than two to a room. We went on picnics to places like the "Remou" on a small mountain overlooking the twenty-five-mile-wide Saint Lawrence with my big, jolly Grandpa. We learned to swim and play golf and tennis and fly-cast for brook trout.

Murray Bay was a very special place for my grandfather. "Big Bill Taft" was the chief justice of the U.S. Supreme Court when I knew him; he had been the president ten years before. But to me he was just a jolly grandfather. He was "patron" of the town despite speaking no French, the language of "habitants." His house was a tourist attraction and the company was always stimulating. Everyone at Murray Bay looked up to him and we all loved to go there.

As I grew from boyhood to manhood I came to realize that my jolly grandfather was a great man, and greatly learned as well. What the reader will find in perusing the pages making up this collection is the basis for my statement about his learning. The subjects of his books ranged from advice to the academic community, including the students, at Yale, to a scholarly study that explained the historic principles of monopoly regulation, to pleas for peace in the world. Grandfather, to be sure, wore learning lightly; after all, he was a man dedicated to serving the public interest. And he was the more successful in that calling because of the wisdom readily discernible in what he wrote. Brought together here for the first time, his writings speak the spirit and the substance of what was best in his America.

Seth Chase Taft

William Howard Taft—An Appreciation

"Mediocrity will not do for Will!"

So said William Howard Taft's father upon learning his son stood only fifth in a large class. Pushed hard by his parents' high expectations, my great-grandfather developed habits of hard work that lasted a lifetime. Yet he displayed a self-deprecating sense of humor, an infectious chuckle, and an ever-present enjoyment of his fellow human beings.

Upon learning of his resignation from the Supreme Court, his fellow justices wrote: "You showed . . . your voluminous capacity for work and for getting work done . . . , your humor that smoothed the rough places, your golden heart that has brought you love from every side."

What stands out as well is Taft's devotion to public service. Indeed he knew little else. At the age of twenty-nine he became a judge in Ohio, at thirty-three the United States solicitor general and the next year a federal circuit court judge. He held public office almost continuously thereafter until his death at the age of seventy-three.

My great-grandfather had a reverence for the law as a means to achieving domestic tranquillity and the peaceful resolution of international disputes. As a diplomat in Cuba, Panama, Japan, and the Philippines, he was a peacemaker as well as a troubleshooter.

His highest achievement came on the Supreme Court, a position he aspired to but had twice declined out of a sense of duty to his unfinished work in the Philippines. As chief justice he reformed the federal judiciary, expedited cases through the court, and got the Congress to approve the freestanding Supreme Court building we visit in Washington today. He sought to speed up justice so it would be less costly and more accessible to all citizens.

I have said little about his four years as president, which is just as he would have wished it. He received scant credit for his accomplishments.

He was often perplexed and frustrated by the political cross-currents he faced while in office. During his later, happier years on the Supreme Court, Taft commented: "In my present life I don't remember that I ever was President."

I was born after my great-grandfather died, yet I feel as if I know him. His warmth and candor shine through his conversations and his writings. I find myself in agreement with Will Rogers who said when Taft died: "Mr. Taft! What a lovely soul! Just as a man and a real honest-to-god fellow . . . it's great to be great but it's greater to be human . . . we are parting with three hundred pounds of solid charity to everybody, and love and affection for all his fellow man."

Bob Taft, Governor of the State of Ohio
and great-grandson of William Howard Taft

Preface to the Collected Works

As with almost every twentieth-century American president, William Howard Taft (1857–1930) left a voluminous literary legacy. There are 750,000 items pertaining to him in the Manuscript Division of the Library of Congress, including state and legal papers, correspondence, diaries, scrapbooks, law lectures, and so on. More germane to this collection, and as with two other learned presidents of his era, Theodore Roosevelt and Woodrow Wilson, Taft wrote a number of books, important in their timeliness, legal and governmental in nature. This edition of his works takes its place alongside scholarly collections of the writings of his presidential compeers. In addition to the books published, a special selection of Taft's court opinions constitutes the final entry in the collection. This assemblage of his writings provides ample evidence of a scholarly and disciplined mind. After the fashion of the presidents of the early republic, John Adams, Thomas Jefferson, and James Madison, whose thinking reflected the influences of the Enlightenment, Roosevelt, Taft, and Wilson were in their policy formulations shaped in critical ways by the scientific revolution of the nineteenth century. If Taft was not as broad based in his learning as Theodore Roosevelt or as intense as Wilson, he nonetheless spoke a highly knowledgeable language, due both respect and admiration. Further, William Howard Taft is the only public man in the nation's history to have served as both chief executive (1909–13) and chief justice (1921–30), thereby bringing experience as an administrator and jurist to his writings. His was a rare combination of theory and practice, as a reading of his work bears out.

The writings of William Howard Taft as they appeared in various forms over his lifetime—books, articles, and speeches, including presidential addresses—command attention because they reflect tellingly on Taft and his times. Depending on the format, Taft comes across as a dedicated student of legal history, as well as a practitioner of the law at the very highest level; as a preacher of the word, demanding of himself and of others honesty and integrity on the part of public servants; and as a keen observer of the contemporary scene, accenting the need for adherence to duty. When his writings are brought together, when they are read as one piece, not only does Taft become fully understandable but the times in which he served the public interest become more accessible. Admirers and critics alike gain fuller knowledge of the man by reading his mind in action and in repose.

With the onset of the twentieth century the American nation underwent profound changes in both its own governmental institutions and its place in world affairs. Taft was at ground zero in both. As the republic's first great proconsul, he helped place the Filipino people on the road to self-government and national independence. Taft was able to temper the new imperialism by his administration of a great island possession, and to put in writing both his awareness of the pitfalls of empire and the need to help recently liberated people on their way to nationhood.

The institution of the presidency took on a new dimension with the new century. If Theodore Roosevelt was the first truly modern president, Taft went on to solidify the power of the office. Furthermore, as no other occupant of the White House before or since, he wrote at length and depth about the powers of the president. His book, *The President and His Powers,* is a gloss that would have stood predecessors in good stead and could have helped many of his successors to discharge faithfully the responsibilities of "the most powerful office in the world."

Taft's writings that deal with attempts to bring about world order in the aftermath of the 1914 war constitute a rich historical vein. The ex-president's hope to establish a league of nations to enforce peace is spelled out in forceful detail. Man of peace that he was, Taft nonetheless took a persuasive stand on the principle that sometimes a nation may need to rely on might to make the right prevail.

The court record of Judge Taft is there for all to read: journal articles, addresses to law societies, lower court rulings, and of course majority and dissenting opinions delivered as chief justice. Taken all in all these writings are primary sources in the history of American law. This collection enables us to connect Taft's thinking and his public philosophy from first to last, from *Four Aspects of Civic Duty* (lectures given at Yale in 1906) down to his considered conclusions as a sitting chief justice years later.

The collection is under the general editorship of David H. Burton. Each volume in the collection is introduced by its own commentator. A foreword by Seth Chase Taft offers some personal impressions of a learned grandfather. Governor Bob Taft of Ohio provides an appreciation of his great-grandfather. *The Collected Works* is intended to be an enduring tribute to William Howard Taft as a legal and political thinker. It makes accessible a full range of Taft's writings and underscores the learned character of leading men of the times.

William Howard Taft's writings are offered unabridged, with only minor modifications made to spelling and punctuation to bring usage into conformity with contemporary practice.

Editing of *The Collected Works of William Howard Taft* has come about largely as a result of the commitment and perceptions of a half dozen scholars who have recognized the need for the collection and have employed their knowledge both of the writings and of the historical context which helps to understand them. The commentaries serving as introductions to each of the books or groupings of writings are an essential and vital part of the undertaking. In so saying I speak not only for myself as general editor but for the Taft family as well. A list of the contributors is to be found at the end of this volume, but it is important to cite them here as well: Donald F. Anderson, A. E. Campbell, Frank X. Gerrity, Francis Graham Lee, Wilson Carey McWilliams, and David Potash. To have enjoyed the support and the friendship of such as these has made the collection not only possible but immensely satisfying.

Allow me to bear witness as well to the encouragement offered me by John S. Monagan and colleagues Elwyn F. Chase, James E. Dougherty, Thomas D. Marzik, Randall M. Miller, and Phillip T. Smith. The staff of Drexel Library at Saint Joseph's University, and especially Chris Dixon and Mary Martinson, have provided assistance whenever called upon.

Thanks must be given as well to the Board on Faculty Research, Saint Joseph's University, for making available funds needed for publication of *The Collected Works of William Howard Taft*. Especially have Executive Vice President Daniel J. Curran and Dean of the College of Arts and Sciences Judith G. Chapman played key roles.

Two Ohioans in particular have supported my work in different ways:

William Ayres, an Ohio congressman, from afar; and his daughter, Virginia Ayres, every step of the way. My wife, Gerri; daughters, Antoinette, Monica, and Victoria; and son-in-law Paul combined to make an ever ready source of encouragement upon which to draw.

The Earhart Foundation of Ann Arbor, Michigan, and the Louise Taft Semple Foundation of Cincinnati, Ohio, have been generous in their support of this collection, which the editor and commentators gratefully acknowledge.

Introduction

William Howard Taft would have been more than pleased to learn that he has been ranked much higher for his accomplishments as chief justice of the Supreme Court than as president of the United States. In the latter category he is never listed among the ten best presidents, although certainly he does not figure among the weakest chief executives in any serious study of his administration. Among the successes Taft achieved while president, for example, one notes that almost twice as many trusts were "busted" in four years as in the seven and a half years of Theodore Roosevelt, the "trust buster," in the White House. And much western land was placed beyond the reach of business interests likely to exploit natural resources for private gain. While president, Taft undoubtedly made mistakes of both commission and omission in matters of tariff reform and executive leadership. In a word, Taft was at times politically maladroit. In his own judgment his greatest failure was the rejection by the Senate of the treaty of arbitration between the United States, Great Britain, and France. All of these are facts well enough known if not always sufficiently understood by the people and pundits alike.

Successes and failures tell a great deal about Taft's public philosophy as it influenced his official statements and his policy moves. Taft was very much a part of Republican progressivism. Theodore Roosevelt first delineated it and gave full expression to its objectives and the means of attaining them as he attempted to recast the Grand Old Party in his own image. But Roosevelt did not succeed by his own actions alone. As Roosevelt's secretary of war, Taft's contributions to the reputation of Roosevelt's presidency were largely confined to diplomacy. It was a diplomacy possessed of progressive instincts seeking to maintain peaceful relations with the new Japan rather than to confront its ambitions in the Far East. This goal was achieved by the Taft-Katsura Agreement of 1905. Taft had played a cool diplomatic hand in dealing with the Japanese, much to TR's satisfaction. It is somewhat ironic that Taft promoted peace by resorting to balance of power arguments and while president pursued the same objective through binding arbitration. Success in the former instance and disappointment in the latter both confirm him as a man of peace, a commitment common to a large body of progressive thinking.

An overview of the provenances of William Howard Taft's public philosophy clarifies the true nature of his public service, from state judge to chief justice. His career years saw the gradual development of what may be termed an American amalgam. It consisted of three disparate elements: traditional values bearing the imprint of Judeo-Christian and Greco-Roman origins; Social Darwinism with its accompanying ethical system based on force, as expressed in the axiom "survival of the fittest"; and pragmatism, the peculiarly American method of problem solving by way of experimentation designed to achieve workability. Pragmatism became the means of rendering a workable relationship between tradition and scientific materialism. Taft's many writings show a person who was steeped in a value system stemming from the old order. Admittedly, that order was hierarchical, but in Taft's usage it took into account rapidly changing ways of thinking and doing. If he was influenced by the law of natural selection preached to him so vigorously by Professor Sumner at Yale, his attachment to the old verities worked to soften its meaning as he met a variety of public responsibilities.

Perhaps the clearest evidence of this is to be found in Taft's endeavors as civil governor of the Philippine Islands. The United States Army under the command of General Arthur MacArthur, the military governor at the time of Taft's arrival in Manila, had made use of *force majeure* to break the back of the Filipino insurrection, which was fighting to gain the islands' independence. Taft deemed this method counterproductive as he replaced the mailed fist with the velvet glove. His purpose was to show that justice rested on time-honored values that proclaimed law and order a matter for legislation and adjudication as opposed to shot and shell. The civil governor set about the awesome task of training the Filipino people in the art of self-government. The result was pacification of the Islands as befit the principles of American constitutional government.

For all of that William Howard Taft was a good Yankee who had a practical turn of mind. Without being self-consciously pragmatic he understood government to be an instrument meant to solve problems of managing an increasingly complex socioeconomy. He was willing to use the Sherman Anti-trust Act as a means of regulating over-concentrations of corporate power, thereby keeping the property rights of the trusts balanced with the interests of the public. Yet there is more.

As president, he used his influence to make a special commerce court a provision of the Mann-Elkins Act of 1910. Such a court was designed to expedite rulings under anti-trust legislation. This innovation indicated Taft's willingness to improve on the instrument of government to meet a particular need. True, Congress chose to eliminate the commerce court within two years, but that decision does not negate the testimony the president had given in support of a proposal to use new ways to solve old problems—in short, a pragmatic touch.

All the elements in this intellectual configuration surface in Taft's writings. But the dominant theme in Taft's thinking, whether in public or in private, resonates with the values of the early national period when government and law were grounded together in the Constitution. John Marshall was in fact Taft's great hero; he believed him to be the single most important man of the generation who brought the states together, forming them into a stable union. Very likely Taft saw himself after the style of Marshall in matters of property rights. When he became chief justice he sought to make the Supreme Court the kind of institution of government that stood for the best interests of the nation as a whole. "Massing the Court" (that is, striving for unanimous or near unanimous rulings), which Taft attempted to do, was his way of emulating the first great chief justice, whose practice was, legend has it, to determine a case and then direct Brother Story to look up the citations. But there is that other legend with which Chief Justice Taft had to contend: Holmes and Brandeis dissenting.

Chief Justice Taft was not the equal of John Marshall, but his understanding of the Constitution was much the same. Taft was a twentieth-century man as well. He fought vigorously for reform of court procedures including the use of certiorari by the justices, a breakthrough which rendered the court's docket more manageable and the court itself more relevant as an institution of governance. When it came to cases before the court, as surely as any of his associate justices Taft was in touch with socio-economic reality. In *Stafford vs. Wallace*, for example, he displayed an understanding of the inner workings of interstate commerce and its deepest implications that no less a critic than Justice Holmes thought masterful. His reasoning pointed the court in the direction of constitutionalizing such controversial New Deal legislation as the Wagner Act. And this by an Ohio Republican supposedly of the old school.

Like Theodore Roosevelt, William Howard Taft was able to orchestrate the competing and ofttimes discordant notes of traditional expectations and scientific assertions into a harmony that moved government forward without cutting its ties to the past. That he did this with imagination and integrity becomes manifest in his written legacy, the *Collected Works.*

FOUR ASPECTS
OF CIVIC DUTY

Four Aspects of Civic Duty

Commentary

David H. Burton

Invited to Yale in 1906 to give a series of lectures on the Dodge Foundation, William Howard Taft, at the time secretary of war in the Theodore Roosevelt cabinet, delivered four talks. As chance would have it, he had met Arthur Twining Hadley, the Yale president, in Saint Louis several weeks before the lectures were scheduled. Hadley suggested that Taft take up certain timely matters of public interest and importance. In succession the lectures examined the viewpoint of recent undergraduates as they took up an active citizenship, the work of the judge on the bench, the responsibilities of the colonial administrator, and the character of the presidential office.

In the first lecture Taft cleared the ground for the subjects of the lectures to follow by enunciating a number of fundamentals. He expressed his concern over the place and function of wealth in American society. Wealth that was earned was far preferable to wealth due to inheritance because "under the spur of necessity" character forms and strengthens. No populist, Taft expressed his belief in rule by the wise, the well born, and the well-to-do. The university graduate, he thought, would quickly learn, once he had passed into the world beyond the university, to moderate the strict rules of political economy and sociology he had been taught in college.

He touched on a number of other points, such as a divinely governed universe, but most significantly Taft preferred to predicate all judgments on a political-philosophical unity. The exercise of private property rights in a free society led to the accumulation of wealth, which was in turn a requisite for advancement, both personal and social. The orchestration of freedom and property in a complex society required some positive action on the part of government. The safest way to achieve and maintain liberty and protect property was to seek resolution of conflicts through party government in the hands of an educated citizenry. It was a public philosophy well enough if briefly stated, one to be built on in the remaining lectures.

Taft was on familiar ground when he turned his attention to the judiciary in his second lecture. He offered a number of observations about law and the judges, revealing a historical awareness of the rule of law as judges placed each case in perspectives of time, kind, and circumstances and always with reference to the law as written, whether in the Constitution or the statutes. A first concern was the jury system. Responding to the rising demand that juries be placed above and independent of the trial judge, Taft reminded his audience that the English Common Law considered the jury and the judge to be a unit. It was the jury and the judge acting together that made for "an admirable tribunal." Taft was to insist this was what was intended in the American Constitution when it referred to trial by jury. This was not an attack on the jury system; among its many advantages it reassured the public that justice would be done.

Taft discerned a number of contemporary challenges to the supremacy of the law and he proposed to deal with them. Laws not capable of enforcement should not be passed, because it was not sound policy to initiate unenforceable legislation. For example, when it came to the prohibition of the sale of intoxicating beverages, he favored local option. On the other hand, a law such as the Sherman Anti-trust Act, however controversial, was nonetheless enforceable. In this second lecture Taft gave a vigorous statement to the effect that the law must be obeyed. Law was the substratum upon which civilization rested. If property was the basis of American civilization, the law was the instrument to maintain and protect it. Law was a living phenomenon responsive to change as change might require. By no means an advocate of sociological jurisprudence, neither was Taft blind to the realities of twentieth-century life.

William Howard Taft was the most experienced and the most successful of American colonial administrators. He had earned the right to a respectful hearing far beyond the boundaries of Yale. His lecture on colonial administration was, however, the least persuasive of his talks. After a brief review of the history of U.S. occupation of the Philippine Islands he went on to fault many of his countrymen who were sympathetic to American colonialism as well as those who advocated independence for the islands. He was against exploitation and independence in equal measure. The only possible justification for continued American control was the opportunity afforded the United States to prepare the Filipino people for self-government at some undetermined date in the future. In this process the former civil governor urged Americans to cultivate the friendship of the islanders, thereby encouraging the people to maintain their allegiance to the insular government. Taft's basic thesis was that only time and experience would ready the Filipinos to master the difficult art of self-rule without fear of foreign interference. In so saying Taft was conscious of the paradox implanted in this American purpose. The greater the American success, the less justification for a presence in the archipelago and with it serious ramifications for American Far Eastern foreign policy. Taft himself had had a hand in the development of that policy—the Taft-Katsura Agreement of 1905. This third lecture tended to exhibit less learning and more polemic.

Finally Taft took under consideration the office of the president. His discussion was more abstract than might have been anticipated in light of his remarks on colonial administration. A reading of this lecture makes it clear what Taft, as secretary of war, had discerned about the office in light of his cabinet experience. He urged the idea that the most powerful of rulers were subject to limitations in the exercise of their office because of circumstances beyond their control. Therefore even Theodore Roosevelt, whom he viewed as the strongest of presidents in action, suffered from limitations imposed on him by the Constitution. A president should, nonetheless, try to surmount obstacles to his use of legitimate power. He should be an active agent pushing new legislation; a president who failed in this regard was a disappointment to his party and to the electorate. Such leadership depended to a considerable degree on a willingness to compromise. Taft worried aloud about the encroachments by Congress on executive privilege. Rather typically, he advocated a balance between the two political branches, saying that investigations and criticisms of one by the other could be important influences toward better government. Ultimately the people would pass judgment on matters of executive leadership as on legislative actions. Describing the American people as "intelligent and keen," Taft was prepared to repose his trust in them.

These lectures clearly imply a paternalism that is, in fact, a fair assessment of William Howard Taft's views as a public man. Taft furthermore shows himself supremely confident as a thinker, convinced of the rightness and the righteousness of America as he wanted it to be. In this respect he was typical of his generation of national leaders. Freshly become a world power, America had, from its beginnings, the best claim to moral leadership among the nations. The American century was upon us, and at home and abroad this was to be treated as a truism. Yet, being Taft, there was to be no boasting and no bravado. America could depend on an inner strength of character, rendering outward swagger incongruous. To be sure, in personal relations Taft might well show a certain jocularity, a trait that won him friends and admirers. But his writings convey the seriousness of purpose that was at the core of his being.

1

The Duties of Citizenship Viewed from the Standpoint of a Recent Graduate of a University

Mr. President, and Gentlemen of Yale:

My occupations within the last month have been so numerous, various, and absorbing that it has been very difficult for me to give thought and proper time of preparation for the series of lectures which, more than a year ago, I was invited to deliver on the Dodge foundation by your alluring secretary—Mr. Stokes. Knowing as I did that it was foolish for me to accept Mr. Stokes's invitation, and knowing that whenever the time came for me to perform my promise it would certainly be the most inconvenient time in the year, I nevertheless yielded weakly, and agreed to come and say something about the duties of citizenship. Of course I could not anticipate that an earthquake would throw additional responsibilities on the War Department; but previous experiences ought to have taught me that something would happen to make it altogether inconvenient and almost impossible for me to comply with a promise so easily given but with such difficulty performed. Still, here I am, and if what I have to say to you proves to be trite or for other reasons lacking in interest, I hope you will bear with me and attribute it to the lack of preparation. I have worried over these lectures a good deal, and have cast about to know what plan for the development of the subject I could properly pursue which might be of assistance to the young men who are about to enter upon what I hope will be useful lives in doing what they ought to do to make this country better and to vindicate its form of government and its capacity for progress and development toward higher civilization. I met President Hadley in St. Louis, and he suggested that I look at the subject from the four standpoints from which, in my personal experience, I have had to look at public matters. He thought that this would give me the advantage of testifying as a witness qualified by opportunities for observation, whether the opportunities were improved or not. Acquiescing, as I always do, in the wisdom of his suggestions, I have therefore taken for the four lectures which I am to deliver the following subjects:

I. The duties of citizenship viewed from the standpoint of a recent graduate of a university.

II. The duties of citizenship viewed from the standpoint of a judge on the bench.

III. The duties of citizenship viewed from the standpoint of colonial administration.

IV. The duties of citizenship viewed from the standpoint of the national executive.

In taking up the first of these heads for discussion I hope I may be pardoned for calling attention to a fact that has not escaped general observation, that there are few conditions of mind more exalted, more comforting, more complacent, than that of the members of the Senior class of a great university like this. The struggle upward from the humility of Freshman year, through the irresponsibility and audacity of Sophomore year, the budding sense of superiority of Junior year, to the beatific appreciation of his own importance in supporting the dignity of the university that every Senior has, are well-known phases in college life. The step downward that has to be taken from the altitude of Senior year to the sense of insignificance that comes quickly to the ordinary graduate in the year succeeding his college life, adds much to his usefulness as a member of the community which he is about to enter. It restores his sense of proportion as to the position that he fills in society, which, in the epitome of life that a four years' course at a university is, had somewhat distorted his views of the extent of the demand which there would be for his presence and services in the community at large.

Of course this humbling change from the estimate of the college world to the estimate of the world at large has a greater effect upon the men who, when they leave college, are thrown upon their own resources and are obliged to earn their own living, than upon those who have money enough and are not dependent upon the assistance of others, or upon the recognition of their ability by employers, by congregations, by clients, or by patients. This is one of the great disadvantages of being born wealthy. The truth is, the wealthy young man, in winning his way to a useful place in the community, has to struggle much more and has to exhibit a moral courage much greater than that of the poor man, if he would make a real success in life and justify his existence as a citizen. The young man most to be congratulated is he who has been given an education as thorough and as useful as he himself wishes to make it, and then under the spur of necessity enters upon a life of work without the temptation to lack of effort and idleness, or to dilettanteism, or to pure pleasure, which a competence always creates. The great accumulations of wealth that we have witnessed during the present generation are, of course, of much benefit to the community in the promotion of art, of music, of charity, and of great educational institutions, as well as in the good they do in the prosecution of industry, the cheapening of the cost of production, and the carrying on of the great enterprises that are needed to make real material and intellectual progress; but, in my judgment, in no one respect can wealth be made more useful from now on than in the support of young men who are willing to devote their attention to politics and public matters, to assume official responsibilities, to follow and preserve the public weal, and by reason of their independence of salaries or office to exercise the beneficent influence of disinterested patriotism and attention to public affairs. There is such a class in England, which has done wonders for their politics and the high tone of their public men. When it comes to be understood in this country, and impressed on the persons to whom it applies, that the man who is wealthy enough to relieve him from any anxiety about supporting his family owes it to society to devote his attention to public affairs, and that one who does not do so is violating his duty, a great step will have been taken in elevating our politics. I think this influence has already shown itself in many directions; but with the increased wealth of this generation the influence of this class ought to become greater and greater. Of course I would not eliminate from our community what I shall hereafter refer to at considerable length, to wit: the motive for gain and accumulation of money, which is the main-spring of nearly all the material improvement which has been so marked in this country; but in such a hoped-for change of motive among the wealthy young men as I have described we are not likely so to reduce the motive for accumulation in the community at large as to affect injuriously our financial and material progress.

So much for the wealthy young man. The poor young man has to earn his own living, but his attention to politics is likely to be much greater in the early years of his business or professional life, when he has only one to support, than when he takes unto himself a wife, and brings into the world a family which gradually absorbs all his energy and takes all his time in earning money enough to provide for its wants. There is a period of ten or fifteen years during which all college graduates, poor as well as rich, have time enough and energy enough and ought to have interest enough to attempt to make the politics of the neighborhood in which they live better; and it is to this period and its obligations that I wish particularly to direct my remarks this evening.

The training in political economy and sociology, and other scientific studies likely to affect one's political views which are pursued in a university curriculum, tends to certainty and severity of view with respect to the issues of the day. As parties and public men fail to square with the views thus formed, there develops in the mind of the young graduate a spirit of criticism and impatience that the Government is so stupidly run, and with so little understanding of the fundamental rules upon which all public affairs ought to be conducted. While I was in college it happened that my father was in the national administration, and I can remember with distinctness my dissatisfaction with his views of public affairs and my impatience that he did not seem to value as fully as I thought he ought the importance of pursuing the up-to-date principles that should govern the policy to be pursued by public men. Now, the step down from Senior year to a struggle for a living, which I have already referred to, has a healthy tendency in moderating this certainty and severity of view formed in the lecture-room and in the abstract study of political science. In such view the graduate is apt to ignore the obstruction by reason of friction in the operation of natural laws. He is apt to ignore, as a negligible quantity, the necessary effect upon the political policies of the existence of popular prejudices and popular emotions. He is apt to treat man as a peculiarly intelligent animal, buying exactly where he can buy cheapest, and selling exactly where he can sell at the highest price; patronizing classes and nations without respect to personal feelings toward them, and moved by purely business considerations, and those which ought to influence him if he properly considers his welfare. Now, I do not mean to say that the professor who instructs, and who is a man of the world, does not know the lights and shadows that should be put into the picture of actual and real political and economic conditions, so as to modify the rigidity of the lines laid down by the strict and theoretical rules which he teaches; but the students ordinarily are much better able to master the main principles than their complicated variation and modification, due to intervening causes. Those they must learn by actual experience. The tendency in my own case, and I think in that of most graduates of my time, was toward the *laissez faire* doctrine that the least interference by legislation with the operation of natural laws was, in the end, the best for the public; that the only proper object of legislation was to free the pathway of commerce and opportunity from the effect of everything but competition and enlightened selfishness; and that that being done, the Government had discharged all of its proper functions. When I graduated we looked upon the Post-office Department of the Government with great suspicion. We felt that it was a departure from proper principles, and that it seemed to offer a pernicious example and suggestion of the extension of governmental interference and initiative into fields which ought to be covered altogether by private enterprise. I do not know what may be taught in this respect now, and I am bound to say that I think these principles, which I may seem to have spoken of in a light way, are still orthodox and still sound, if only the application of them is not carried to such an extreme as really to interfere with the public welfare. Experience will show that there are fields of business action which the Government can better cover than private enterprise; and there are also fields over which, because of probability of abuse by private enterprise, the Government should assume control, not by way of initiation and administration but by way of effective regulation. This topic, however, involves too many considerations to justify its discussion further tonight.

On the other hand, there are, in addition to those of the *laissez faire* school, a few graduates of universities whose substratum of common sense and whose sense of proportion, with reference to things as they are, are so lacking, and whose poetic and emotional temperament is so overwrought, that they are led to contemplate only the injustice and the abuses that occur under the existing social order, and fail utterly to note the tremendous advance, the immense progress which has been made under the present guaranties of life, liberty, and property; who yearn for an entirely different system and radical change, in which men are to be governed solely by love and not by any motive of gain. In their eyes selfishness can never be enlightened, and they finally acquire a state of mind so morbid that the only happiness they have is the contemplation of human misery as an argument for the immediate abandonment of the principles lying at the basis of modern society. When such theories proceed from men who have really suffered, men to whom equality of opportunity seems to have been denied, men who live under a weight of misfortune and poverty and disease and the other ills that flesh is heir to, there ought to be much sympathy with their feeling. It is entirely natural that they should be lacking in the sense of proportion which a man not so oppressed may have in respect to the advantages of our present social and economic system. But when one encounters a graduate of a university, of means and opportunity for public usefulness, who allows his emotional side to overcome his judgment so that he develops into a parlor socialist, without really understanding anything about the real springs of material and intellectual progress in this world, then we have a result with which it is difficult to be patient. I think this class is, for the time, on the increase, but I am glad to think that among educated men the class is only that of faddists and will fade away as the Millerites did. The spectacle of men who enjoy all the luxuries of life, with trained servants and costly establishments of all kinds, declaiming against the social order and the injustice done to the poor and suffering in the community, is not one to attract the sympathy of sensible men. The truth is that an argument in favor of a first cause, or a divine plan of the universe, finds no better or stronger illustration than in the progress of the world under the impulse of men toward personal freedom and the right of property. The right of property has played quite as important a part in the development of the human race as the right of personal liberty. Indeed, the two rights are so associated in the struggle which man has had to make in taking himself out of the category of the lower animals and lifting himself to his present material and spiritual elevation that it is hard to separate them in a historical discussion. After man became his own master, the next step in his progress was the conception and establishment of the right of private property. When he began to live in a social state with his fellows, he recognized, dimly at first, but subsequently with greater clearness, that the laborer should have and enjoy that which his labor produced. As his industry and self-restraint grew, he made by his labor not only enough for his immediate necessities, but also a surplus which he was able to save for use in aid of future labor. By use of this surplus, the amount which each man's labor would produce was thereafter increased. As the advantage of the principle that the laborer should enjoy his own product came to be recognized, so it came to be at a later time equally well recognized that he whose savings from his own labor increased the product of another's labor was entitled to enjoy and share in the joint result; and the adjustment of their respective shares was the first settlement of the ever-recurring controversy between labor and capital. What one had the full right to enjoy he had the right to give to another to enjoy; and so it happened that when a man was about to die he assumed, and was accorded, the privilege of giving to those whom he wished to enjoy it that which was his. As the natural parental instinct dictated provision for those whom he had brought into the world, it first became custom and then law that if he made no express disposition of that which he had the right to enjoy, it should become the property of those for whose existence he was responsible. In this way the capital saved in one generation was received by succeeding generations, and its accumulation for producing purposes was made much more probable. The certainty that a man could enjoy as his own that which he produced or saved, and that it could be enjoyed after his death by those to whom he was bound by ties of natural affection, furnished the strongest motive for industry beyond what was merely adequate to obtain the bare necessities of life, and was the chief inducement to economy and self-control. The institution of private property with all its incidents is what has led to the accumulation of capital in the world. Capital represents and measures the difference between the present condition of society and that which prevailed when men lived by what their hands would produce without implements or other means of increasing the result of their labor; that is, between the utter barbarism of prehistoric ages and modern civilization. Without it the whole world would still be groping in the darkness of the tribe or commune stage of civilization, with alternating periods of starvation and plenty, and no happiness but that of gorging unrestrained appetite. Capital increased the amount of production. The cheaper the cost of production, the less each one had to work to earn the absolute necessities of life, and the more time he had to earn its comforts. As the material comforts increased, the more possible became happiness, and the greater the opportunity for the cultivation of the higher instincts of the human mind and soul. This material progress in the human race, covering cycles of time in the slow process of evolving as an essential principle in the development of the race the right of private property, was attended by violence and fraud and cruelty and oppression; but in the end it had a profound educational effect upon the human race and established in the human heart and soul the virtues that have made man the superior being that he is. The struggle implanted in the human breast the virtue of providence, the restraint of the appetite of the present, in order that there may be left that with which the future can be enjoyed; the lesson that the pains and thoroughness with which a work is done increase the product and enlarge the source of future supply; and finally, the recognition of the fact that the only peaceable way by which a man can really enjoy the fruits of his own labor is to recognize this as a right of every other man. This struggle thus gave us the virtues of providence, of industry, and of honesty, and with these basic elements of character all the other traits and virtues that we admire in man have been developed. Of course, I would not ignore or minimize the influence of religion on the development and uplifting of human character; but the industrial virtues I have described, when instilled by hard experience, certainly offer a greater opportunity for the effective working of religious influences. The whole human race has had to fight its way upward to modern civilization and its beneficent incidents by a struggle so arduous and so long continued that we can no more appreciate it than we can realize the time taken to create the geological formations. This operation of the natural laws, leading to the wonderful development of modern society out of the prehistoric man, we are told that man must change by law; that we must abolish the right of property and the motive for gain, divide up the wealth, and distribute it according to the sense of justice of the socialist committees of organization and control.

While we may find a few shining examples of such dreamers and impracticable and morbid thinkers among the graduates of universities of this country, we may be confident that substantially all the sane graduates of our universities will set their faces like flint against the spirit of any such foolish doctrine; and that they will find their chief reasons for discrediting the premises and the conclusions advanced in favor of socialism in the wholesome principles of political economy and sociology which they have imbibed at the most formative period of their lives and characters in the lecture and recitation rooms of their *alma mater.*

But now, assuming the political and economic sanity of the recent college graduated—not, I think, a violent assumption—what should be expected of him politically? Well, in the first place he ought to learn where the polling-place is in his ward and precinct where he can cast a ballot. I think it might be rather humiliating to some graduates of several years' standing if a close examination were made into their knowledge of this simple fact; and if the investigation were to proceed farther, to find out where the primaries and the preliminary political meetings for organization are held, the amount of ignorance in respect to these details on their part would be still more embarrassing. Perhaps, however, before they go either to the polls or to the primaries they ought to select a party. I know there is a disposition on the part of the free-born American graduate from an institution of learning, full of admiration for independence of thought and a desire to maintain his independence of action, to hold himself aloof from party regularity and vote for the best men if he can find them, and thus teach the party organization that it must beware of the influence of the independent voter. I think this tendency on the part of the recent college graduate is much modified as he acquires experience and a knowledge of conditions. Whether he will become a Republican or a Democrat or a Mugwump will depend on many circumstances. He may yield to the natural tendency to inherit his politics, and so become a Democrat or a Republican because his father was. He may find that his views upon the main issue between the parties at the particular time when he comes first to exercise his franchise and discharge his electoral duty are such that on principle he selects one of the parties and thereafter identifies himself with it. He may find that his pecuniary interests are affected by the success or defeat of a particular party, and select the one or the other in accordance with those interests. Whatever turns him in the direction of one party or the other, he will after a while learn that there is much to be said in favor of party regularity if that be not carried to an extreme. The modern government of a people of 80,000,000, reaching from the Atlantic to the Pacific and from Canada to Mexico, is very complicated. It has long been a principle, enunciated, but "honored more in the breach than in the observance," that the less government has to do, the less government there is, the better for the people; but in recent years there have been so many functions which it is impossible for private business to maintain and undertake that even the most orthodox of the *laissez-faire* school must admit that the legitimate functions of the modern government constitute it a very complex machine. The difficulties of its management are greatly increased if, instead of leaving the control to one man, as in Russia, or to a small group of men, as in the ancient aristocracy, we commit its control to all males over the age of twenty-one, and call it a popular government. The real advantage of a popular government, in securing the greatest good to the greatest number, is that experience has shown that individuals and classes of men of reasonable intelligence are better able to look after their own interests or those of their class, and secure equality of opportunity and equal protection for themselves or persons similarly situated, if they are given a voice in the government, than if this duty is left to some one else, however altruistic. How is it possible so to reduce the varying wishes and views of the entire population of 80,000,000 people, or 14,000,000 adult males, to one resultant executive force, which shall carry on this complex machine of government effectively, as it should be carried on in the public interest and for the public weal? The problem has been solved in the growth and the establishment of popular government by the institution of parties among the people. A useful party cannot be formed unless those who are members of it, with a sense of responsibility for the successful and unobstructed continuance of the administration by that party, yield their views on the less important and less essential principles, and unite with respect to the main policies for which the party is to become responsible. The resultant solidarity of opinion is necessary to secure unity of action.

The sense of responsibility for the successful operation of the Government must furnish a power of cohesion which shall prevent the breaking off from the party of a sufficient number of its members to make its arm nerveless and to take away from it its power of initiative and action. That party is the more efficient party, therefore, in which the members are more nearly united on the great principles of governmental policy. I do not for a moment intend to depreciate the good effect of having in the community persons not affiliated with parties, whose unbiased judgment will lead them to vote sometimes for one party and sometimes for another; for it may well be that the power of cohesion in a party, growing out of its traditions or the desire for office or some other motive not the highest, shall lead it into apparent unanimity upon a course detrimental to the Government and from which nothing can save the Government but the withdrawal of support by the independent voter. Be this as it may, and however useful the independent voter may be, the existence of parties, their maintenance, and their discipline are essential to the carrying on of any popular government. The difficulty with the politics of France has frequently been the inability of the leaders to form parties large enough to maintain a government. There are too many small groups, and the administration is thus likely continually to change.

It is difficult to classify parties in this country as conservative and radical, because the facts do not always justify such a classification; but generally it will be found that the more efficient party in administration is the more progressive and more affirmative—more radical, therefore, in its policies. The opposing party is usually negative, declining to initiate new reforms, looking back to a probably non-existent condition of simplicity and purity and honesty in public affairs, and offering in effect, when successful, a conservative and do-nothing administration. Now, young men will select their parties, other things being equal, according to the natural tendencies of their minds. Some men are in favor of progress, affirmative action, and radical reforms—a change of the existing arrangements for something better. Other men naturally prefer the ills we have than to fly to those we know not of, and with their conservative tendencies they will find a home in the more conservative party. The independent, refusing to subordinate himself to the views of either party, first votes for one ticket and then for another, and thus seems to exercise a more decisive influence than the regular members of either party. Indeed, it is true that as a mass the independent voters are generally of great importance and influence for the betterment of political and governmental conditions. As individuals, in the exercise of individual influence and to accomplish useful purposes, they do not play so important a part. If a man goes into public life and wishes to secure an influence for good, he may properly be chary of breaking his political ties with the party of his affiliation, because the only real opportunity, the only real avenue that he can follow to accomplish permanently useful results is by influencing the course and policy of his party. As this is a party government, and as measures are controlled by party decisions, the real progress must be made along party lines; and if a man separates from his party he loses altogether any influence he may exert in determining those policies. I do not at all advocate that a man should adhere to party against high principle and conviction, but this life is all a series of compromises by which little by little, and step by step, progress toward better things is made. All the good in the world cannot be attained at one breath. We must achieve what we can at the time we can, and must let other aims and objects of the highest good abide a different opportunity for their attainment. While, therefore, we may not agree with all the principles adopted into legislation or into executive policy by a party with which we are affiliated, we should ordinarily not destroy our usefulness and power for good in influencing the party in the right direction, by withdrawing from it on issues not the most important, if, on the whole, we believe that more good can come from its success than from that of its opponent.

Having selected his party and found his polling-place and the place for the meeting of the primaries, and having ascertained who are the men in the precinct and the ward who exercise influence over the people, the graduate of a university who takes life as seriously as he should, who appreciates his responsibility as a citizen, will spend as much time as he can in learning the local situation; in becoming acquainted with the precinct and ward leaders, in consulting them as far as he can, in making himself acquainted not only with the well-to-do and well-educated persons in his precinct and ward, but also with the laborers, the artisans, the storekeepers, the saloon-keepers, in order that he may understand what are the controlling influences in the primaries and elections of that precinct and ward. This will bring him, doubtless, into contact with some people whom he would not wish to have as permanent associates and companions. It is not generally elevating to associate with saloon-keepers, and yet there is a word to be said upon this subject and with respect to them. There are among them honest, hard-working men, rising early in the morning and staying up late; in the great cities they are the proprietors of the social clubs of the neighborhood for the poor people, and naturally they exercise a very considerable influence in the discussion of public matters that go on among the wage-earners and persons of small means. The college graduate is not made of sugar, and he ought to be sufficiently strong to resist any evil influence which might some time arise from such political associations if they were to become permanent. But if a college graduate is to exert any influence at all for good among the people, especially when as a young man he can exert his influence only or chiefly through personal contact, he must convince those whose votes he wishes to control and use for good purposes that he does not hold himself above them; that he is a real democrat and recognizes that he has only one vote, as they each have but one vote, and that he has no right to exercise influence over them except as his opportunities for information and his knowledge of public affairs justify him in speaking on such subjects. He must stand on an exact equality with men of less education and less advantages and must familiarize himself with the exact conditions that prevail in local municipal and broader politics. In many respects the college graduate has as much to learn from the working-man and the business man who have not enjoyed a college education as they have to learn from him. It cannot but broaden his sympathies and make him understand his country and its needs with more certainty if he associates in political and other ways with those who make up the large body of our American citizens. He will cease by such association to assume the attitude of a dilettante closet critic, and will understand the motives and the emotions and the real feelings of the great mass of the American people. As I have already suggested, there is a tendency on the part of those having a college education, of the class known as "the scholar in politics," to ignore the element of sentiment, of patriotic emotion, and to assume that everything ought to be and will be ultimately determined by nicely reasoned processes like those which are often postulated in the class-room of the professor of economics and political economy. Now, without in the slightest minimizing the importance of straight thinking in accordance with the great principles of political economy and sociology, it seems to me wise to emphasize the necessity for college men who wish to be useful in political life to go into the humblest political movements and find out the views, the prejudices it may be, and the real needs of their less fortunate fellow-citizens.

The tendency of recent years toward reorganization and the economic use of means and instrumentalities to secure efficiency, shown in the production of material things, has manifested itself in politics also, and has led to much more effective political machines, in municipal politics particularly, than ever existed before. There are in the governments of many municipalities striking examples of the use of official patronage to establish and maintain a machine from which it is impossible for the voters of the party to wrest its power, and which for a time seems to be able by the thoroughness of its organization even to defy the people at the polls. Every once in a while the people rise and defeat the machine ticket and then pat themselves upon the back and retire again, while the machine in a short time resumes its power. It is idle to hope that the people may be roused at every political contest and defeat machine slates unless there are counter organizations made up of younger men actuated by the disinterested patriotic desire to select only good candidates for office. Such young men, and among them certainly ought to be all university graduates, should maintain an organization the year round, so that they may keep in touch with the continually changing local situation and call upon members for action when action is necessary. Eternal vigilance is the price of good government. The professional machine politician is always at work, and he can be defeated and discouraged only by an organization which can be called together like the Minute Men, and may know how and when to strike for good government. Politics ought to be neither distasteful nor degrading, and men who enter them for the purpose of keeping them pure and making them better are engaged in the highest duty. We must meet the conditions as they exist. In this country, where nearly every adult male has a vote and suffrage is exercised by all sorts and conditions of men, suitable and proper means must be used, adapted to reach the better nature of the electors and rouse them to their duty to secure good government by the exercise of their suffrages at the primary and at the polls. Organization by good men is one of the suitable and proper means for achieving this purpose. When the people know that agencies exist through which they can secure good government, they will be much more certain to take an interest and support such agencies. I would not, of course, exclude men of any age from the burden of carrying on this work of organization, but young men must naturally be more active in it.

It will be entirely natural, especially for those who are well-to-do and do not need to earn a livelihood, to become candidates for public office, and the more that such men offer themselves for office the better for good government. Of course, in the ideal condition of things the office should seek the man; but we do not have an ideal condition of things, and we never will have. Politics are practical, and while it may often occur that in an organization of good men, for the purpose of lifting politics out of the slough, a man may be drafted for office against his will, it is exceptional. There is no real objection to a good man's seeking office when he feels himself competent to discharge its duties, has a high ideal as to how they ought to be discharged, and a commendable ambition to serve his country. Certainly, men less qualified and with less high ideals will seek it, and why should the public lose the benefit of a personal motive on his part to gratify his desire to be of use?

But I have talked longer than I ought. I close by urging upon the men of Yale their duty, immediately upon leaving college, to take a deep interest in local politics, to learn what they are, to study the actual conditions that prevail with respect to the electorate, and to affiliate themselves with local political movements in order that they may find for themselves opportunities for usefulness. If the country is not to avail itself of the intelligence, patriotism, and disinterestedness of its educated men, and especially of those who can devote a large part of their time to public matters, it will lose the benefit of the progress that we hope we are making by extended higher education.

2

The Duties of Citizenship Viewed from
the Standpoint of a Judge on the Bench

Mr. President, and Gentlemen of Yale:

The subject for this evening is the second on the list—The Duties of Citizenship from the Standpoint of a Judge on the Bench.

I went on the State bench when I was twenty-nine years old, and served three years; subsequently, at thirty-two, I went upon the Federal bench, where I served for nine years. As I look back, I am sure that my knowledge of law when I went on the bench was very limited. I commend to those who have an opportunity a term on the bench as one of the best law schools I know. It is true that in this way one gets his legal education at the expense of the public, and tries his "'prentice hand" on the litigants as victims; but after a time, if he is at all apt and anxious and earnest, the public makes a good judge of him. If he can be kept on the bench after that, he sometimes makes a better judge than an older man, with much more experience at the bar; for there are men, and not a few, who succeed admirably at the bar as counsel and advocates, but who, when elevated to the position of a judge, cannot drop the habits of a lifetime or forget that they are advocates. Still, I do not urge the appointment of young men to judicial positions, and do not favor a system by which judges are given their judicial learning after they are called to the bench.

The first duty of a citizen which is impressed on the mind of the judge of first instance, who has to try the usual class of cases, is his duty to sit on the jury, and to spend the time necessary, when properly drawn, to make up the tribunal which the common law and the Constitution make necessary for the determination of issues of fact in common-law civil cases and criminal cases. Service on the jury is, of course, just as much a part of one's public duty as the obligation to pay taxes under the law, or the obligation to respond to the call of the Government to act in the posse of the sheriff, or to testify as a witness when duly summoned, or to shoulder a gun when drafted into the military service in an emergency. The success of a jury system is utterly impossible among a people who are not, on the average, intelligent and above undue influences. Hence a jury system must tend to failure if the intelligent and honest men of the community regard the service as such a burden that they evade it by excuses, and leave for selection only the unintelligent and those subject to venal motives.

On a pure question of fact, controverted by witnesses on both sides and presented to the jury with full argument and the comment of the court, a jury of intelligent, conscientious men is a most satisfactory tribunal. Taken from different walks of life, containing within the panel men of experience in many directions, united they make up a tribunal of men of force, who are quite as well able as the judge to make their inferences from the evidence as it has been drawn out by examination and cross-examination, and reach a conclusion of fact, not necessarily unerring, but of very considerable accuracy and certainty. But I beg to impress upon you the fact which seems frequently to have been lost sight of, especially in legislation with respect to the procedure of State courts, that the tribunal contemplated by the common law was not the jury alone, but it was the court and jury, and that the ultimate decisions rested not on the verdict of the jury only, but on the verdict as approved by the judge holding the court. The method of reaching a conclusion at common law was after the hearing of the evidence and argument of counsel, and after a charge by the court; in which the court did not hesitate to assist the jury in commenting on the evidence, even to the point of intimating an opinion as to the proper conclusion to be drawn from the evidence. Thus constituted, the jury and the court do make an admirable tribunal, if the intelligence of the jury is equal to the average intelligence of the community at large. There has been a dangerous tendency in the legislation in the Southern and Western States in regard to the control which the judge in the court may exercise over the jury. His instructions to the jury are frequently limited to a written charge, made before the argument of counsel on the facts, in which he is not permitted to comment in any way on the facts or to assist the jury, except by laying down abstract and hypothetical questions of law. In other words, the legislation has tended to eliminate the judge as far as possible from the influence he was wont to exercise in the decision of the tribunal as it was when the Constitution made it an essential part of our judicial system. With this change from the old common-law use of a jury, much greater power is vested in the panel than ever before, and in many instances the power is abused, because the jury takes it into its head that it is not only a tribunal to arrive at a decision upon a sharp issue of facts presented by the evidence, but that it is, in a sense, a legislator to reach natural justice without much regard to the law; and in suits against corporations, and in many instances in spite of the absence of legal liability by the corporation, it will act as an almoner of its charity, and mulct it in a large sum to meet an alleged liability, which in fact and in law does not exist. Under such circumstances the obligation of the good citizen to discharge his duty as a juror is even of higher importance than when the power of the jury was more subject to the control of the experienced judge who presided over the trial of which it is a part. The truth is that the law is not so carefully followed, and property rights and other rights are not so well safeguarded, and criminals are not punished with the same certainty as formerly in communities in which the jury has had the reins thrown on its back, and practically been given a discretionary power in its decisions that was wholly wanting under the common-law system.

The common-law system is preserved in its purity in the Federal courts. There the judge still maintains the power which he had at common law, and which he exercises in English courts today, not of controlling or directing the verdict, but of aiding and instructing the jury in respect to the decision which it should reach, in commenting on the evidence, and in taking much more complete control of the trial than a judge in a Western State is now permitted to exercise. And what is the result? It is seen that everybody in the South and West who is anxious to have a law enforced, and is anxious to have the guilty punished under it, devises ways and means by which the offence can be denounced under a Federal statute and brought for trial into the Federal courts. There it is known that if a man is guilty he probably will be convicted. There it is understood that the wiles of the criminal lawyer, his dramatic resources, and the obstructing policy of delays can ordinarily not prevent the law from overtaking the offender. Of course this distinction between State and Federal courts in the general estimation does not obtain in the older and more conservative States of the East, where there is usually less departure from the common-law system of trial than in the newer and more radical jurisdictions. The jury system ought never to be abolished in an Anglo-Saxon country in criminal cases or, indeed, in sharp and simple issues of fact in civil cases, though there are many complicated issues of fact involved in accounts and other matters (as, for instance, the question of invention in a patent) with respect to which a jury trial is not at all useful. The great advantage of a jury trial in a popular government is that it gives the public confidence that in criminal cases which involve the liberty or life of a citizen and the public, he can be assured that there will intervene in the consideration of his cause twelve impartial and indifferent persons, selected by lot, as a tribunal to decide upon his guilt; and that danger from prejudice against the accused whom the Government is prosecuting, which might be suspected in a judiciary appointed by the Executive of the Government, will be eliminated. The jury system popularizes the court, and gives the people to understand that they have not only an interest, but also a part in the administration of justice.

A jury system requires a panel of individuals who are able to assume a judicial attitude on the issue between two litigants, and to banish from their minds all influence of prejudice of any character with respect to the parties or the subject matter. This judicial quality, this sense of fair play, has been developed in the Anglo-Saxon mind, more than in any other race perhaps, by long training in jury trials. Among the Latin people the power of suppressing one's prejudices and one's preconceived notions in sitting as judges to determine an issue of fact, even under the sanction of an oath, seems not natural, and is hard to develop. This quality is, of course, better developed, other things being equal, in a man of education than in one who has not enjoyed that advantage; and this suggests another reason why the obligation on the educated man is greater than it is in the case of his less fortunate fellow-citizens.

One of the great reasons why jury duty is evaded by good men is because of the delay, and unnecessary delay, that arises in the disposition of causes in jury trials in our courts. In trying to understand what the common-law trial was, we may well look to the English method of disposing of cases. Under that system the lawyers are so well trained and the judge so skilled in pushing the trial that cases which take in this country three and four weeks are disposed of there in a day or a day and a half. Lawyers are not there permitted to introduce myriads of witnesses on the same point and to be guilty of great prolixity in their examinations or in their discussions before the jury. The main and substantial points are dwelt upon, both in the evidence of witnesses and in the argument of counsel, and the counsel are not permitted to divert the attention of the jury to irrelevant circumstances and to absurd theories. The judge retains control and pushes the trial, both because it usually results in a juster judgment and also because neither the time of the court nor the time of the jury ought to be taken up with the histrionic exhibitions of counsel for either side, or with the dragging, tedious, and often irrelevant and unnecessary cross-examinations of supposedly important witnesses. A juryman sitting in a panel and listening to such drawn-out controversy, which as a business man he thinks ought to be settled in the course of a day or a day and a half, will, the next time he is called upon, naturally seek to avoid a duty which is not a pleasure, but a mere bore by reason of the prolixity of the hearing.

A most important principle in the success of a judicial system and procedure is that the administration of justice should seem to the public and the litigants to be impartial and righteous, as well as that it should actually be so. Continued lack of public confidence in the courts will sap their foundations. A careful and conscientious judge will, therefore, strive to avoid every appearance from which the always suspicious litigants may suspect an undue leaning toward the other side. He will give patient hearing to counsel for each party, and however clear the case may be to him when stated, he will not betray his conclusion until he has heard in full from the party whose position cannot be supported. More than this, it not infrequently happens, however clear his mind in the outset, that argument, if he has not a pride of first opinion that is unjudicial, may lead him to change his view.

This same principle is one that should lead judges not to accept courtesies like railroad passes from persons or companies frequently litigants in their courts. It is not that such courtesies would really influence them to decide a case in favor of such litigants when justice required a different result; but the possible evil is that if the defeated litigant learns of the extension of such courtesy to the judge or the court by his opponent he cannot be convinced that his cause was heard by an indifferent tribunal, and it weakens the authority and the general standing of the court.

I knew of one judge who indignantly declared that of course he accepted passes, because he would not admit, by declining them, that such a little consideration or favor would influence his decision. But in the view I have given above a different ground for declining them can be found than the suggestion that such a courtesy would really influence his judgment in a case in which the railroad company giving the courtesy was a party.

Another duty of citizenship which impresses itself on the mind of the judge is that of maintaining the supremacy of the law. Ours is a government by law; not by rule of thumb, but by rules of conduct which have equal application to all. Any exception to the equal operations of the law upon individuals is necessarily most injurious to the future operation of that law for the public good, because one exemption from its operation is certain to lead to others. The public detriment arising from violations of law, followed by immunity from prosecution or punishment, can hardly be overstated. It is, of course, the duty of the legislator in the enactment of laws to consider the ease or difficulty with which, by reason of popular feeling or popular prejudice, laws after being enacted can be enforced. Nothing is more foolish, nothing more utterly at variance with sound public policy than to enact a law which, by reason of the conditions surrounding the community in which it is declared to be law, is incapable of enforcement. Such an instance is sometimes presented by sumptuary laws, by which the sale of intoxicating liquors is prohibited under penalty in localities where the public sentiment of the immediate community does not and will not sustain the enforcement of the law. In such cases the legislation is usually the result of agitation by people in the country who are determined to make their fellow-citizens in the city better. The enactment of the law comes through the country representatives, who form a majority of the legislature; but the enforcement of the law is among the people who are generally opposed to its enactment, and under such circumstances the law is a dead letter. This result is the great argument in favor of so-called local option, which is really an instrumentality for determining whether a law can be enforced before it is made operative. In cases where the sale of liquor cannot be prohibited in fact, it is far better to regulate and diminish the evil than to attempt to stamp it out. By the enactment of a drastic law and the failure to enforce it there is injected into the public mind the idea that laws are to be observed or violated according to the will of those affected. I need not say how altogether pernicious such a loose theory is. General Grant said that the way to secure the repeal of a bad law was to enforce it. But when the part of the community which enacts the law is not the part affected by its enforcement, this is not a practicable method. The constant violation or neglect of any law leads to a demoralized view of all laws, and the choice of the laws to be enforced then becomes as uncertain as the guess of a political executive in respect to public opinion is likely to make it. Such a policy constantly enlarges in the community the class of men with whom the sacredness of law does not exist.

Last June, in this very hall, I delivered an address on the administration of the criminal law, and attempted to point out its present inadequacy and to explain the reasons why there was such a discouraging failure to bring violators of the law to justice by reason of the defects of our criminal procedure.

I observe in the public prints a report that a distinguished graduate of this university, in his well-founded indignation at the present maladministration or non-administration of the criminal law in this country, is represented as justifying, or at least as palliating, lynch law. I confess this seems to me to be a most dangerous doctrine. It is doubtless true that the instances of lynch law have been prompted and greatly increased by the defects and failures to punish malefactors under the lawful procedure in courts. But it is far better that violators of the law go free than that we should introduce such a barbarous and altogether demoralizing and un-controllable practice; first, because it too often results in the punishment of innocent persons, and, second, because it makes chaos of our government by law. Nothing can be more detrimental to the public interest than for any part of the people to take the law into their own hands. Assembled in a mob, they soon lose their conscience; the spirit of the mob, different from that of any individual, enters the crowd; and the desire for vengeance prompts it to acts of violence and of the most fiendish cruelty.

The only way to remedy the evil in which lynch law is supposed to find a justification is by strengthening the hands of the court by repealing the absurd laws that give to every defendant too much chance to escape just punishment and make it as difficult as possible for the State to secure a conviction. It should be provided, as has been recommended a number of times, that no error in the record of a criminal case carried to the Court of Appeals should lead to the reversal of the judgment, unless it affirmatively appears that but for the error a different verdict would have been reached. In the United States courts and in the courts of England for many years there never was an appeal allowed in a criminal case. In the trials in the Federal court and in England there is little opportunity for playing a game, pursued by counsel for the defence in all courts where the judge retains but little control of the trial. He is not permitted to befuddle the jury and defeat a verdict of conviction by a dramatic diversion of the minds of the jury from the real points at issue; nor is he permitted, after an adverse verdict, to reverse the judgment of the trial court by fine and technical points which it was impossible, in the hurry of the trial, for the court below to consider or properly to decide. The emotional and untrue doctrine that it is better that ninety-nine guilty men should escape than that one innocent man should be punished has done much to make our criminal trials a farce. This has come about through popular demand, without a full understanding on the part of the legislatures and the people as to its logical effect. And now that the result has come, we find a popular tumult on the other side in favor of lynch law because the present criminal procedure is inadequate to punish men who should be punished.

It is possible that a remedy for this evil may be worked out through a development of the present accumulation of wealth and the abuses which have followed the concentration of much wealth in comparatively few hands and corporations. The arrogance that this has produced on the part of some successful men has led them to a willingness to evade and escape the laws of the country in their pursuit of wealth. In what I had to say last night in regard to the right of property and the benefit to the world from the accumulation of capital, I hope I will not be thought to be blind to the abuses that grow out of the possession of great wealth by unscrupulous men. Such men are quite apt to think that laws are not made for the purpose of restraining them; that they are, in a sense, above the law; that they can, by the employment of able and acute counsel, who shall advise just what the law is and just how its effects can be evaded, find some way to be exempt from its restrictions.

The Sherman anti-trust law was a law enacted for the purpose of preventing agreements in restraint of interstate trade and preventing monopoly of trade. It was directed to the restraint of the so-called trusts—associations of men who, by use of various instrumentalities, constituted a system of unfair and oppressive trade, and induced and finally compelled the public to deal with them rather than with their helpless competitors. The definition of the offences described in the statute, and the proof of the circumstances tending to make out the offence, are both difficult; and in meeting prosecutions against wealthy corporations and their managers under this law, as well as under the law with reference to interstate commerce forbidding discriminations and secret rebates in favor of certain shippers, the protection which has long been afforded to the ordinary criminal, and the leniency with which the law treats an accused, have inured greatly to the benefit of these wealthy and powerful violators of the law. With the immense fund at their disposal for the purpose of defence they are able to secure the most acute counsel and make every possible point that the looseness of the present criminal procedure affords. When this occurred in the prosecution of the ordinary criminal the public seemed incapable of being roused to the necessity for a change. But now that the defects in the procedure and administration of the criminal law are becoming apparent in the case of the arrogant and wealthy violators of the law who seem to defy the public, we may hope that a full examination will be made into the reason why it is that, if a man has money enough to employ counsel, it is so difficult to bring him to justice under the system now in force.

May the day be speeded in the reform of our administration of the criminal law! If the escape of the ordinary criminal leads to lynch law, what may we expect from the escape of the wealthy malefactor in these days of unrest, when the complaints against accumulated wealth and its abuses are so many, if the administration of the criminal law fails as to them?

I do not for a moment sympathize in the view that everything is corruption and that all the picture should be dark and black. I think that we have had during our last ten years a decade of prosperity never before known in the history of the country; and in the immense sums which have been made for the benefit of all of us in the prosperity that we all have enjoyed, there are some who have taken a larger and an ill-gotten share, and who are attempting to maintain and increase this share by methods that should be reprobated and punished. It is impossible that such abuses should not have occurred in prosperity so unprecedented. But the abuses furnish but little reason for condemnation of the system unless it can be first shown that the prosperity has not been general, and unless it can be further shown that the abuses of the concentration of much wealth in a few hands are a greater detriment than the general prosperity is an advantage.

Just at present we have been passing through a siege of attacks upon our social and political system by gentlemen whom President Roosevelt has properly denominated "the men with the muck-rake." Either in order that they may sell their articles, or in order that for political purposes they may stir a spirit of unrest, they exaggerate the abuses thought to exist in political and business life, and give a distorted and therefore a false view of actual conditions. They attribute corrupt motives without proof; and by dwelling only on instances of evil they destroy, or they seek to destroy, the sense of proportion of their hearers and readers in a general condemnation of society at large. There never was a time in the history of the world when there was more virtue, more charity, more sense of brotherly affection, than there is today. Could anything be more inspiring than the bounteous out-giving of money, provisions, and labor for the benefit of our fellow-men which was evoked by the disaster in California? The truth is that the denunciations of these muck-rakers have reached such a point that a reaction has set in, and they find that their wares are not as salable as they were. They have overdone the picture. Their eyes have become so dulled that they have not realized that everything they say now is discounted by the public, as born not of a desire to present a just picture but of a desire to be sensational at the expense of fact and the expense of justice. It is true that there is corruption in many of our munipical corporations. It is true also that there are on foot substantial and most encouraging movements to stamp out the evils that we find in municipal government. It is not true that there is great corruption in the national Government. Nearly every one who has been at all familiar with the national capital for the last twenty-five years will admit that there has been a very decided improvement in the disinterestedness of legislators and the freedom from venality and corruption in Congress and the executive departments. But let us concede that there have been abuses, as undoubtedly there have been, both in the violations of law by great corporations, railway and others, and in the evasion of the anti-monopoly and trust laws. What is the remedy? Is it not in taking measures to secure the maintenance and supremacy of the law? Is it not in looking to those instrumentalities by which such violations can be properly suppressed and punished? And that is what so emphasizes the importance of an improvement in our judicial procedure in this respect. Any suggestion that there is any other remedy possible for preventing the violation of law and these abuses than in the training and character of the individual on the one hand, and in the strengthening of the arm of the law by judicial procedure on the other, is vicious.

It may be that the enormous accumulation of money in the hands of individuals has reached such a point that it would be wiser to discourage its continuance in the next generation by heavy inheritance tax or other methods. Neither at the common law nor under the Constitution is the right of descent of property or of devising it an inalienable right. It depends wholly upon the legislature; and, therefore, if the legislature sees fit to give a tendency to the division of fortunes, and prevent their greater accumulation in the second and third generations, there are ample means under our present system, and without revolutionary methods, to bring this about.

But the point which I wish most to emphasize at present is the duty of every one to discountenance at every point the suggestion that the people at large are to take the law into their own hands, and accomplish something by violent and radical illegal action against the evils of present society. This would be to substitute chaos for a government of law. Law must be enforced through the lawful executive and through the lawfully constituted courts.

I fear that we must admit that there is not so strongly developed among our people the reverence for law and the demand for its enforcement as there is among our Anglo-Saxon brethren across the sea. Personal liberty and the rights of property are rather more protected under the English system than under ours. Newspaper libel is much rarer in England than here, for Englishmen seem to regard it as their duty to carry such a case into court, and the newspaper is usually mulcted if any license is taken with their reputations. In this country the abuse of the privileges of the press, in holding up to unjust criticism and sensational condemnation many respectable members of the community, has reached such a point that the injured pass it over, accept it as a burden they must bear, and decline to go into court. The delays that the courts permit in working out the rights of a litigant, and the length of time and the worry that are taken up in litigation, all tend to frighten the man out of court who has a just cause, and to make him feel that it is better to abandon his cause than to subject himself to the nervous strain and the bitter disappointment of trying to secure a prompt hearing and decision.

The remedy for these defects is both legislative and executive. The defects exist less in the Federal courts, as I have explained, than in the State courts; and that is sufficient to indicate that the nearer our State courts approximate to the Federal courts in procedure and in the power of the judge, the more certainty is there of an improvement in the judicial administration in this country. The courts are the background of our civilization. The Supreme Court of the United States is the whole background of the Government. It is the body to determine whether Congress is acting within its constitutional limitations; to determine whether the Executive has exceeded his legal authority. It is the last resort and the final tribunal. Its power rests not upon its marshals or its constables, not upon an army under its control or a navy whose battleships it may summon; but its power and precedent rest upon the supremacy of the fundamental law which it is its duty to declare and to preserve, and which it is the duty of every citizen to maintain at all hazards. It is possible for the intelligent members of the community to bring to bear their influence upon legislatures to reduce, by a few well-drawn amendments to the existing procedure, the chances of escape of criminals through the technical meshes of the law. It is possible for intelligent members of the community to exert, at all times and everywhere, an influence against the frequently advanced proposition that lynch law is justifiable. It is possible to create among the good men of the community a public sentiment, expressing itself through the ballot-box and in other ways, in favor of the supremacy of the law and in favor of the punishment of wrong-doers. The exercise of such an influence is one of the highest duties of citizenship.

3

The Duties of Citizenship Viewed from
the Standpoint of Colonial Administration

Mr. President, and Gentlemen of Yale:

My subject tonight is, "The Duties of Citizenship from the Standpoint of Colonial Administration." I shall treat this subject by reference to the Philippine Islands, with which I am familiar, which form the most important dependency we have, and present the most difficult problems for solution.

The first Americans to land in the Philippines were the army and navy, together with those venturesome business spirits that thrive best in times of trouble and excitement, when the opportunities for making money quickly are good. The experiences of our army and navy with Aguinaldo's forces, the contempt which the Filipino army manifested toward the American troops before the beginning of hostilities between them, and the subsequent guerrilla warfare, all tended to create a bitterness of feeling on the part of our soldiers toward their Filipino opponents that could not but be shared by the Americans who were on the islands at that time. It was natural that every defect and every weakness of the Filipino character should be dilated upon by the American soldiers and by those who accompanied them. The exigencies presented by the guerrilla warfare required an increase in the American forces, until in July, 1900, there were upward of 65,000 American soldiers on the islands, and they were stationed at 500 different posts. Their presence in the islands created so large a demand for American supplies of food and drink and other things, that the few American merchants, the only ones familiar with the needs and demands of the American soldiers, found themselves with a business on their hands that they could hardly take care of. Their profits were large. They had no need, therefore, to look for other trade or patronage. The necessity for cultivating the goodwill of the Filipinos for business purposes was wholly absent, and the fact that their profitable patrons were deeply imbued with hostility and contempt toward the native population put the American merchants in the same frame of mind. It was natural that the American newspapers, whose editorial staffs were composed of men recently in the battlefield, whose subscribers were chiefly the soldiers, and whose advertisers were the American merchants, should in their attitude toward the Filipinos reflect the opinions of their readers and patrons. The American soldier knew little of the Spanish language, and still less of the dialects of the country—the Tagalog, the Visayan, and the Ilocano. His opportunity for communication with the native was exceedingly restricted. He said what he meant and meant what he said. His manners were those of the Anglo-Saxon, abrupt and blunt. The Filipino, on the other hand, with a timidity born of years of subordination under the Spanish régime, with the Oriental tendency to speak that which his auditor wishes to hear, and with the courtesy which is innate in the race and has been increased by the Spanish influence, used expressions which, interpreted by Anglo-Saxon standards, were false and deceitful, but which, interpreted by men who understood the race, were nothing more than courteous commonplace. And so it was that the American enlisted man, together with many American officers and merchants, looked upon every effort to cultivate the good-will of the natives as love's labor lost; and, if pursued by the Government, as likely to result in weakness and to invite treachery.

The progress of the army in subduing the insurrection and establishing civil government enabled us in two years to reduce the American soldiers on the islands from 65,000 to about 15,000. The Americans on the islands, outside of the army and the civil servants, have not increased much in number since 1900. The demand for American goods and supplies from merchants on the islands has therefore been much reduced with the withdrawal of the army. The opportunity for large profit on the part of the American merchants, so long content with American trade only, has passed. The only possible source of real business and real trade which our merchants living on the islands can now have is with the Filipino people. The promotion of their material and intellectual welfare will necessarily develop wants on their part for things which in times of poverty they regard as luxuries, but which as they grow more educated and wealthier become necessities.

The cultivation of the good-will of the Filipinos, who thus may be made good customers, is the one course which can create any market among the people on the islands for American goods and American supplies; and, if this be true, a policy which embitters and renders a whole people hostile to the American merchants must necessarily defeat all hopes of increasing the American business. A merchant who sneers at his customer, who calls him names, who turns his back upon him, is not likely to keep him long as a customer. It hardly needs a business man to see this; a layman may predict it with the utmost confidence. Under these conditions in the Philippines it is not strange that right under the noses of the American merchants Spanish merchants, English merchants, German merchants, and Swiss merchants do business with the Filipinos. They are engaged in selling goods to the Filipino peoples and in exporting their agricultural products from the islands. The American merchants, feeling the pinch of a loss of business, have been disposed to charge it to the policy of the Government in declaring in favor of the policy of "the Philippines for the Filipinos." They have been looking for a scapegoat for their lack of success in business, and they have selected the Government and its policy as the chief object of criticism.

This condition of affairs has been held up by anti-imperialists as evidence of the utter unfitness of the American to attempt colonial administration. With the engendering of this spirit, it is urged that we cannot hope to create the belief among the Filipinos that we are attempting to do them good, and that we ought to give up the experiment. But while such temporary manifestations are not encouraging, it is full of consolation to read in the lives of Lord Macaulay and Lord John Lawrence and Lord Canning of the very great bitterness with which all their policies for the amelioration of the native Indian were attacked by the Englishmen who had settled in Calcutta; who in their supreme self-satisfaction regarded the interest of their class, numbering not more than 4,000 or 5,000, as of much greater importance than the interest of the 300,000,000 East Indians.

I am not, however, discouraged by this first attitude of the American merchants in Manila and elsewhere on the islands toward the Filipinos, because a change to a more sensible view is already at hand. There is now the strongest motive for the American merchant to seek the good-will of the Filipinos, in order to secure their business. It is colossal egotism on the part of the American who goes to the Philippines to suppose that the Government of those islands must have its policy affected solely by his interests. The United States is attempting a solution of a most complex and difficult problem. It has been forced into the position of becoming a guardian of the archipelago for the benefit of seven or eight millions of people. It has felt it necessary in the discharge of this trust to take charge of the islands and create a government and maintain it. Its only possible justification for this course, according to its own traditions and the principles upon which its own structure rests, is that the people of the islands are not now fit for self-government; that it owes a duty to them of maintaining a government until the time when they as a people, by actual sharing in the government and by education, shall become completely fitted to run their own political affairs. In other words, the chief characteristic of the trust which we involuntarily assumed is that we must conduct affairs in the Philippines with a view solely to the interest of the Filipinos.

This is as far as possible from saying that Americans may not go to the islands, may not engage in industry of any kind, may not be induced by hope of good profits to invest as much capital as possible in enterprises tending to develop their resources. Such a course is in the interest of the islands, and should be encouraged by the Filipinos themselves; and if the American on the islands will only see his own real interest, he will unite with the Government in an attempt to conciliate the Filipinos as far as possible. It of course interferes with the success of the Government in convincing the Filipinos that the United States is really not moved by selfish motives, but anxious to promote the interest of the Filipino in every way, to have the resident representatives of that country occupy a position of hostility and contempt toward the natives. I should say, therefore, *that the first duty of the American citizen* who goes to the Philippine Islands and lives there is to make himself as well acquainted with the Filipinos as he can; to cultivate their good-will; to have them understand that the interests of the Filipinos are paramount in determining the policy of the United States toward the islands.

The next class of citizens whose duties we may consider are the Filipinos themselves. By the fundamental act of the Philippine Islands they are made citizens of the Philippines. This is to distinguish them from citizens of the United States, who are entitled to certain constitutional privileges *for the exercise of which the Filipino is not ready.* With reference to his treatment by every foreign government, the Filipino occupies exactly the same position and is entitled to exactly the same protection from our Government as an American.

What is the duty of the Filipino citizen of the Philippine Islands toward the insular Government? He owes allegiance to the Government, and is subject to the duties that citizens ordinarily owe to the government that gives them protection and looks after their governmental needs. It may be admitted that there are many Filipinos who would be very glad to have the rule of the American Government end, and a period of absolute independence ensue. The people of the islands have no disposition to come under Japanese rule, as has sometimes been suggested. The truth is, the unfounded report that the United States expected to sell the islands to Japan aroused such indignation as to show that the people much preferred the United States to Japan as a guardian. The poor and ignorant among the Filipinos, who number in all about ninety percent, are not particularly interested as to what kind of a government they have, provided they be let alone. They are easily influenced by the educated of their own race and easily aroused to follow the teachings of any Filipino of influence and standing. But taken as a class, if some one does not seek to excite them they are quiet, peaceable, law-abiding, and not interested in politics or government.

In the other ten percent, however, there are to be found educated persons who deem themselves entirely fitted to carry on a government and to rule the ninety percent which I have described. What ought a citizen of the

Philippine Islands, with these views, to do in respect to the Government? Legally, of course, there is no doubt that he ought to support the Government, or at least not attempt to overthrow it; but in the interest of his people, and released from the obligations that the law imposes upon him, how ought he to act? Is it necessarily patriotism for him to plan to arouse his people to an insurrection and destroy or make as difficult as possible the government of the islands by the United States, or is it his duty to uphold the hands of the representatives of the United States in doing the work which they are sent there to do, to wit, that of guiding the islands to peace and prosperity? Of course it is difficult for an Occidental to put himself in the place of the Oriental, but I have had a good deal of opportunity to study the Filipino people and to understand in a dim but still somewhat comprehensive way the characteristics of the race. I do not hesitate to say that the strong man among them believes that the worst thing that could happen to his country would be to have the United States abandon it; that it is far better to go on as proposed by us, under the sovereignty of the United States, with a gradual extension of the electorate to the people who show themselves qualified, and of the governing power to the electorate. It cannot be hoped that a purely Filipino government by the educated ten percent would pursue a policy to lift the other ninety percent into the ruling class and share with them the political power which the educated ten percent expect to wield. Indeed, that is exactly what many of the educated ten percent wish to avoid. They are in favor of an oligarchy.

In an examination of the committee of the so-called Independence party, conducted by the Senators and Congressmen who took the Philippine trip last summer, the leaders did not hesitate to say that in their judgment the Philippine people were quite ready for self-government, because the ninety percent were an obedient serving class, while the ten percent were a directing or governing class, in every way competent to act as such, and thus were able to carry on an excellent government. I need hardly say that such a government would not meet the views that we have as to what a government ought to be. The ninety percent would not be educated or trained to become self-governing citizens, but would remain in the status which they now occupy. It is absolutely true that most of those who advocate independence, most of those whose voices we hear echoed in Boston and elsewhere in the demand for freedom for the Philippines, are persons who have not the slightest idea of maintaining in the islands a *popular government.*

But it is said the oligarchical government is the only kind of government for which the people of the islands can ever be adapted. Even supposing this to be a plausible view, it is likewise true that we could not depend on any stability in such a government. The difficulty is that the governing class fall out so easily among themselves that were we to permit the ten percent to take charge of the Government, we should find that there was no cohesion in the governing class; that it would divide up into factions; and that almost before the Americans had left the islands there would be internecine warfare and chaos that would require the Americans to return. This is the reason why the conservative members of the community are satisfied with the fact that the American Government has control over the islands, for they realize that no other government in the world could be as generous and as disinterested in its management of the archipelago. Under such circumstances it seems to me to be the duty of a lover of his race—a citizen of the Philippine Islands—to hold up the hands of the Americans engaged in attempting to prepare all the people for the exercise of gradually increasing political control.

The truth is that even the ten percent of the Filipinos who long for an oligarchy are in many respects wholly unfitted to assume the great responsibilities of government. They have had very little experience, their views are expressed in abstract principles. One witness of this class, whom I summoned early in the days of our stay on the islands, I asked to assist us in the matter of the tax laws and to say from what particular class and out of what particular property taxes ought to be raised. He said he had never given any consideration to that subject, because he considered it a mere detail. Another body of men of the Independence party, some of whom appeared before the Congressmen, had at an earlier day come to see me to secure permission to organize a party for the obtaining of independence by peaceable means. I attempted to dissuade them from the task at that time because there were still guerrillas and robbers in the field. I was afraid that in the organization of such a party a great many physical-force men would become incorporated as members, and that ultimately these very good gentlemen who made the proposition to me might be brought under suspicion of the Department of Justice. They said to me that they desired to present an argument in favor of their plan of independence. They said, in writing, that they were fit for self-government because they had counted over the number of offices—central, provincial, and municipal—and had found that while the number was great, they were able to select from the people of the islands enough educated men to fill every office twice; in other words, that if one shift failed for any reasons to meet the requirements of office, then there was another shift that could take their places; and with these two shifts they regarded it as entirely practicable to carry on any sort of a complicated government. The force of a sound, safe public opinion they regarded as of slight importance.

The men who are in favor of independence are not the practical Filipinos. Ordinarily, men of property, men of business, men who by the virtues of providence and self-restraint and foresight have succeeded in laying up fortunes, are convinced, as I have said, that it would be the worst blow possible to the islands to have the Americans leave them now. But the uncertainty in this country as to what course the Government intends to pursue—the impression in the islands that the opposition party intends, when it gets into control of this Government, to let the islands go—has the effect of making every native in the islands, who would otherwise speak out in favor of a continuance of the present arrangement, anxious lest a change may occur, and fearful of taking such a position that he may suffer when independence is granted.

Finally I come to the question, What is the duty toward the Philippine Islands of the American citizens making up the American electorate? I have heard it stated that our people are getting tired of the burden of governing those islands; that the business which has come from them has not been sufficient to justify the outlay that we have made; and that any method of ridding us of the responsibility for their government will be adopted by the people. I differ from this view. I think the American people know that they did not seek the burden of carrying on the government of the Philippine Islands, but that circumstances were such that they could not escape it, and that their honor as a people requires that they discharge the duties that it involves. We are a great and a prosperous nation. Here are eight millions of people in the tropics, differing very much from our own, yet with a capacity for development that justifies our making the experiment of educating them—of leading them on in governmental practice to see if they cannot at length safely walk alone.

We have already done a great deal for the Filipinos. We have organized a good government there; we have given them partial representation in it, and we expect to give them a larger representation next year by the election of a popular assembly which shall be one branch of the governing legislature; we have been educating and are now educating in the English language a half million of the youth of the islands; we have introduced health laws and enforced them; we have suppressed ladronism, which was the bane of the islands in Spanish days; we have eliminated the question of the friars' lands. Owing to causes beyond our control, we have not been able to bring about a period of great prosperity there; and of course in hard times it is difficult to convince the people that the Government is not in some way responsible for this. But we have given the islands a good sound gold-standard currency; we have given them extended telegraph and mail communications; and we are just now about to begin, with Government encouragement, the construction of some seven or eight hundred miles of railway.

It is the duty of the citizen to look at this experiment from the right standpoint; to understand that we are not in the Philippines for the purpose of making trade, but that we are there to discharge the highest duty that one nation can toward another people. It is very probable that the trade between the Philippines and the United States will increase to such proportions as to make that particular trade useful to both countries. But we cannot base our conduct or action on such a motive. What we do in the Philippines must rest on our national duty—a duty which is the greater because of our prosperity and ability to discharge it.

This policy has been sustained in two national elections, and the question therefore arises, What is the duty of the other citizens of the United States who have heretofore held aloof from such a policy and denounced it? Ought they not now to hold up the hands of the Government and assist in every way to make the experiment which, against their will and against their express vote, the Government entered upon? Why should the anti-imperialists, so called, now attempt to make what we do in the Philippines a failure? Is it not a small policy and an unpatriotic one? In the beginning the attitude of the anti-imperialists and their extreme statements and their

45

apparent rejoicing at American defeats undoubtedly continued the war of the insurrection a number of months and probably a year beyond what it would have been had the insurgents thought the whole people was behind the Government.

It is frequently said that Congress cannot give the time necessary for governing the Philippines; that it cannot consider their many needs; and therefore that our government is not one adapted to governing dependencies. I differ from this view; and certainly the conduct of Congress toward the Philippines does not justify the criticism. A number of important acts have been passed which have conferred power to govern the islands on the Philippine Commission, subject only to supervision by the Secretary of War. Congress has been generally wise to put the power where it ought to be—in Manila.

The truth is, considering the many obstructions which we have had to overcome in building up the Philippine Government and the Philippine people, considering the dreadful agricultural depression in the islands and the consequent financial depression, the present condition of the islands is remarkable. One cannot hope to be successful in government unless there comes every little while a period of prosperity. We have not had such a period since we have been in the islands. One must feed a man's belly before he develops his mind or gives him political rights. The pendulum must swing in favor of the islands and prosperity of some kind must come. It will be greatly aided if free trade between the United States and the islands should be established. Whether this will happen in the present Congress, I do not know. That it will come ultimately, I am confident. That it ought to come at once, I am sure. When it does come, the people of the islands will realize how much America has done for them. Until that time we must expect to be blamed for everything in the shape of ill that comes to the islands and we must expect to encounter complaints and criticism from the Filipinos. But their attitude ought not in the slightest degree to affect ours or to take from us the sense of obligation that we should put them on their feet.

The great principle to guide us is that we are to govern the Philippine Islands in accordance with the maxim "the Philippines for the Filipinos." If in the course of a decade or a quarter of a century an examination of all the legislation of Congress shall reveal, as I hope it may, that this was the motive which governed substantially every act passed by that body, then it will form a great exception in the history of the control of dependent possessions by great nations. No one has more admiration than I have for the thorough and effective method of government pursued by England with respect to her colonies, both those which are quasi-independent and those which are crown colonies absolutely under the control of an appointed government. But generally it will be found that in those governments England has pursued a policy of enlightened selfishness; has, so far as she could, recouped herself for any expenditures by the home Government; and has held them primarily with a view to the improvement of English trade. Her opium policy with respect to Oriental colonies has not been controlled by the highest and purest motives; and a large part of the income which has done so much to improve their material conditions, to build roads and construct public works, can be traced directly to this source. The spread of the use of opium among her Oriental subjects is quite discouraging, and a change in that part of her policy ought to made. I do not mean to say that England has not generally looked well after the material comfort and growth and prosperity of her subjects in tropical colonies, or that her governments have not always made for better civilization, justice, and security of life and property. She has established and conducted excellent governments, maintained fine order, built magnificent roads, and in every way made her countries fair to look upon. I think it can hardly be said, however, that she has given great time to the improvement of the individual among her tropical peoples. She has not devoted as much money or as much time as she should have devoted to the education of her subjects and their preparation to take part in governmental matters. In this respect her policy is exactly the opposite of that which we have pursued in the Philippines; and it is supported by the argument, drawn from the experiences of men long accustomed to deal with tropical races, that it is much wiser to keep them in ignorance, to keep them subject to control, than to give them by education ideas of taking part in the government, which will merely foment discussion and agitation which do not work for the good of the whole number.

The most altruistic experiment which England has attempted in the management of tropical races is what she has done in Egypt, under Lord Cromer; and there she has worked wonders for the people of Egypt. She has improved marvellously the prosperity of the fellaheen by public works; she has encouraged agriculture; she has introduced schools and made some attempt at the education of the Egyptians. The admiration of people who have visited Egypt for Lord Cromer's policy and methods is certainly no greater than has been justly deserved; but in the Philippines the principle of our policy is far more advanced than that of Lord Cromer's or of England's anywhere. It may be that it is too far advanced; it may be that it is an experiment that is doomed to failure; but at any rate it is an experiment that it is wise for us to make. We can afford to make it; and if it be a failure, we can afford to accept the responsibility for the failure. That experiment is the preparation, by education and by the gradual extension of practice in governmental matters, of a tropical people who heretofore have not had any practical experience in saying how they shall themselves be governed. In beginning this experiment and carrying it on, it must be understood that there are certain things very much in our favor, and that there are others which constitute very serious obstacles to our success.

In the first place, we have a people, a tropical people, to deal with, who as a people are the only Christians in the Orient. That is, there are seven millions out of eight millions who are Christians, and have been Christians under the influence of Spain and the Roman Catholic Church for upward of 250 years. This fact turns them naturally to Europe and to America for their ideals of virtue and of thought, and for their aims and ambitions. This makes them far more subject to Western influence than the Mohammedans or the Buddhists, both of whom regard the Christian religion with contempt and are to that extent proof against the civilizing ideas of modern Europe and America.

Secondly, though the people are in a state of Christian pupilage, of almost total ignorance, they have an ambition, that it is easy to cultivate, to take advantage of education. Nothing is more inspiring, nothing gives more hope of the success of what we are doing, than the interest which the poor Filipinos, the "taos" as they are called, manifest in having their children receive an education in English. We have not now funds enabling us to educate more than twenty-five percent of the youth of school age in the islands; but I am hoping that prosperity will increase the funds available for education, and that Congress, out of the abundance of this country, will be willing to contribute as much as the Philippine Government itself

48

contributes, thus doubling the educational facilities. The great needs are primary education and industrial education. Industrial education is of greater importance there than in this country, because it has a tendency to correct a feeling which was left by the civilization of Spain, and which is the greatest obstacle that has to be overcome—the idea that labor is degrading and an evidence of slavery. Industrial education dignifies labor.

The parts of the earth which have been retarded, the places where there is the greatest field for progressive work, both material, intellectual, and moral, are in the tropical countries. The discoveries of medical science, the knowledge of conditions that promote health, have improved to such a point that it is much more practicable now for people of the temperate zone to live an extended period in the tropics without injury to health than it was a decade or two decades ago. The land of the temperate zones is rapidly being absorbed. Profit lies in the improvement of the tropical countries; agriculture, mines, and other sources of revenue are there; and it is inevitable that in the next century the great progress of the world is to be made among tropical peoples and in tropical countries. Therefore what we are doing in the Philippines is merely a precursor of what will be done in other lands near the equator; and if we demonstrate that it is possible for people purely tropical to be educated and lifted above the temptations to idleness and savagery and cruelty and torpor that have thus far retarded the races born under the equatorial sun, we shall be pointing another important way to improve the civilization of the world.

Hence it is that the value of the work we are doing in the Philippines rises far above the mere question of what the total of our exports and imports may be for this year or for next year or hereafter, or whether they are at present a burden. The Philippine question is, Can the dominion of a great and prosperous civilized nation in the temperate zone exercise a healthful and positively beneficial influence upon the growth and development of a tropical people? What we have to do is in a sense to change their nature; it is to furnish, by developing their physical and intellectual wants, a motive for doing work which does not exist under their present conditions. That this can be done I have no doubt, from what has already been done in the islands. But it is a question of time and patience. The tropical peoples cannot lift thenselves as the Anglo-Saxons and other peoples of the cold and temperate zones, where the inclemency and rigors of the climate

49

demand effort and require labor, have lifted themselves. The struggle that these tropical peoples must go through in reaching better things is far more difficult; and its outcome must depend, in my judgment, on the outside aid of friendly and guiding nations. The principle which our anti-imperialists seek to apply, that people must acquire knowledge of self-government by independence, is not applicable to a tropical people. We cannot set them going in a decade and look to their future progress as certain. We must have them for a generation or two generations, or perhaps even three, in order that our experiment with reference to education, primary and industrial, shall have its effect, and that our guiding hand, in teaching them commonsense views of government, shall give them the needed direction. It is supposed that if the Democratic party comes into power it will give up the islands and turn them over to the control of the people who inhabit them. I venture to predict—although prediction is dangerous—that the Democratic party, should it come into power, would not assume this responsibility, but would proceed on practically the same lines as have been followed hitherto. Such a result would be desirable, because then it would be shown that both political parties were in favor of the policy which has been instituted, and that the people of our country would unite in a great and successful effort for the benefit of humanity.

4

The Duties of Citizenship Viewed from
the Standpoint of the National Executive

Mr. President, and Gentlemen of Yale:

The subject of my remarks this evening is, "The Duties of Citizenship from the Standpoint of the National Executive."

The administration—the President and his cabinet officers and others who are part of it—naturally thinks that the first duty of a citizen with reference to the national Executive is to hold up its hands and support all of its policies, and be properly tender and gentle in dealing with its defects, suspected or proven. It is easy for the administration to fall into the view that criticisms of its policy and misrepresentations with respect to what it has done, or has not done, seriously affect the work of the Government and interfere with doing it well. When a man has great executive responsibility, and finds that his plans are more or less interfered with by what he regards as the extravagances and injustices of the press, there is an unconscious disposition on his part to believe that a restriction of the license of the press would be a very excellent thing, and that it would prevent the driving away from his moral support of the sympathy and assistance of the public, which are essential to the ultimate success of the plans that he has made for the public good. These demands for restriction of the press are likely to be more unreasonable and extreme in such a place as the Philippines or Puerto Rico, where misrepresentations and criticisms are of vastly more importance, because in those places the views of the native population of particular matters affect the success of governmental measures more directly than they can in this country. We are anxious, of course, to impress the Filipinos with our disinterestedness and desire for their good. The American press of Manila has frequently been bitter in its denunciation of the entire Philippine people, and has stirred up among them a feeling that we are hypocrites, and that there is no real friendliness on our part toward them. Yet every effort to secure by legal proceedings a restraint of the license of the press, or the extravagances and misrepresentations of an irresponsible editor or newspaper proprietor in Manila, is a great deal worse than the evil from which the complaint arises; because it dignifies the issue at once into that of freedom of the press, and makes the man who is prosecuted or in any way brought into court a martyr for the cause of free speech. It is vastly better, if the Executive only realizes the truth, that the injustice, comment, and unjust criticism, and the deliberate misrepresentations that sometimes do characterize articles in the newspapers, should be left to lose their effect by the gradual discovery of the actual facts, and of the injustice of the criticism, in the events which follow. This duty of citizenship not to criticise public servants unjustly and not to misrepresent the character of their commissions and omissions is of course an important one; a violation of it is frequently a serious hindrance to the accomplishment of valuable results from a patriotic and governmental standpoint; but while headlines seem outrageous, and while articles seem to be fraught with great and vicious results, because they are untruthful and exaggerated and sensational, the evil neutralizes itself. Our people are intelligent and keen. They are able after experience to gauge the importance to be attached and the confidence to be accorded to statements so extreme that they bear between their lines the refutation of what they express. The press is essential to our civilization and plays an unofficial but vital role in the affairs of government. The discipline of a fear of publicity, the restraining and correcting influence of the prospect of fearless criticism, are of much value in securing a proper administration of public affairs. The exercise of power without danger of criticism produces an irresponsibility in a public officer which, even if his motives are pure, tends to negligence in some cases and arbitrary action in others.

Speaking from a Washington standpoint, the standard of newspaper correspondents at the national capital, representing all the great dailies and all the press associations, is on the whole a high one; higher, I think, than that of any other newspaper men, as a class, that I know. Such men, when they have established the right to have it, as most of them have, share the confidence of Senators, of the leading members of Congress, of the Cabinet, and even of the President himself; and they are most careful to observe the lines which are laid down in these confidences, restraining the extent of their publication. The amount of information that the Washington correspondents have which they do not give to the public would surprise most men not familiar with affairs in the nation's capital. The truth is that the partisan character of despatches that are seen in some newspapers is determined rather by instructions from headquarters that by any disposition of the correspondents themselves to give a colored account of the facts.

Another topic that perhaps deserves consideration here, in discussing the duty of the citizen toward the national administration, is the suppression of personal feelings in questions of foreign policy. How far, when this nation is dealing with other nations, either in making treaties, or in matters likely to lead to a war, or in actual war, ought a citizen, disregarding all party considerations, to stand by his own government and hold up its hands in achieving a successful result? It would be going very far to say that no matter how unjust a war there ought to be no criticism by American people of the conduct of the administration in such a crisis. In a free government the right and duty to criticise that which is plainly wrong obtain and ought to obtain, no matter how critical the situation with respect to an international controversy. But I submit that the natural attitude of the partisan toward the administration, at times when the country's welfare in war or in approaching war is at stake, should be laid aside; that the presumption should be indulged that our country is right in its contentions and that its opponent is wrong, unless the attitude of our country is so indefensible that it is impossible to avoid condemnation of those who are responsible for it. Nothing so interferes with the success of a nation in carrying out international matters as a fire in the rear by part of its own people. Everything that is said of that character is at once repeated in the newspapers and public prints of the opposing nation, and strengthens it in its unyielding attitude toward our contentions. I remember that in an article on this subject Secretary Olney deprecated the spirit of partisanship that was developed in many of the newspapers and magazines of this country in international matters as compared with the conduct of opposition newspapers in such crises in England. Of a similar character is the position taken by some with respect to our attempt to set up and maintain a government for the benefit of the Filipinos in the Philippines. This I mentioned last night. If our policy there is to be unsuccessful—as I hope and believe it will not be—this result can be charged largely to the agitation, unreasonable, bitter, partisan, altogether unjust, of the so-called anti-imperialists; who seek not merely to criticise and bring to the public mind most unfair statements of the defects of our policy and its failure, but deliberately to embarrass us with the people of the Philippine Islands in everything that we attempt to do. There are instances in which the spirit of opposition to the policy of the Government was originally roused by entirely sincere and proper motives, but in which there has been developed a bitterness of feeling until all fair judgment has disappeared and there is substituted an intense desire that the arguments in opposition to the policy shall be vindicated by the proof of abuses and by failure of the policy. This attitude, which I may call unjudicial and unpatriotic, interferes materially with our success in conciliating the Filipino people, because they are very responsive to any report and have no sense of proportion in judging of the credibility and weight to be given to such partisan statements. In this country any such attitude or course of conduct is unpopular, and is generally rebuked at the polls.

One of the chief reasons for the misjudging of the characters of rulers of nations is the failure of the critics, the historians, and the people themselves fully to appreciate the actual limitations and restrictions upon the exercise of a supposedly unlimited governing power. The most absolute monarch has limitations upon his freedom of action that are little understood except by those who are on the ground and close enough to him and his daily walks of life to understand how the circumstances hem in the exercise of his discretion, limit him in that which he would like to do, and prevent absolutely his carrying out the ideals which as a free man he would be glad to follow. The same thing is in a much greater degree true of the power of the President and of the members of the administration. Take for instance the appointing power. A member of a community remote from the capital, studying politics from the standpoint of entire indifference, with the critical faculty well developed, wonders that a president, with high ideals and professions of a desire to keep the government pure and have efficient public servants, can appoint to an important local office a man of mediocre talent and of no particular prominence or standing or character in the community. Of course the President cannot make himself aware of just what standing the official appointed has. He cannot visit the district; he cannot determine by personal examination the fitness of the appointee. He must depend upon the recommendations of others; and in matters of recommendations as indeed of obtaining office, frequently it is leg muscle and lack of modesty which win, rather than fitness and character. The President has assistance in making his selection, furnished by the Congressmen and the Senators from the locality in which the office is to be filled; and he is naturally quite dependent on such advice and recommendation. He is made the more dependent on this because the Senate, by the Constitution, shares with him the appointing power. It is true that strictly and technically speaking he has the initiative and the Senate only the ratifying or confirming power; but practically, because of the knowledge of the Senators of the locality, the appointing power is in effect in their hands subject only to a veto by the President; and the Senators in turn are hampered, first, by the fact that many competent and prominent men will not accept the places, and again by the fact that under our political system there is much pressure on them to recognize the party services of men who are more active as politicians than they are successful as business men. On the whole, I think the character of the Federal employees the country over is excellent; but of course there are exceptions, and it is the exceptions upon which the criticism of an administration is based, and properly based, because the number of the exceptions determines the care with which all such appointments are made.

This naturally leads to the consideration of a limitation upon the policies which the President may favor or undertake. Under our system of politics the President is the head of the party which elected him, and cannot escape responsibility either for his own executive work or for the legislative policy of his party in both Houses. He is, under the Constitution, himself a part of the legislature in so far as he is called upon to approve or disapprove acts of Congress. A president who took no interest in legislation, who sought to exercise no influence to formulate measures, who altogether ignored his responsibility as the head of the party for carrying out ante-election promises in the matter of new laws, would not be doing what is expected of him by the people. In the discharge of all his duties, executive or otherwise, he is bound to a certain extent to consult the wishes and even the prejudices of the members of his party in both Houses, in order that there shall be secured a unity of action by which necessary progress may be made and needed measures adopted. I need hardly point out, for I have already referred to it in my first lecture, the absolute necessity of parties in a popular government, and the fact that efficiency of government, other things being equal, is greatly promoted by party uniformity and solidarity of opinion. In order to attain this unity of party action, in order to make any progress for the better, the administration is obliged to give up or hold in abeyance measures that it would, other things being equal, heartily approve; and, in a series of compromises, it is bound to sacrifice some of its aims in order to accomplish others more important. Now it by no means follows that this is on the whole not a useful condition in government. Popular government must be a series of compromises. The resultant mean is often better than the extreme which would be reached if an administration were able to carry out all its views. A conservative course is the result of the very limitation imposed on the projected policies of the administration by the necessity for conciliating the many different people and interests that constitute controlling factors in a party. It is doubtless true that under our government of the people things are not done that ought to be done; but on the other hand, if these restraining influences were absent, we might be led into extreme measures which would be disastrous in their results.

The policy of those responsible for the national administration in any respect must be judged as a whole, after sufficient time has elapsed to measure properly what has been done. It is a very unsafe and unfair thing to judge a single act and its probable bearing on the rest of a policy of the administration; and fortunately the people understand this fact. In the end, the judgment of the people is probably as safe and fair as any judgment could be, for they take the administration of public affairs by and large;

and while they do not always credit men with the highest and purest motives, and recognize that there is much human nature in man, they are not searching for reasons for distrusting the good faith and the desire for good government in their public servants.

One of the encouraging experiences of men who live in Washington and are close to the mainsprings of national policy, both in Congress and in the Executive, is to find how much less influential are private interests in the matter of legislation and executive action than is generally held by critics who are not familiar with the situation. The hard work that is done by men whose bugles are not blown, the effort that there is on the part of legislators and executive officials to subserve the public interest, cannot be known except by intimacy with public affairs. I do not mean to deny that at times private and special interests do, in fact, exercise an influence to the extent of defeating needed legislation; but in the end, though it may take one or two or three Congresses, the sense of public duty and the clearness of vision that discussion and deliberation give ultimately bring about the kind of legislation which the people want, formulated by those whose interest in the public welfare is sincere.

Of course there is a kind of influence at Washington that disfigures legislation and retards executive action of general importance and interest; an influence exercised by those who prefer what they suppose to be the interest of a locality or district to the interest of the nation at large. The people of congressional districts and of States compete with each other through their representatives in Congress and in the Senate to shape national legislation for local advantage; to secure the investment of national funds in public works and the construction of military posts and other great governmental institutions in one part of the country instead of another. It is impossible that these influences should not be exerted, and they do more or less affect the efficacy of measures adopted for a national purpose. But these are incidents inevitable in the character of the government that we have; they are inherent in our system; and with the great benefits that proceed from the popular basis of our government, we may well put up with some inconveniences and minor obstacles to the most efficient national administration.

One of the facts that is not often made prominent is that in our Government at Washington there is an entity distinct in many ways from the

President and Cabinet officers charged with the responsibility of the executive policies, and distinct from Congress charged with the responsibility of the legislative policies. For one hundred and thirty years, since the beginning of the Constitution, we have been perfecting the administrative departments of the Government. Most of the positions in these departments now are filled by selection under the civil-service law or by promotions from positions thus filled. We have a complicated structure, which has grown with the needs of the Government; it is an enormous machine, so officered and adjusted that it would run itself with great efficiency without a President and without a Cabinet and without Congress, except for the lack of the appropriation of the money necessary to pay the cost. It is an organization whose members have been trained by long experience, and now, under the civil-service law which prevents their being made the football of politics and secures to them a permanent tenure of office, are put in a position of impartiality and indifference to other considerations than those of the efficiency of governmental work. They are, it is true, affected more perhaps than they need be by the traditions as to how governmental work has been done from the beginning, but my experience with this machine in two departments is that generally this routine part of the life of the Government (and it makes up ninety-five hundredths of that life) is carried on by men who have an eye single to the interests of the Government and to the conduct of its affairs according to law and according to the public interests. The civil-service law has now been in operation more than a quarter of a century, and, although violated at first, it has come to be more and more regarded as essential to the life of the Government; and it has finally made the organization to which I refer indifferent to party changes and unaffected by them, and has greatly increased the certainty of proper administration.

I do not mean by what I have said to minimize the importance of the position of the President or of the heads of the departments in the administration of public affairs. The heads have to determine in many instances important questions of broad policy; but the aggregate of these questions is quite small in proportion to those which arise every day and have to be decided by men who from long training are even better able to decide them than their superiors who control the administration. Of course the influence that the heads of an administration may have upon the whole civil service is very great, if the determination of the heads of the Government that the administration shall be pure and shall not be affected injuriously by partisan or other undue influence is well understood. It strengthens the body of permanent civil servants in their good work and secures from them a closer adherence to the public interests and to the best traditions of the service.

This Government, as you know, is divided into three departments—the executive, the legislative, and the judicial. It is frequently charged that the tendency of the modern Executive is to usurp the functions of Congress by seeking to control and influence legislation in violation of the spirit of the Constitution. I have already pointed out the constitutional participation in legislation by communications to Congress and by the exercise of the veto power, with which the Executive is expressly vested; and I have also attempted to show what, under our system of politics, are the position and obligation of the President as head of the party through whose instrumentality he must accomplish any progress dependent on affirmative legislation. The party traditions not only justify but require him to take an active interest in it, and so to unify the members of his party as to secure that solidarity without which initiative for good is quite impracticable.

History does not bear out the charge that there is any usurpation by the Executive of legislative functions. On the contrary the tendency is exactly the other way. Congress in its legislation has frequently failed to recognize a thing which the Constitution certainly intended, to wit: freedom of discretion in executive matters for the Chief Magistrate and his subordinates. I need not go back of the Tenure of Office Act, passed Congress in the administration of President Johnson, by which it was attempted to limit materially the power of appointment that the President certainly has under the Constitution. The act was repealed after Mr. Johnson went out of office, and I think it is generally recognized now that it was an undue stretch of legislative power. I do not mean to deny that the line between proper legislative limitation upon the mode of exercise of executive power and unconstitutional restriction is sometimes very difficult to draw; but the danger that the Executive will ever exceed his authority is much less than the danger that the Legislature will exceed its jurisdiction. The Commons of England won freedom and brought about a popular government through its insistence upon holding the purse-strings; and the Congress of the United States has exactly that control over the Executive which enables it at all times to restrain the exercise of executive power by withholding the appropriations absolutely necessary to the exercise of executive power at all. With that dependence upon Congress, the executive branch can never be untrammelled in the conduct of public affairs. It is always responsible to Congress to explain what it has done with the money already appropriated, and it must always make a showing of the money needed for executive work during the next ensuing year. In other words, the Executive is always a petitioner at the door of Congress for the money necessary to carry on public affairs; and as long as that relation exists the frequently expressed fear that the Executive is overshadowing the Legislature is merely imaginative—useful for glowing periods and party platforms, but for nothing else.

Life in Washington leads most men who are impartial and who take broad views of affairs to a condition of reasonable optimism as to the progress toward better things. The account that one receives of the defects of earlier administrations and the corruption that at times prevailed shows that we have made great improvement; and it is not unfair to say that there is a high standard of morality and public conduct throughout all the departments and the executive and legislative branches of the Government. I do not mean to deny that there are individual instances of neglect of public duty and possibly of corrupt methods; but, on the whole, one who is familiar with the workings of the Government at Washington may well take heart and courage at the general level of good and honest legislation. Efficiency of administration has been greatly promoted by the widening of the application of the civil-service law; which has so reduced the calls upon the time of the heads of the departments and the President that they are able to give to matters of public interest a great deal of time which before the enactment of this law was taken up in discussing the merest details as to the selection of clerks.

There has been a question mooted whether it would not be wiser to allow Cabinet officers to take part in the debates of Congress, as do the English parliamentary executive leaders, who are really elected as legislators to begin with and are selected as executives afterward. I am inclined to think that it might aid much the deliberations of Congress if such a policy were adopted, but there are inconveniences connected with it that perhaps will forever prevent a change of this character.

The disposition of the Legislature to investigate and criticise executive action is one of the most important influences toward a better government that exists in our system. Investigating committees of Congress are always at work; and the fear of such investigations, the fear of just criticisms on the floor of either House, has a most salutary and restraining effect upon the naturally wasteful and somewhat arbitrary disposition of human nature in the exercise of power. On the whole, when one looks into the system of government at Washington and regards it from the standpoint of an impartial, tolerant citizen and critic, taking into consideration all the limitations of structure and constitution which prevent any government from becoming a perfect machine, he cannot but reach the conclusion that we are a fortunate people, who have progressed far in the development of an efficient public service and in vindicating the theory of popular sovereignty.

PRESENT DAY PROBLEMS

A Collection of Addresses

Delivered on Various Occasions

Present Day Problems

Commentary

A. E. Campbell

*P**resent Day Problems* was first published in 1908, the year in which Taft, running as Theodore Roosevelt's chosen successor, easily won the presidency, delivering to the hapless William Jennings Bryan the most emphatic of his three emphatic defeats. The book is not quite what the simple title might suggest. It is not an ordered statement of what is wrong with the country and what Taft proposes to do about it. It is not even—like, say, Woodrow Wilson's *The New Freedom*—the distilled essence of a campaign. It is, as the subtitle honestly makes clear, "A Collection of Addresses Delivered on Various Occasions," and, as it might have added and as will become apparent, to various audiences. Most of the fifteen addresses date from 1907 or 1908, but by no means all; the earliest (though placed late in the volume) was delivered in 1895, when Grover Cleveland was still president. That the book was nevertheless worth publishing tells us a good deal about the author, about the state of politics in 1908, and even about the Progressive movement.

Since the book does not have any unity imposed by occasion or by date, the considerable unity it does have is provided, for good and ill both, by the personality of the author. It is hard to avoid the sense that Taft's political character, political opinions, political prejudices even, were formed early and thoughtfully, and thereafter changed little. The Taft recorded here is, of course, Taft before the campaign of 1908 began, but the presidential campaign of 1908 was on the Republican side decorous enough; small need for adaptability or fast footwork then. Rather it was Taft's task to appear presidential, the sound man, the man of experience opposed yet again by the wild radical. The principles and policies he was defending were, after all, not his but Roosevelt's, the task—a relatively easy one—to show that they would be safe in Taft's hands. To that task these addresses contribute well enough, and if they leave the reader with the uneasy impression that Taft was following an intellectual path already well trodden, hindsight may be doing its insidious work.

One purpose of the collection was to show the range of Taft's experience, which was, of course, exceptional. If one address probably missed its mark, it is so lightweight that it can be passed over quickly. In his capacity as secretary of war, Taft spoke at the dedication of General Grant's mausoleum in New York on May 30, 1908. Though of course he spoke admiringly he felt it necessary to refer to Grant's drinking problem before the Civil War, and for that he was attacked by some newspapers and individuals. In reprinting the address, evidence perhaps of a certain stubbornness, he defended himself in a foreword, reminding his readers that his father had served in Grant's cabinet. It is clear that the younger Taft had intended no disrespect for Grant—rather the reverse—but he took the opportunity to emphasize Republican credentials already long established; his own service in the national government had begun as solicitor general under Benjamin Harrison.

Among Taft's credentials was experience overseas, at a time when Theodore Roosevelt had begun to argue that the United States must play an appropriate part in the world. The experience seems an odd byway in the career of a man who, as all his biographers agree, most wanted to be a judge. By 1900 he was well established as a judge on the Sixth Circuit, a post he could combine with teaching at the Cincinnati Law School. He gave that up in order to head the commission to establish civil rule in the Philippines, and there he stayed until February 1904, resisting even TR's effort to appoint him to the Supreme Court. The first two pieces in this volume are his inaugural address as civil governor of the Philippines, appropriately enough delivered on July 4, 1901, and a speech when he returned for the inauguration of the Philippine Assembly in October 1907. With the last, we may bracket two addresses from the same trip, delivered in Shanghai and Tokyo, dealing respectively with Chinese and Japanese relations with the United States. Those relations were then almost entirely commercial, as Americans always wished them to be, though the sore point of Asiatic immigration into California had to be touched on. So it was, but so tactfully that the reader will be hard put to it to discern what the issues were.

These four addresses set a tone which later pieces sustain. In a sense Taft only has one tone, whomever he is addressing. There is never any exhortation, and still less is there any lightness of touch. There is only calm, reasoned exposition, always clear if sometimes ponderous, based on the belief that when presented with the facts fairly stated, reasonable men will agree. Unreasonable men therefore can and must be opposed. Taft was a success as governor, proving himself a sound administrator and winning the regard of many Filipinos. There is nothing here to suggest—though there is a hint or two later in the volume—that he was not optimistic about the islanders' capacity for self-government. His well-known description of them as "our little brown brothers" captures neatly both affection and patronage. But he spoke to his little brown brothers in a tone of grave instruction, as he spoke to everyone else.

The bland, even-handed character of Taft's prose, though it must strike any reader of this book, does not do the man justice. In spite of his bulk, his reputation both for energy and for universal competence was growing. Only a few months after he had successfully resisted appointment to the Supreme Court, he was summoned back to Washington to succeed Elihu Root as secretary of war. In that office he retained some general supervision of the Philippines, and though the army was his principal responsibility, he found time to take temporary charge of affairs in Cuba and to supervise the planning of the Panama Canal. On Cuba this volume is silent, but the army was the topic on which he chose to speak to the Board of Trade of Columbus, Ohio, in April 1908, and the canal that with which he favored the Ohio State Bar Association a couple of years earlier in July 1906, venturing one of his few mild jokes, to the effect that he had chosen the subject because he had forgotten most of the law he knew. That talk shows a careful mastery of the arguments for and against the several possible routes and of the engineering problems. His audience probably learned more than they cared to about the canal, and for this piece the reader would be grateful for the maps and plans that Taft clearly had available when he gave it.

By 1906 talk of Taft both as chief justice and as president
had become so general as to be embarrassing. There is no
doubt that what Taft wanted was to be not merely a justice of
the Supreme Court but chief justice—several times he might
have had the junior appointment—and there is as little
doubt that Mrs. Taft wanted her husband to be president.
Fate, and the determination of Chief Justice Fuller to cling
to office, tipped the scales in her direction. The remaining
addresses here presented, whatever their date, serve appropriately as election addresses—of a kind. There is no hint in
them anywhere of a desire for office, no fighting talk. Taft,
let us remember, won the presidency perhaps in the only way
in which he could have won it, certainly in the only way in
which he would have wanted to win it. With Roosevelt behind him, he was nominated overwhelmingly on the first
ballot at the Republican convention and then needed to do
almost nothing to ensure his crushing victory. Characteristi-
cally, it was after his election and not before it that he under-
took a national tour during which he made 266 speeches.

Nevertheless, in these speeches Taft dealt thoroughly
with all the main issues of the election, and laid down some
very plain principles of policy. As an expositor of Roosevelt-
ian Progressivism he had few equals. First, his line was simply to write off the Democratic party, at least as led by Bryan.
Taft valued a two-party system, but contended that the
Democrats had moved so far away from the mainstream that
they had destroyed it. They could offer only socialism, anarchy, and violence. For such men—as he depicted them—
Taft had nothing but contempt. Of course Taft knew that
no one could be elected by the rich alone and that many
voters were working men or farmers. He commonly dealt
briefly with the panaceas that sometimes attracted these voters. Free silver, indeed, was dead, but he tackled schemes for

the removal of tariff protection or for the breaking up of trusts. Having disposed of these, he then dealt more thoroughly with what, in his mind, were the real issues—not protection as such but, in some instances, excessive or improper protection; not trusts, but trusts corruptly organized against the public interest. When he drew these distinctions, it was to insist with the force of deep conviction that the law, the courts, an independent judiciary, were fully equal to seeing fair play among competing interests. State courts could often act effectively, but when they could not, the federal courts were there to step in. Taft might have said with Gilbert's Lord Chancellor, "The law is the true embodiment of everything that's excellent." He did not, of course, think that the law as it stood was excellent or even adequate. It could be and where necessary should be changed by legislation—Taft's view of the Constitution allowed legislators plenty of scope—but, often enough, all it needed was sound interpretation by realistic courts. For example, Taft was by no means hostile to organized labor. He recognized the absurdity of the idea that an individual working man could face his employer on equal terms. But, since he was totally opposed to labor violence, he recognized also that the law must protect labor rights and that, if necessary, laws must be modified to do that. He, and the other right-thinking men who agreed with him, were qualified and able to hold the balance.

This very idea implies that there is a balance to be held. Where did Taft think that it fell? Perhaps the single truth to which he held most firmly, other than the necessary supremacy of the law, was that property rights were sacred. The right to hold property was next only to liberty in the great pantheon of American rights, and the two were so intimately linked that they could hardly be disentangled. Unless a man had security in his property, he could hardly be said to have liberty in any sense. Here Taft may be thought a profound conservative, and certainly he would readily have admitted as much in opposition to the madmen of the left whom he scorned. But he thought it right to keep a very close eye both on the means by which a man acquired his property—hence, for example, his regard for workers' right to claim injury compensation against employers, which he was ready greatly to extend—and on what he did with his property once he had acquired it—hence his readiness to look closely into the behaviour of monopoly trusts. Self-interest, vital though it was as the engine of all progress, must always be checked by social responsibility. This was the creed of conservative Progressives, and in holding it, Taft did not differ much from the man who was then still his mentor, Theodore Roosevelt. The great and, as time was to prove, critical difference was that TR and Taft each played to his strength. TR insisted, knew, that force of personality mattered. Taft profoundly believed that, where reason reigned, it should not. There was in his make-up a strong streak of paternalism. It made him an excellent administrator, a conscientious reformer, a careful expositor of the Republican credo. It did not make him a politician.

The two longest pieces in the volume, one delivered in Idaho in November 1906, the other in Ohio in August 1907, are surveys of the work and achievements of the Roosevelt administration from 1904 onwards, and of the principles on which Taft thought they were based. There follow three on more narrowly defined topics. One, delivered in Boston, is on the panic of 1907, for which Taft is, of course, concerned to acquit the administration of any blame. Economics in his day was still a primitive science, the gold standard was still in place and its maintenance a central tenet of the Republican faith, but if dressed in more technical language, his views on the nature of "monetary panic" would have much in common with received wisdom today. The second, delivered in Kentucky, is on the place of the South in national politics. He argues, persuasively enough, that obsession with the race issue should no longer determine party allegiance—at least in the upper South. Sensible Southerners, like other sensible men, belong in the Republican party; if they are not there it is "merely because of the traditions of the past and the ghost of a former issue." Even if much of Taft's argument rests on the compelling need to reject the Democratic party of Bryan, he is here clearly right—but it took another half-century to lay that ghost. The third, delivered in New York at the tail end of the 1907 panic, is perhaps Taft's best and fullest statement not only of what he thought the proper relations between "Labor and Capital" (his title) should be; it deals with the abuses on both sides, sets out, of course, his view of the value of the injunction in labor disputes—the very center of the debate—but ends with a sentence that is the essential Taft: "I earnestly hope that a more *conservative and conciliatory* attitude on both sides may avoid the destructive struggles of the past" (italics added). The next piece deals again with Republicanism, but here Taft is speaking among friends, addressing the Young Men's Republican Club of Missouri, before he turns to his final themes of "Criticism of the Federal Judiciary" (an early piece of 1895) and of "Administration of Criminal Law," delivered at Yale Law School in 1905.

What holds such diverse addresses, given to such diverse audiences, together? One quality, already discussed, is the steady, sturdy, perhaps not very imaginative but essentially generous, character of Taft himself. But there is another. The "problems" with which Taft was concerned were not merely those of 1908. They were those of a longer period, the whole Progressive era, extending from perhaps the turn of the century up to—though Taft could not then know this—the coming of the First World War. Remarkably little in an address given in 1895 was out of date thirteen years later. Moreover, that period was in general, in spite of 1907, one of optimism. Let the reader make what allowance he will for a touch of Dr. Pangloss in Taft, it remains true that the problems to which he drew attention were manageable, and true also that, so far as they were world problems, problems deriving from the crooked timber of humanity, American institutions were capable of dealing with them and the United States was in the lead in trying to meet them. Some American self-satisfaction, to which Taft was ready to appeal, was legitimate.

One might go further. Much about our modern society, whether in the United States or in other western countries, Taft, an essentially decorous nineteenth-century gentleman, would have detested, would even, perhaps, have failed to understand. Yet a great many of the problems with which we wrestle remain in essence those with which he was concerned and, even if many of them are now perceived as global rather than national, American power still requires American attention to them. Take the attempt to spread honest, limited government to other countries. Political correctness now limits what can be said, but the task has not greatly changed. Now, as in 1908, some are more willing than others to undertake it. Or the maintenance of a sound currency which meant, until very lately indeed, the avoidance of inflation. The gold standard has gone; the underlying goal has not. Or the sense that enormous concentrations of wealth in private hands are a potential danger, and that the state must find ways of controlling them without damaging economic activity or legitimate property rights. Or the danger of too great a gap between rich and poor. Or the need to develop a fair international trading system, allowance made for competing interests within the United States. The list might be much extended, but one gets the sense that Taft would bring to *our* present day problems the same shrewd, considering mind that he brought to his own, and that he would remain much what he was, a moderate, reforming Republican, even perhaps, in the words of another Roosevelt of another party, "a little left of center."

Only one important omission stands out. There is nothing in the entire book on education. In one sense, of course, the Progressives were keenly interested in education, and the paternalistic Taft here described was as interested as others. But they saw it as a means to competence. Immigrants needed education. Filipinos needed education. Even the sort of poor whites to whom Bryan appealed needed education. That was obvious but, in 1908, it was not a problem. Of our own obsession with education as a means to self-awareness and self-criticism there is not a trace. Taft knew where he stood and where his country stood. That underlying self-confidence is as much a quality of the Progressives as their reforming zeal, and it sets them apart from us, their successors.

1

Inaugural Address as Civil Governor of the Philippines

Manila, Philippine Islands, July 4, 1901

My Fellow-Countrymen: This ceremony marks a new step toward civil government in the Philippine Islands. The ultimate and most important step, of course, will be taken by the Congress of the United States, but with the consent of the Congress the President is seeking to make the Islands ready for its action. However provisional the change made today, the President by fixing the natal day of the Republic as its date has manifested his view of its importance and his hope that the day so dear to Americans may perhaps be also associated in the minds of the Filipino people with good fortune. The transfer to the Commission of the legislative power and certain executive functions in civil affairs under the military government on September first of last year, and now the transfer of civil executive power in the pacified provinces to a civil governor, are successive stages in a clearly formulated plan for making the territory of these Islands ripe for permanent civil government on a more or less popular basis. As a further step in the same direction, on September first next, at the beginning of the Commission's second legislative year, there will be added as members to that body by appointment of the President, Dr. Trinidad H. Pardo de Tavera, Señor Don Benito Legarda and Señor Don José Luzuriaga. The introduction into the legislature of representative Filipinos, educated and able, will materially assist the Commission in its work by their intimate knowledge of the people and of local prejudices and conditions. On September first, also, the executive branch of the insular government will be rendered more efficient by the establishment of four executive departments. There will be a department of the interior, of which Commissioner Dean C. Worcester will be head; a department of commerce and police, of which Commissioner Luke E. Wright will be the head; a department of justice and finance, of which Commissioner Henry C. Ide will be the head, and a department of public instruction, of which Commissioner Bernard Moses will be the head. The foregoing announcements are made by direction of the Secretary of War.

Since the above was written, in confirmation of the statement of the President's purposes with respect to the people of these Islands, I have this morning received the following telegram from the President of the United States:

Washington, July 3—3.45 p.m.

Taft, *Manila:*

Upon the assumption of your new duties as civil governor of the Philippine Islands I have great pleasure in sending congratulations to you and your associate commissioners and my thanks for the good work already accomplished. I extend to you my full confidence and best wishes for still greater success in the larger responsibilities now devolved upon you, and the assurance not only for myself but for my countrymen of good will for the people of the Islands, and the hope that their participation in the government which it is our purpose to develop among them, may lead to their highest advancement, happiness and prosperity.

William McKinley.

The extent of the work which the Commission has done in organizing civil governments in towns and provinces is considerable, but its scope and effect may easily be exaggerated by those not fully acquainted with the situation. Twenty-seven provinces have been organized under the general provincial act; but it has not been possible to fill the important office of supervisor in eight or nine of them because a supervisor must be a civil engineer. We have sent to America for competent persons, whose arrival we look for this month. As the supervisor is one of the three members of the governing provincial board, his absence necessarily cripples the administration. Of the twenty-seven provinces organized, four, possibly five and small parts of two others in which armed insurrection continues, will remain under the executive jurisdiction of the military governor and commanding general. There are sixteen provinces or districts in which there is entire freedom from insurrection which the Commission has not had time to organize. Of the unorganized provinces and districts, including Mindoro and Paragua, the latter just occupied by the army, there are four that are not ready for civil government. In the organized provinces nearly all the towns have been organized under the municipal code; and some towns have been similarly organized in unorganized provinces. It was not supposed that either the municipal code or the provincial government act would form perfect governments, though it was possible to make the former much more complete than the latter, for there had been two experiments in municipal government under the administration of General Otis and General McArthur before the Commission began its legislative work. The provincial government act was tentative. The result of the southern trip of the Commission was a substantial amendment and there will doubtless be others. Government is a practical, not a theoretical, problem and the successful application of a new system to a people like this must be brought about by observing closely the operation of simple laws and making changes or additions as experience shows their necessity. The enactment of the law in its first form and appointments under it are but one of several steps in a successful organization.

The conditions under which the municipal and provincial governments of the Islands are to have their first real test are trying. The four years' war has pauperized many, and its indirect effect in destroying the habits of industry of those who have been prevented from working in the fields, or who have been leading the irresponsible life of guerrillas, is even more disastrous. Not only war, but also the death from disease of a large percentage of the carabaos which are indispensable to the cultivation of rice and are greatly needed in all agriculture, has largely reduced the acreage of rice and other staple products. Then the pest of locusts has been very severe. In one province, and perhaps more, gaunt famine may have to be reckoned with. Poverty and suffering in a country where ladronism has always existed are sure to make ladrones.

With the change made today, the civil governments must prepare to stand alone and not depend on the army to police the provinces and towns. The concentration of the army in larger garrisons where, in cases of emergency only, they can be called on to assist the local police may be expected; but the people must be enabled by organization of native police under proper and reliable commanders to defend themselves against the turbulent and vicious of their own communities.

The withdrawal of the army from the discharge of quasi-civil duties of police will be accompanied also by the ceasing of the jurisdiction of military commissions to try ordinary criminal cases. They have been most useful in punishing and repressing crime. We have enacted a judiciary law and appointed judges under it who will succeed to this work. But the adoption of a new civil code of procedure, a new criminal code and code of procedure, all of which are ready, may be delayed somewhat by the needed public discussion of them. Until they are all adopted, we shall not feel that the chief step has been taken toward securing the blessings of civil liberty to the people of the pacified provinces, the protection of life, liberty and property.

The difficulties of official communication between provinces on the sea and between towns of the same province similarly situated must be met by a properly organized fleet of small steamers or launches which shall, at the same time, assist in the revenue or postal service. Provincial governments, in many cases, without such means of communicating with their numerous towns, are greatly impeded in their functions.

Congress, in its wisdom, has delayed until its next session provision for the sale of public lands, of mining rights and the granting of franchises. All are necessary to give the country the benefit of American and foreign enterprise and the opportunity of lucrative labor to the people. Commercial railroads, street railroads, mortgage-loan companies or land banks and steamship companies only await Government sanction to spring into being. These may remedy the poverty and suffering that a patient people have now to bear.

The school system is hardly begun as an organized machine. One thousand American teachers will arrive in the next three months. They must not only teach English in the schools, but they must teach the Filipino teachers. Schoolhouses are yet to be built; schoolrooms are yet to be equipped. Our most satisfactory ground for hope of success in our whole work is in the eagerness with which the Philippine people, even the humblest, seek for education.

Then there is another kind of education of adults to which we look with confidence. It is that which comes from observation of the methods by which Americans in office discharge their duties. Upon Americans who accept office under the civil government is imposed the responsibility of reaching the highest American standard of official duty. Whenever an American fails; whenever he allows himself to use his official position for private ends, even though it does not involve actual defalcation or the stealing of public property or money, he is recreant to his trust in a far higher degree than he would be were he to commit the same offense in a similar office at home. Here he is the representative of the great Republic among a people untutored in the methods of free and honest government, and in so far as he fails in his duty, he vindicates the objection of those who have forcibly resisted our taking control of these Islands and weakens the claim we make that we are here to secure good government for the Philippines.

The operation of the civil-service Act and the rules adopted for its enforcement have been the subject of some criticism; but I think that when they are fully understood, and when the Filipino, in seeking a position in executive offices where English is the only language spoken, fits himself, as he will with his aptness for learning languages, in English, he will have nothing to complain of either in the justice of the examination and its marking or in the equality of salaries between him and Americans doing the same work. The civil-service Act is the bulwark of honesty and efficiency in the government. It avoids the most marked evil of American politics, the spoils system. Without it success in solving our problem would be entirely impossible. Complaints of its severity and its unfortunate operation in individual instances may give plausibility to attack upon it, but those who are responsible for appointments can not be blinded to the fact that its preservation is absolutely essential to the welfare of these Islands.

If I have understood the decision of the Supreme Court in the recent so-called Puerto Rico cases, the question of what duties shall be levied on imports into these Islands from the United States and on exports from these Islands into the United States is committed to the discretion of Congress. Without assuming to express an opinion on the much-mooted issue of constitutional law involved, I venture to say that the result is most beneficial to the people of these Islands. It seems to me that a decision that the same tariff was in force in these Islands as in the United States, and must always be so, would have been detrimental to the interests of the Islands. They are 7,000 miles from the coast of the United States. The conditions prevailing in them are as different as possible from those in the United States. The application to them of a high protective tariff carefully prepared to meet trade and the manufacturing conditions in the United States would have been a great hardship. It is true that to sugar and tobacco planters would have been opened a fine market, but it would have greatly reduced all trade between the Philippines and China and other Oriental countries and all European countries, and it would have necessitated a heavy internal tax to pay the expenses of the central government. Now the people may reasonably entertain the hope that Congress will give them a tariff here suited to the best development of business in the Islands, and may infer from the liberal treatment accorded in its legislation to Puerto Rican products imported into the United States that Philippine products will have equally favorable consideration.

The finances of the insular government are at present in a satisfactory condition, though changes in laws made or about to be made may affect them considerably. There is now in the insular treasury a sum of money exceeding $3,700,000 in gold unappropriated. The engineers in the Manila harbor work have been authorized to make contracts involving a liability of $2,000,000 beyond the $1,000,000 already appropriated, but this is the only liability of the government and it will not accrue for two years at least. The insular income, which is now about $10,000,000, gold, a year, is likely to be reduced more than $1,000,000 by the provision of the provincial act which applies the proceeds of the internal-revenue taxes to the support of the provincial governments. Moreover, a new customs tariff is soon to be put in force, the immediate result of which may be to reduce the total amount of duties collected. It reduces the import tax on necessities and increases it on luxuries and roughly approximates, as nearly as a tariff of specific duties can, to a purely revenue tariff of 25 percent ad valorem. In addition to this, the cost of the insular government is bound to increase as the establishment of peace and civil government is extended through the Archipelago and the skeleton bureaus and departments now recognized in the law are enlarged and given a normal usefulness. Still the increase of business due to returning peace and prosperity will doubtless keep pace with the needs of the government.

The conduct of the civil and military branches of a military government under independent hands is necessarily a delicate matter. It depends, as the President in his instructions says, upon the fullest coöperation between the military and the civil arms, and I am glad to be able to say that I believe that there will be the same coöperation in the future as there has been in the past; that the possible friction which may arise between the subordinates of the respective arms will have no encouragement from those in whom is the ultimate responsibility. There is work enough and to spare for all who are concerned in the regeneration of these Islands.

The burden of the responsibility which, by taking the oath this day administered to me, I assume, I shall not dwell upon, except to say that no one, I think, realizes it more keenly than I do. While I am profoundly grateful to the President of the United States for the personal trust he has expressed in appointing me to this high office, it is with no exultant spirit of confidence that I take up the new duties and new task assigned to me. I must rely, as I do, upon the coöperation, energy, ability and fidelity to their trust of those with whom I am to share the responsibility now to be presented, upon the sympathetic and patriotic patience of those educated Filipino people who have already rendered us such tremendous aid, and upon the consciousness that earnest effort and honest purpose, with a saving of common sense, have in the past solved problems as new, as threatening and as difficult as the one before us.

The high and sacred obligation to give protection for property and life, civil and religious freedom and wise and unselfish guidance in the paths of peace and prosperity to all the people of the Philippine Islands is charged upon us, his representatives, by the President of the United States. May we not be recreant to this charge which, he truly says, concerns the honor and conscience of our country. He expresses the firm hope that through our "labors all the inhabitants of the Philippine Islands may come to look back with gratitude to the day when God gave victory to American arms at Manila and set their land under the sovereignty and protection of the people of the United States." God grant that in spite of all the trials and perplexities, the disappointments and difficulties, with which we are sure to be confronted, we may live to see this fervent hope made a living fact in the hearts of a patriotic people linked within the indissoluble ties of affection to our common and beloved country.

2

The Inauguration of
the Philippine Assembly

Manila, Philippine Islands, October 16, 1907

Gentlemen of the Assembly: President Roosevelt has sent me to convey to you and the Filipino people his congratulations upon another step in the enlargement of popular self-government in these Islands. I have the greatest personal pleasure in being the bearer of this message. It is intended for each and every member of the Assembly, no matter what his views upon the issues which were presented in the late electoral campaign. It assumes that he is loyal to the government in which he now proposes, under oath of allegiance, to take part. It does not assume that he may not have a wish to bring about, either soon or in the far future, by peaceable means, a transfer of sovereignty; but it does assume that while the present government endures, he will loyally do all he lawfully can to uphold its authority and to make it useful to the Filipino people.

I am aware that, in view of the issues discussed at the election of this Assembly, I am expected to say something regarding the policy of the United States toward these Islands. Before attempting any such task, it is well to make clear the fact that I can not speak with the authority of one who may control that policy.

The Philippine Islands are territory belonging to the United States, and by the Constitution, the branch of that Government vested with the power, and charged with the duty, of making rules and regulations for their government is Congress. The policy to be pursued with respect to them is, therefore, ultimately for Congress to determine. Of course, in the act establishing a government for the Philippine Islands passed by Congress July 1, 1902, wide discretion has been vested in the President to shape affairs in the Islands, within the limitations of the act, through the appointment of the Governor and the Commission, and the power of the Secretary of War to supervise their work and to veto proposed legislation; but not only is the transfer of sovereignty to an independent government of the Filipino people wholly within the jurisdiction of Congress, but so also is the extension of any popular political control in the present government beyond that conferred in the organic act. It is embarrassing, therefore, for me, though I am charged with direct supervision of the Islands under the President, to deal in any way with issues relating to their ultimate disposition. It is true that the peculiar development of the government of the Islands under American sovereignty has given to the attitude of the President upon such issues rather more significance than in most matters of exclusively Congressional cognizance. After the exchange of ratifications of the treaty of Paris in April of 1899, and until the organic act of July 1, 1902, Congress acquiesced in the government of the Islands by the President as Commander in Chief of the Army and Navy without interference, and when it passed the organic act it not only confirmed in every respect the anomalous quasi-civil government which he had created, but it also made his instructions to the Secretary of War part of its statute, and followed therein his recommendation as to future extensions of popular political control. This close adherence of Congress to the views of the Executive in respect to the Islands in the past gives ground for ascribing to Congress approval of the Philippine policy, as often declared by President McKinley and President Roosevelt. Still, I have no authority to speak for Congress in respect to the ultimate disposition of the Islands. I can only express an opinion as one familiar with the circumstances likely to affect Congress, in the light of its previous statutory action.

The avowed policy of the National Administration under these two

Presidents has been and is to govern the Islands, having regard to the interest and welfare of the Filipino people, and by the spread of general primary and industrial education and by practice in partial political control to fit the people themselves to maintain a stable and well-ordered government affording equality of right and opportunity to all citizens. The policy looks to the improvement of the people both industrially and in self-governing capacity. As this policy of extending control continues, it must logically reduce and finally end the sovereignty of the United States in the Islands, unless it shall seem wise to the American and the Filipino peoples, on account of mutually beneficial trade relations and possible advantage to the Islands in their foreign relations, that the bond shall not be completely severed.

How long this process of political preparation of the Filipino people is likely to be is a question which no one can certainly answer. When I was in the Islands the last time, I ventured the opinion that it would take considerably longer than a generation. I have not changed my view upon this point; but the issue is one upon which opinions differ. However this may be, I believe that the policy of the Administration as outlined above is as definite as the policy of any government in a matter of this kind can safely be made. We are engaged in working out a great experiment. No other nation has attempted it, and for us to fix a certain number of years in which the experiment must become a success and be completely realized would be, in my judgment, unwise. As I premised, however, this is a question for settlement by the Congress of the United States.

Our Philippine policy has been subjected to the severest condemnation by critics who occupy points of view as widely apart as the two poles. There are those who say that we have gone too fast, that we have counted on the capacity of the Filipino for political development with a foolish confidence leading to what they regard as the disastrous result of this election. There are others who assert that we have denied the Filipino that which is every man's birthright—to govern himself—and have been guilty of tyranny and a violation of American principles in not turning the government over to the people of the Islands at once.

With your permission, I propose to consider our policy in the light of the events of the six years during which it has been pursued, to array the difficulties of the situation which we have had to meet and to mention in some detail what has been accomplished.

The Civil Government was inaugurated in 1901 before the close of a war between the forces of the United States and the controlling elements of the Philippine people. It had sufficient popular support to overawe many of those whose disposition was friendly to the Americans. In various provinces the war was continued intermittently for a year after the appointment of a Civil Governor in July, 1901. This was not an auspicious beginning for the organization of a people into a peaceful community acknowledging allegiance to an alien power.

Secondly, there was, in the United States, a strong minority party that lost no opportunity to denounce the policy of the Government and to express sympathy with those arrayed in arms against it, and declared in party platform and in other ways its intention, should it come into power, to turn the Islands over to an independent government of their people. This not only prolonged the war, but when peace finally came, it encouraged a sullenness on the part of many Filipinos and a lack of interest in the progress and development of the existing government, that were discouraging. It offered the hope of immediate independence at the coming of every national election by the defeat of the Administration at the polls. This was not of assistance in carrying out a policy that depended for its working on the political education of the people by their cordial participation, first, in the new municipal and provincial governments, and finally in the election of a National Assembly. The result has been that during the educational process there has been a continuing controversy as to the political capacity of the Filipino people. It has naturally been easy to induce a majority of the electorate to believe that they are now capable of maintaining a stable government. All this has tended to divert the people's attention from the existing government, although their useful participation in that must measure their progress toward fitness for complete autonomy.

The impatience of the popular majority for further power may be somewhat mitigated as the extent of the political control which is placed in the hands of the people increases, and as they become more familiar with the responsibilities and the difficulties of actual power. The difference between the attitude of an irresponsible critic who has behind him the easily aroused prejudices of a people against an alien government, and that of one who attempts to formulate legislation which shall accomplish a definite purpose for the good of his own people, is a healthful lesson for the ambitious statesman to learn.

Other formidable political obstacles had to be overcome. There still remained present in the situation in 1901 the smoldering ashes of the issues which had led the people to rebel against the power of Spain—I mean the prospective continuance of the influence of the regular religious orders in the parochial administration of the Roman Catholic Church in the Islands and their ownership of most valuable and extensive agricultural lands in the most populous provinces. The change of sovereignty to a Government which could exercise no control over the Church in its selection of its agents made the new régime powerless, by act or decree, to prevent the return of the friars to the parishes, and yet the people were disposed to hold the Government responsible whenever this was proposed. It would have been fraught with great danger of political disturbance. It was also essential that the religious orders should cease to be agricultural landlords in order to eliminate the agrarian question arising between them and sixty thousand tenants which had played so large a part in the previous insurrections against Spain. These results were to be attained without offending, or infringing upon the rights of, the Roman Catholic Church, the influence of which for good in the Islands could not be denied. Other political difficulties attending the transfer of a sovereignty from a Government in which the interests of the State and the Church were inextricably united to one in which they must be absolutely separated, I need not stop to elaborate. The religious and property controversies arising out of the Aglipayan schism, and the disturbances caused, added much to the burden of the Government.

The novelty of the task for the United States and her people, the lack of the existence of a trained body of colonial administrators and civil servants, the dependence for a time upon men as government agents who had come out in a spirit of adventure to the Islands and some of whom proved not to be fitted either by character or experience for the discharge of responsible public duties, gave additional cause for discouragement.

Another great difficulty in working out our policy in these Islands has been the reluctance of capitalists to invest money here. Political privileges, if unaccompanied by opportunities to better their condition, are not likely to produce permanent contentment among a people. Hence the political importance of developing the resources of these Islands for the benefit of its inhabitants. This can only be done by attracting capital. Capital must have the prospect of security in the investment and a certain return of profit before it will become available. The constant agitation for independence in the Islands, apparently supported by the minority party in the United States, and the well-founded fear that an independent Philippine government now established would not be permanent and stable have made capitalists chary of attempting to develop the natural resources of the Islands. The capital which has come has only come reluctantly and on terms less favorable to the public than would have been exacted under other conditions.

Another difficulty of the same character as the last in preventing material progress has been the failure of Congress to open the markets of the United States to the free admission of Philippine sugar and tobacco. In every other way Congress has shown its entire and generous sympathy with the policy of the Administration; and in this matter the popular branch of that body passed the requisite bill for the purpose by a large majority. Certain tobacco and sugar interests of the United States, however, succeeded in strangling the measure in the Senate committee. I have good reason for hope that in the next Congress we may be able to secure a compromise measure which shall restore the sugar and tobacco agriculture of the Islands to its former prosperity, and at the same time by limitations upon the amounts of importation allay the fears of injury on the part of the opponents of the measure. Still, the delay in this much-needed relief has greatly retarded the coming of prosperous times and has much discouraged supporters of our policy in America who have thought this indicated a lack of national purpose to make the present altruistic policy a success.

But the one thing that interfered with material progress in the Islands, more than all other causes put together, was the rinderpest which carried away from 75 to 80 percent of the cattle that were absolutely indispensable in cultivating, reaping and disposing of the agricultural products upon which the Islands are wholly dependent. The extent of this terrible disaster can not be exaggerated and the Islands have not yet recovered from it. Attempts to remedy the evil by the importation of cattle from other countries have proved futile, and the Islands can not be made whole in this respect except by the natural reproduction of the small fraction of the animals that escaped destruction. This is not a matter of a year, or of two years or of three years, but a matter of a decade. Then, too, there were in these years surra, locusts, drought, destructive typhoons, cholera, bubonic plague and smallpox, ladronism and pulajanism. The long period of disturbance, of guerrilla warfare and unrest, which interfered for years with the carrying on of the peaceful arts of agriculture and made it so easy for those who had been used to work in the fields to assume the wild and loose life of predatory bands claiming to be liberating armies, all made a burden for the community that it was almost impossible for it to bear.

When I consider all these difficulties, which I have rehearsed at too great length, and then take account of the present conditions in the Islands, it seems to me that they present an occasion for profound satisfaction and that they fully vindicate the policy which has been pursued.

How have we met the difficulties? In the first place, we have carried out with entire fidelity the promises of Presidents McKinley and Roosevelt in respect to the gradual extension of political control in the Government as the people should show themselves fit. In 1901 the Commission adopted the Municipal Code, which vested complete autonomy in the adult male citizens of every municipality in the Islands, except that of Manila, which for special reasons, like those which have prevailed with respect to the government of the city of Washington, was preserved for control by the Central Government. The electorate was limited to those who could speak English or Spanish, or who paid a tax of P15 a year, or who had filled municipal office under the Spanish régime, and did not exceed 20 percent of the total adult males of the population. Very shortly after this a form of provincial government was established in which the legislative and executive control of the province was largely vested in a provincial board consisting of a governor and treasurer and supervisor. Provision was made for the election of a governor and the appointment under civil-service rules of a treasurer and supervisor. Subsequently it was found that the government was too expensive and the office of supervisor was finally abolished, and after some four years the board was made to consist of a governor and treasurer, and a third member elected as the governor was, thus effecting popular autonomy in the provincial governments. And now comes the Assembly.

It is said by one set of critics, to whom I have already referred, that the franchise is the last privilege that ought to be granted in the development of a people into a self-governing community, and that we have put this into the hands of the Filipinos before they have shown themselves to be industrially and in other ways capable of exercising the self-restraint and conservatism of action which are essential to political stability. I can not agree with this view. The best political education is practice in the exercise of political power, unless the subject is so ignorant as to be wholly blind to his own interests. Hence the exercise of a franchise which is conferred only on those who have qualifications of education or property that prove intelligence and substance, is likely to teach the electorate useful political lessons. The electorate under the Philippine law are sufficiently alive to their own interests to make the exercise of political power a useful training for them, while the power to be exercised is subject to such limitation as not to be dangerous to the community. More than this, the granting of the franchise was most useful in producing tranquillity among the people. The policy has been vindicated by the fact.

The importance of the agency of the Army of the United States in suppressing insurrection I would not minimize in the least; but all who remember clearly the succession of events from 1901 to 1903 will admit that the return to peace and the acquiescence of the Filipino people in American sovereignty were greatly influenced and aided by the prospect held out to the Filipinos of participation in the government of the Islands and a gradual extension of popular self-control. Without this and the confidence of the Filipino people in the good purposes of the United States and the patience with which they endured their many burdens that fate seemed to increase, the progress which has been achieved would have been impossible.

Let us consider in some detail what progress has been made:

First. To repeat what I have said, the Islands are in a state of tranquillity. On this very day of the opening of the National Assembly, there has never been a time in the history of the Islands when peace and good order have prevailed more generally. The difficulties presented by the controversies arising with and concerning the Roman Catholic Church have either been completely settled or are in process of satisfactory adjustment on a basis of justice and equity.

Second. Most noteworthy progress has been made in the spread of general education. One of the obstacles to the development of this people speaking half a dozen or more different native dialects was a lack of a common language, which would furnish a medium of sympathetic touch with modern thought and civilization. The dense ignorance of a very large proportion of the people emphasized the necessity for a general educational system. English was the language of the sovereign power, English was the business language of the Orient, English was the language in which was thought and written the history of free institutions and popular government, and English was the language to which the common people turned with eagerness to learn. A system of education was built up, and today upward of half a million children are being taught to read, write and recite English. It is not an exaggeration to assert that now more native Filipinos speak English than Spanish, although Spanish was the language of the ruling race in these Islands for more than two hundred and fifty years. English is not so beautiful as the Spanish language, but it is more likely to prove of use to the Filipinos for the reasons I have given. The strongest basis for our confidence in the future of the Filipino people is the eagerness with which the opportunities extended for education in English have been seized by the poor and ignorant parents of these Islands for their children. It is alike pathetic and encouraging.

I am not one of those who believe that much of the public money should be expended here for university or advanced education. Perhaps one institution merely to form a type of higher education may be established at Manila or at some other suitable place in the Islands, and special schools to develop needed scientific professions may be useful, but the great part of the public funds expended for education should be used in the spread of primary education and of industrial education—that education which shall fit young men to be good farmers, good mechanics, good skilled laborers, and shall teach them the dignity of labor and that it is no disgrace for the son of a good family to learn his trade and earn his livelihood by it. The higher education is well for those who can use it to advantage, but it too often fits a man to do things for which there is no demand, and unfits him for work which there are too few to do. The enlargement of opportunity for higher education may well await private beneficence or be postponed to a period when the calls upon the Island Treasury for other more important improvements have ceased. We have laid the foundation of a primary and industrial educational system here which, if the same spirit continues in the Government, will prove to be the most lasting benefit which has been conferred on these Islands by Americans.

Third. We have introduced here a health department which is gradually teaching the people the necessity for sanitation. In the years to come, when the great discoveries of the world are recited, that which will appear to have played as large a part as any in the world's progress in the current hundred years will be the discovery of proper sanitary methods for avoiding disease in the Tropics. The introduction of such methods, the gradual teaching of the people the simple facts affecting hygiene, unpopular and difficult as the process of education has been, will prove to be another one of the great benefits given by Americans to this people.

The efforts of the Government have not been confined to preserving the health of the human inhabitants of these Islands, but have been properly extended to doing what can be done in the matter of the health of the domestic animals which is so indispensable to the material progress of the Islands. The destruction by rinderpest, by surra, and by other diseases to which cattle and horses are subject, I have already dwelt upon. Most earnest attention has been given by men of the highest scientific attainment to securing some remedy which will make such widespread disasters in the future impossible. Much time and effort and money have been spent and much has been accomplished in this matter. The people are being educated in the necessity for care of their cattle and for inviting in public aid at once when the dread rinderpest shows its presence. Serums have been discovered that have been effective to immunize cattle, and while the disease has not disappeared, it is not too much to say that such an epidemic as that which visited the Islands in 1900, 1901 and 1902 is impossible.

Fourth. A judicial system has been established in the Islands which has taught the Filipinos the possibility of the independence of a judiciary. This must be of enduring good to the people of the Islands. The personnel of the judges is divided between Americans and Filipinos, both for the purpose of aiding the Americans to learn and administer civil law and of enabling the Filipinos to learn and administer justice according to a system prevailing in a country where the judiciary is absolutely independent of the executive or legislative branches of the Government. Charges have been made that individual judges and particular courts have not been free from executive control and have not been without prejudices arising from the race of the particular judge who sat in the court, but on the whole an impartial review of the six years' history of the administration of justice will show that the system has been productive of the greatest good and that right has been sustained without fear or favor. It is entirely natural that a system which departs from the principles of that in which one has been educated should at times attract his severe animadversion, and as the system here administered partakes of two systems, it is subject to the criticism of those trained in each.

Another agency in the administration of justice has been the Constabulary. When I was here something more than two years ago, the complaints against that body were numerous, emphatic and bitter. I promised, on behalf of the Philippine government and the Washington Administration, that close investigation should be made into the complaints and that if there was occasion for reform, that reform would be carried out. It gratifies me on my return to the Islands now to learn that a change has come, that the complaints against the Constabulary have entirely ceased, and that it is now conceded to be discharging with efficiency the function which it was chiefly created to perform, of sympathetically aiding the provincial governors and municipal authorities of the Islands in maintaining the peace of each province and each municipality, and that there is a thorough spirit of coöperation between the officers and men of the Constabulary and the local authorities.

In respect to the administration of justice by justices of the peace, reforms have been effected, but I am not sure that there is not still great room for improvement. This is one of the things that come home close to the people of the country and is a subject that will doubtless address itself to the wise action and consideration of the National Assembly.

Fifth. We come to the matter of public improvements. The port of Manila has been made into a harbor which is now as secure as any in the Orient, and which, with the docking facilities that are now being rapidly constructed, will be as convenient and as free from charge and burden as any along the Asiatic coast. The improvements in Iloilo and Cebu harbors, the other two important ports of the Islands, are also rapidly progressing. Road building has proceeded in the Islands, both at the instance of the

Central Government and through the agency of the provinces. The difficulties of road building and road maintaining in the Philippines are little understood by those not familiar with the difficulty of securing proper material to resist the enormous wear and tear caused by the torrential downpours of the rainy season. Progress in this direction must necessarily be gradual, for the Islands are a poor country, comparatively speaking, and roads are expensive.

Early in the history of the Islands we began the construction of a road from Pangasinan to the mountains of Benguet in order to bring within the reach of the people of the Islands that healthful region where the thermometer varies from 40 to 80 degrees, and in which all the diseases of the Tropics are much more easily subject to cure than in the lowlands. Had it been supposed that the road thus to be constructed would involve an expense of nearly two millions of dollars, the work would not have been begun, but, now that the road has been constructed, I would not undo what has been done even if it were possible. As time progresses, the whole Province of Benguet will be settled; there will be made the home of many educational institutions, of many sanitariums, and there will go, as transportation becomes cheaper, the Filipino people to obtain a change of air and acquire a renewed strength that is given to tropical peoples by a visit to the temperate zone.

When the Americans came to the Islands there was one railroad 120 miles long, and that was all. In spite of circumstances, which I have already detailed, making capital reluctant to come here, contracts have now been entered into, that are in the course of fulfillment, which in five years will give to the Islands a railroad mileage of 1,000 miles. The construction of these roads will involve the investment of twenty to thirty millions of dollars, and that in itself means an added prosperity to the country, additional demands for labor, and the quickening of all the nerves of trade. When the work is finished, it means a great additional profit to agriculture, a very great enlargement of the export capacity of the Islands, and a substantial elevation of the material condition of the people.

In the matter of municipal improvements, which directly concern the people, that which has taken place in Manila is most prominent. The improvement of the streets, the introduction of a satisfactory street railway system 35 miles in length, the improvement of the general appearance of the city and its hygienic condition, the construction of new waterworks and a new sewage system, all strike one who knew the city in 1900. The improvements of other municipalities in the Islands have not kept pace with those in Manila, and of course they were not so imperatively needed; but the epidemics of cholera and plague and smallpox which have prevailed have convinced those in authority of the necessity of bettering the water supply of all municipalities and for improving this by the sinking of artesian wells and other means, so that bad water, that frightful source of the transmission of disease, should be reduced to a minimum.

The government now maintains and operates a more complete system of posts, telephones and telegraphs than ever before in the history of the Islands. Seventy-five percent of the 652 municipalities now established in these Islands have post-offices, in 235 of which there are now opened for business postal savings banks. The telegraph or telephone now connects all of the provincial capitals with Manila and more than 90 offices are now open for business. Appropriation has been made to provide for a system of rural free delivery. In less than one year of operation the Postal Savings Bank has deposits exceeding 600,000 pesos, and the number of Filipino depositors now exceeds 1,000, and the proportion of their deposits is steadily increasing.

Sixth. We have inaugurated a civil service law for the selection of civil servants upon the merit system. On the whole it has worked well. It has grown with our experience and has improved with the disclosure of its defects.

One of the burning questions which constantly presents itself in respect to the civil service of a Government like this is, how far it shall be American and how far Filipino. In the outset it was essential that most of the civil servants of the government should be Americans. The government was English speaking, and the practical difficulty of having subordinates who did not speak that language prevented large employment of Filipinos. Then their lack of knowledge of American governmental and business methods had the same tendency. The avowed policy of the government has been to employ Filipinos wherever, as between them and Americans, the Filipinos can do equally good work. This has given rise to frequent and bitter criticism, because it has been improperly assumed that every time there has been a vacancy, it could be filled by a Filipino. There are two great advantages in the employment of Filipinos—one is that this is the government of the Filipinos and they ought to be employed where they can be, and the other is that their employment is a matter of economy for the government, because they are able to live more cheaply and economically in the Islands than Americans and so can afford to receive less salary. There has therefore been a constant reduction of American employees and an increase of Filipinos. This has not been without its disadvantage because it makes competent American employees feel an uncertainty of tenure, and materially affects their hope of promotion and their interest in the government of which they are a part. This disadvantage I believe can be largely obviated.

There are many American civil servants in this government who have rendered most loyal, difficult and efficient service, in season and out of season, through plague and epidemic, in sickness and in health, in full sympathy with the purposes and policy of the government. Without them our government would have been a complete failure. They will never receive adequate reward. Their interest in their work has prevented their return to their native land, where the same energy and efficiency would have earned them large return. They are most valuable public servants who have done a work that, had they done it in the English colonial service or at home, would have been certain to secure to them a permanent salary and entire freedom from anxiety as to the future. I would be glad to see adopted a system of permanent tenure and retirement on pensions for the small and higher classes of civil employees. Their continuance in the government indefinitely is a public necessity. I sincerely hope the Philippine Assembly will exhibit its spirit of justice and public interest to the point of concurring in such a measure even though this, at present, will be of benefit to more Americans than Filipinos.

Seventh. In the progress which has been made, I should mention the land system, the provision for homestead settlement, for free patents, and for perfecting of imperfect titles by land registration. The homestead settlements under the law were very few for several years, but I am delighted to learn that during 1907 they reached 4,000 and the free patents applied for were 10,600. It is probable that the machinery for land registration, though necessary, is too expensive, and it will be for you to decide whether, in view of the great public benefit that good land titles will bring to the country, it may not be wise to reduce the cost of registration to the landowner and charge the expense to the government. Capital will not be advanced to the farmer unless his title is good, and the great benefit of an agricultural bank can never be realized until the registration of titles is greatly increased.

This naturally brings me to the subject of the Agricultural Bank. After much effort Congress was induced to pass an act which authorizes the Philippine Government to invite the organization of such a bank with private capital by guaranteeing an annual income of a certain percentage on the capital invested for thirty years. Negotiations have been opened and are pending with some American capitalists in the hope of securing the establishment of such a bank.

The condition of agriculture in the Islands, while generally much improved in the last three years, is still unsatisfactory in many parts of the Islands, due not only to the continued scarcity of cattle but also to the destructive effect of the typhoon of 1905 upon the hemp culture. This has properly led to the suspension of the land tax for another year and the meeting of half the deficit in provincial and municipal treasuries thus produced, out of the central treasury.

The production of rice has, however, materially increased. It is also a source of satisfaction to note that the exports from the Islands, which are wholly agricultural, are larger in value by half a million gold dollars than ever in the history of the Islands. One of the chief duties of this Assembly is to devote its attention and practical knowledge to measures for the relief of agriculture.

Eighth. The financial condition of the Philippine government is quite satisfactory, and so, too, is the state of the money and currency of the Islands. There is a bonded indebtedness for the purchase of the friar lands amounting to $7,000,000, for the waterworks and sewage of Manila of $3,000,000, and for public works amounting to $3,500,000. Sinking funds have been established for all of these. The price paid for the friar lands was a round one and may result, after the lands are disposed of, in some net pecuniary loss to the Government, but the political benefit of the purchase was a full justification. The lands will be disposed of to the tenants as rapidly as the public interest will permit. The only other permanent obligation of the government is the contingent liability on the guaranty of interest for thirty years on the bonds issued to construct 300 miles of railroad in the

Visayas. We may reasonably hope that this obligation will soon reduce itself to nothing when the roads come into successful operation. The Governor-General reports to me that the budget for 1908 will show an income and surplus from last year, without any land tax, from which it will be possible to pay all the interest on the bonds and guaranties, all the insular expenses, the proper part of the expenses of Manila, $2,000,000 in permanent improvements, and still have on hand for contingencies $1,000,000. I am further advised that the condition of most of the provinces is excellent in respect to income and surplus.

It has been necessary to reduce the silver in the Philippine peso to keep its intrinsic value within the value of 50 cents, gold, at which it is the duty of the government to maintain it, and this change is being rapidly carried through without much difficulty. The benefit to the people, and especially the poorer and working classes, in the establishment of the gold standard is very great. It eliminates a gambling feature from the business of the Islands that always worked for the detriment of the Philippine people. We are just carrying through a settlement with the Spanish-Filipino Bank which I hope will provide a means of safely adding to the currency of the country and increasing its elasticity.

In recounting these various evidences of progress in the last six years, I am not unmindful that the business of the Islands is still far from prosperous. Indeed, it is noteworthy that so much progress has been made in the face of continued business depression due to the various causes I have elsewhere enumerated; but it is a long lane that has no turning and I look forward to the next decade in the history of the Islands as one which will be as prosperous as this one has been the reverse. Business is reviving, the investment of foreign capital is gradually increasing and only one thing is needed to insure great material improvement, and that is the continuance of conservatism in this Government. I feel confident that the inauguration of this Assembly, instead of ending this conservatism as the prophets of evil would have it, will strengthen it.

Before discussing the Assembly, I wish to give attention to one report that has been spread to the four corners of the globe, and which, if credited, might have a pernicious effect in these Islands. I refer to the statement that the American Government is about to sell the Islands to some Asiatic or

European power. Those who credit such a report little understand the motives which actuated the American people in accepting the burden of this Government. The majority of the American people are still in favor of carrying out our Philippine policy as a great altruistic work. They have no selfish object to secure. There might be a grim and temporary satisfaction to those of us who have been subjected to severe criticism for our alleged lack of liberality toward the Filipino people and of sympathy with their aspirations, in witnessing the rigid governmental control which would be exercised over the people of the Islands under the colonial policy of any one of the powers to whom it is suggested that we are about to sell them; but that would not excuse or justify the gross violation, by such a sale, of the implied obligation which we have entered into with the Filipino people. That obligation presents only two alternatives for us—one is a permanent maintenance of a popular government of law and order under American control, and the other, a parting with such control to the people of the Islands themselves after they have become fitted to maintain a government in which the right of all the inhabitants to life, liberty and property shall be secure. I do not hesitate to pronounce the report that the Government contemplates the transfer of these Islands to any foreign power as utterly without foundation. It has never entered the mind of a single person in the Government responsible for the Administration. Such a sale must be the subject of a treaty, and the treaty power in the Government of the United States is exercised by the President and the Senate, and only upon the initiative of the President. Hence an Executive declaration upon this subject is more authoritative than an Executive opinion as to probable Congressional action.

Coming now to the real occasion of this celebration, the installation of the National Assembly, I wish, for purposes of clearness, to read the section of the organic act under which this Assembly has been elected:

That two years after the completion and publication of the census, in case such condition of general and complete peace with recognition of the authority of the United States shall have continued in the territory of said Islands not inhabited by Moros or other non-Christian tribes and such facts shall have been certified to the President by the Philippine Commission, the President upon being satisfied thereof shall direct said Commission to call, and the Commission shall call, a general election for the choice of delegates to a popular assembly of the people of said Territory in the Philippine Islands, which shall be known as the Philippine Assembly. After said Assembly shall have convened and organized, all the legislative power heretofore conferred on the Philippine Commission in all that part of said Islands not inhabited by Moros or other non-Christian tribes shall be vested in a legislature consisting of two houses—the Philippine Commission and the Philippine Assembly. Said Assembly shall consist of not less than fifty nor more than one hundred members, to be apportioned by said Commission among the provinces as nearly as practicable according to population: *Provided*, That no province shall have less than one member: *And provided further*, That provinces entitled by population to more than one member may be divided into such convenient districts as the said Commission may deem best.

Public notice of such division shall be given at least ninety days prior to such election, and the elections shall be held under rules and regulations to be prescribed by law. The qualification of electors in such election shall be the same as is now provided by law in case of electors in municipal elections. The members of Assembly shall hold office for two years from the first day of January next following their election, and their successors shall be chosen by the people every second year thereafter. No person shall be eligible to such election who is not a qualified elector of the election district in which he may be chosen, owing allegiance to the United States, and twenty-five years of age.

The Legislature shall hold annual sessions, commencing on the first Monday of February in each year and continuing not exceeding ninety days thereafter (Sundays and holidays not included): *Provided*, That the first meeting of the Legislature shall be held upon the call of the Governor within ninety days after the first election: *And provided further*, That if at the termination of any session the appropriations necessary for the support of the government shall not have been made, an amount equal to the sums appropriated in the last appropriation bills for such purposes shall be deemed to be appropriated; and until the Legislature shall act in such behalf the Treasurer may, with the advice of the Governor, make the payments necessary for the purposes aforesaid.

The Legislature may be called in special session at any time by the Civil Governor for general legislation, or for action on such specific subjects as he may designate. No special session shall continue longer than thirty days, exclusive of Sundays.

The Assembly shall be the judge of the elections, returns, and qualifications of its members. A majority shall constitute a quorum to do business, but a smaller number may adjourn from day to day and may be authorized to compel the attendance of absent members. It shall choose its Speaker and other officers, and the salaries of its members and officers shall be fixed by law. It may determine the rule of its proceedings, punish its members for disorderly behavior, and with the concurrence of two-thirds expel a member. It shall keep a journal of its proceedings, which shall be published, and the yeas and nays of the members on any question shall, on the demand of one-fifth of those present, be entered on the journal.

I can well remember when that section was drafted in the private office of Mr. Root in his house in Washington. Only he and I were present. I urged the wisdom of the concession and he yielded to my arguments and the section as then drafted differed but little from the form it has today. It was embodied in a bill presented to the House and passed by the House, was considered by the Senate, was stricken out in the Senate, and was only restored after a conference, the Senators in the conference consenting to its insertion with great reluctance. I had urged its adoption upon both committees, and, as the then Governor of the Islands, had to assume a responsibility as guarantor in respect to it which I have never sought to disavow. I believe that it is a step and a logical step in the carrying out of the policy announced by President McKinley and that it is not too radical in the interest of the people of the Philippine Islands. Its effect is to give to a representative body of the Filipinos a right to initiate legislation, to modify, amend, shape or defeat legislation proposed by the Commission. The power to obstruct by withholding appropriations is taken away from the Assembly, because if there is not an agreement as to appropriations between the Commission and the Assembly, then the appropriations of the previous year will be continued; but the power with this exception, absolutely to veto all legislation and initiate and shape proposed laws, is a most substantial one. The concurrence of the Assembly in useful legislation can not but command popular support for its enforcement; the discussion in the Assembly and its attitude must be informing to the executive and to the other branch of the legislature, the Commission, of what are the desires of the people. The discharge of the functions of the Assembly must give to the chosen representatives of the Philippine electorate a most valuable education in the responsibilities and difficulties of practical government. It will put them where they must investigate not only the theoretical wisdom of proposed measures, but also the question whether they can be practically enforced, and whether, where expense is involved, they are of sufficient value to justify the imposition of a financial burden upon the people to carry them out. It will bring the members of the Assembly as representatives of the people into close relations with the Executive, who will be most anxious to preserve a harmony essential to efficient government and progressive, useful measures of reform.

Critics who do not sympathize with our Philippine policy, together with those who were reluctant to grant this measure of a legislative assembly to the Philippine people at this time, have not been slow to comment on the result of the election as an indication that we are going too fast. I differ entirely from the view of these critics as to the result of this election and the inferences to be drawn from it.

The small total vote as compared with the probable number of the total electorate shows that a considerable majority of those entitled to vote did not exercise the privilege. This indicates either an indifference or a timidity that we would not find in a people more used to the wielding of political power; but it affords no reason for supposing that as the Assembly proves its usefulness and important power, the ratio of votes to the total electorate will not rapidly increase.

The election was held without disturbance. In many districts there were bitter controversies, but the complaints of fraud, violence or bribery are insignificant. Although the Government was supposed to favor one party, and was subject to much criticism in the campaign, no one has been heard to say that the power of the Executive was exerted in any way improperly to influence the election. This furnishes a good object lesson.

A popular majority of those who exercise the franchise have voted for representatives announcing a desire for the immediate separation of the Islands from the United States. This majority is a small one when the returns are carefully considered and is much less than the ratio between the party representatives in the Assembly would lead one to suppose. However, assuming a decided majority for immediate independence, the result is one which

I thought possible even while I was urging the creation of the Assembly. It is not a disappointment. If it indicated that a majority of the representatives elected by the people were a body of irreconcilables determined to do nothing but obstruct the present government, it would indeed be discouraging; but I am confident from what I know and hear of the gentlemen who have been elected that while many of them differ with me as to the time in which the people of the Islands will become fit for complete self-government, most of them have an earnest desire that this government shall be carried on in the interests of the people of the Philippines and for their benefit, and shall be made for that purpose as effective as possible. They are thus generally conservative. Those whose sole aim is to hold up the government to execration, to win away the sympathy of the people in order to promote disturbance and violence, have no proper place in this Assembly. Had the Filipino people sent such a majority, then I should have to admit that the granting of the Assembly was a mistake and that Congress must abolish it.

It has been reported in the Islands that I was coming here for the purpose of expressing, in bitter and threatening words, my disappointment at the result of the election. Nothing could be further from my purpose, nothing could be less truly descriptive of my condition of mind. I am here, filled with a spirit of friendship and encouragement for these members, who now enter upon a new field in which they have much to learn, but where everything can be learned and this duty most efficiently discharged if they are led by an earnest desire to assist and guide the government in aiding the people. I have no right to appeal to the membership of this Assembly to conduct themselves in the discharge of their high duties in a manner to vindicate me in the responsibility I assumed in urging Congress to establish this Assembly, because they should find a stronger reason for so doing in their sworn duty; but it is not inappropriate for me to touch on this personal feature of the situation, because my attitude has been misconstrued and my sympathetic interest in, and hope for, the success and usefulness of this National Assembly have not been properly stated.

I venture to point out a number of things that you will learn in the course of your legislative experience. One is that the real object of a legislature is to formulate specific laws to accomplish specific purposes and reforms and to suppress specific evils; that he makes a useful speech who studies the question which he discusses and acquires and imparts practical information by which the remedies offered can be seen to be applicable to the evil complained of; that the office of a legislator for a great country like this is one that can be discharged conscientiously only by the use of great labor, careful, painstaking investigation and hard work in the preparation of proposed measures. One of the most necessary traits in a successful legislator or executive is patience. Where the sudden change in that which is regarded as a wrong system may paralyze a necessary arm of the government, ways and means must be devised to bring about the change gradually. There will be a temptation to take up measures which will invite the support of popular prejudice rather than measures which will really accomplish good for the body politic. Such a temptation exists in older legislative bodies than this, and we can not hope that it will be absent from here; but, in the end, the man who exerts the most influence in this body and among the people will be the man who devotes most conscientiously his time to acquiring the information upon which legislation should be based and in explaining it to his colleagues and his people. The man who is seeking to put his adversary or the government in an embarrassing situation may win temporary triumph; but the man who himself feels responsibility of government, and who, while not concealing or failing to state the evils which he considers to exist in the government, is using every effort to reform those evils, will ultimately be regarded as the benefactor of his country.

I have not the time and doubtless not the information which would justify me in pointing out to the Assembly the various subjects-matter to which they may profitably devote their attention with a view to the formulation of useful legislation. They will properly feel called upon to devote their attention to public economy in the matter of the numerous governmental bureaus which have been made the subject of criticism. It is quite possible that they may find in their investigations into these matters reasons for cutting off officers and bureaus, but I sincerely hope that no such effort will be made until a full investigation is had into the utility of the functions which the bureau performs and the possibility of dispensing with them. I can remember that while I was Governor there was much outcry against the extravagance of maintaining certain bureaus which in subsequent crises in the public welfare proved their great usefulness beyond cavil. Of course we shall encounter in this investigation and discussion a radical difference between legislators and others as to the function which a government in these Islands ought to perform. It is entirely easy to run an economical government if all that you do is to maintain order and if no steps are taken to promote health, to promote education and to promote the general welfare of the inhabitants. It is of course the object of the person charged with the duty of governing a country to reach the golden mean— that is, to make governmental provisions for the welfare of the people without imposing too great a tax burden for the purpose. The taxes in this country are imposed partly by the legislature and partly by Congress. The former will constantly have your attention. In so far as the welfare of the country is affected by the latter, to wit, the customs duties, and can be improved by a change of them, it would be wise for the Legislature to devote much time and thought to recommendations to Congress as to how they should be changed, for I doubt not that Congress will be willing and anxious to take such steps as may commend themselves to the people of the Islands in the matter of adjustment of duties, having regard to the raising of sufficient revenue on the one hand and to as little interference with useful freedom of trade as possible on the other.

As you shall conduct your proceedings and shape your legislation on patriotic, intelligent, conservative and useful lines, you will show more emphatically than in any other way your right and capacity to take part in the government and the wisdom of granting to your Assembly, and to the people that elected you, more power. There are still many possible intervals or steps between the power you now exercise and complete autonomy. Will this Assembly and its successors manifest such an interest in the welfare of the people and such clear-headed comprehension of their sworn duty as to call for a greater extension of political power to this body and to the people whose representative it is? Or shall it, by neglect, obstruction and absence of useful service, make it necessary to take away its existing powers on the ground that they have been prematurely granted? Upon you falls this heavy responsibility. I am assured that you will meet it with earnestness, courage and credit.

In closing, I can only renew my congratulations upon the auspicious beginning of your legislative life in a fair election, and to express to you my heartfelt sympathy in the work which you are about to undertake, and my confidence that you will justify in what you do, and do not do, the recommendations of those who are responsible for that section in the organic act that has given life to this Assembly.

3

China and Her Relations
with the United States

Delivered at a Banquet Tendered by the American Association
of China, Shanghai, October 8, 1907

Mr. Chairman and Gentlemen: For the courtesy and hospitality evidenced by this beautiful banquet, I wish to express to you my grateful acknowledgment. It is a great opportunity and pleasure to meet the prominent citizens and residents of this great city. Shanghai is the business center and in some respects the political center of the Empire of China.

On my way to the Philippines, as a representative of the President of the United States, to signify the importance which he attaches to another step in the extension of popular self-government in those Islands, I am here only by the way as a traveler, accredited with no official authority or duty or message in respect of China. What I am about to say in respect to China, therefore, is said as an American citizen and not as a representative of the American Government.

Attitude towards the Philippines

One word in respect to the Philippines before I come to America's relation to China. Americans interested in Oriental and Chinese trade naturally look to the Philippine policy of the Government as having a bearing upon the attitude of America toward the Orient in general. Reports have been circulated with an appearance of authority throughout this part of the world that the United States intends to sell the Philippines to Japan or some other country. Upon that point I do not hesitate to express a decided opinion. The Philippines came to the United States by chance, but that Government assumed a duty with respect to them and entered into an implied obligation affecting them, with the people of the Philippines, of which it would be the grossest violation to sell the Islands to any other Power. The only alternatives which the United States can in honor pursue with respect to the Philippines are either permanently to retain them, maintaining therein a stable government in which the rights of the humblest citizen shall be preserved, or, after having fitted the people for self-government, to turn the Islands over to them for the continuance by them of a government of the same character. It is enough to say here that there is not the slightest danger of a sudden cessation of the present relation of the United States to the Philippines, such as would be involved in a sale of those Islands, and that for our present purpose the attitude of the United States toward China must be regarded not alone as a country interested in the trade of China, but also as a Power owning territory in China's immediate neighborhood.

The Policy of the Open Door

The policy of the Government of the United States has been authoritatively stated to be that of seeking the permanent safety and peace of China, the preservation of Chinese territorial and administrative entity, the protection of all rights guaranteed by her to friendly Powers by treaty and international law, and, as a safeguard for the world, the principle of equal and impartial trade with all parts of the Chinese Empire. This was the policy which John Hay made famous as that of "the open door." By written memorandum, all the great Powers interested in the trade of China have subscribed to its wisdom and declared their adherence to it. The Government of the United States has not deviated in the slightest way from its attitude in this regard since the policy was announced in 1900.

I am advised by Mr. Millard, who has written much and well on the

Far East and has given close attention to the statistics of the trade between China and the various countries of the world, that the trade, both export and import, between China and the United States is second only to that of Great Britain. He says there is much difficulty in fixing the exact amount of trade because of the long-established custom of treating every piece of merchandise that comes from Hongkong as an importation from British territory. It is certain, therefore, that the American Chinese trade is sufficiently great to require the Government of the United States to take every legitimate means to protect it against diminution or injury by the political preference of any of its competitors. It cannot, of course, complain of loss of trade effected by the use of greater enterprise, greater ingenuity, greater attention to the demands of the Chinese market and greater business acumen by its competitor, but it would have the right to protest against exclusion from Chinese trade by a departure from the policy of the open door. The acquiescence in this policy by all interested nations was so unhesitating and emphatic that it is hardly worth while to speculate as to the probable attitude of the United States were its merchants' interests injured by a violation of it.

How far the United States would go in the protection of its Chinese trade no one of course could say. This much is clear, however, that the merchants of the United States are being roused to the importance of their Chinese export trade, that they would view political obstacles to its expansion with deep concern, and that this feeling of theirs would be likely to find expression in the attitude of the American government. Domestic business in the United States has expanded so enormously, and has resulted in such great profits, as to prevent American business men from giving to the foreign trade that attention which it deserves and which they certainly would give, but for more profitable business at home. As the population of the United States increases, as its territory fills and its vast manufacturing and agricultural interests become greater, its interest in foreign trade is certain to increase. The manufacturers now take little care to pack their goods or to give them the sizes as desired by Chinese purchasers, but this stiff-necked lack of business sense is disappearing. We shall soon find the same zeal and the same intense interest on their part to induce purchasers in foreign markets that now characterize the manufacturers of other nations whose home business is not so absorbing as that of the manufacturers of the United States. While we have been slow in rousing ourselves to the importance of a trade which has grown without government encouragement and almost without business effort to its present important proportions, I feel sure that in the future there will be no reason to complain of seeming government indifference to it.

Development of the Empire

The United States and others who favor the open door policy sincerely will, if they are wise, not only welcome, but will encourage this great Chinese Empire to take long steps in administrative and governmental reforms, and in the development of her natural resources and the improvement of the welfare of her people. In this way she will add great strength to her position as a self-respecting Government, may resist all possible foreign aggression seeking undue, exclusive or proprietary privileges in her territory, and without foreign aid can enforce the open door policy of equal opportunity to all. I am not one of those who view with alarm the effect of the growth of China with her teeming millions into a great industrial empire. I believe that this, instead of injuring foreign trade with China, would greatly increase it, and while it might change its character in some respects, it would not diminish its profit. A trade which depends for its profit on the backwardness of a people in developing their own resources and upon their inability to value at the proper relative prices that which they have to sell and that which they have to buy, is not one which can be counted upon as stable or permanent.

Monetary Reform

I may stop a moment in this connection to say that the Monetary Commission headed by Professor Jenks, which was sent at the expense of the United States to adopt a gold standard, sought to effect a reform that would have inured greatly to the benefit of the Chinese people. The example of Japan and the Philippines justifies this statement. While the recent rise in the price of silver has reduced somewhat the difficulty of the two standards, the elimination from business of the gambling element involved in the fluctuations of exchange due to the difference between the gold and the silver standard would be ultimately of great benefit to the merchants and the common people of China, and to the stability and fairness of Oriental business. I am sincerely hopeful that it will not be many years before such a reform is brought about.

China for the Chinese

For the reasons I have given it does not seem to me that the cry of "China for the Chinese" should frighten anyone. All that is meant by that is that China should devote her energies to the development of her immense resources, to her industrious people and to the enlargement of her trade and to the administrative reform of the Empire as a great national Government. Changes of this kind could only increase our trade with her. Our greatest export trade is with the countries most advanced in business methods and in the development of their particular resources. In the Philippines, we have learned that the policy which is best for the Filipinos is best in the long run for the countries' which would do business with the Islands.

Reform in Administration in China

It is a pleasure to know that the education of Chinese in America has had much to do with the present steps toward reform begun by the Government in China. It is not to be expected that these reforms shall be radical or sudden. It would be unwise if they were so. A nation of the conservative traditions of China must accept changes gradually, but it is a pleasure to know and to say that in every improvement which she aims at, she has the deep sympathy of America, and that there never can be any jealousy or fear on the part of the United States due to China's industrial or political development, provided always that it is directed along the lines of peaceful prosperity and the maintenance of law and order and the rights of the individual, native or foreign. She has no territory we long for, and can have no prosperity which we would grudge her, and no political power and independence as an Empire, justly exercised, which we would resent. With her enormous resources and with her industrious people the possibilities of her future can not be overstated.

The Boycott Ended

It is pleasant to note a great improvement in the last two years in the relations between the United States and China. In the first place, through the earnest efforts of President Roosevelt, the administration of the Chinese immigration laws of the United States has been made much more considerate. The inquisitorial harshness to which classes properly admissible to the United States under the treaty between the two countries were at one time subjected, has been entirely mitigated without in any way impairing the effectiveness of the law. The boycot, which was organized ostensibly on the ground of such harshness of administration, proved in the end to be a double-edged knife, which injured Chinese even more than Americans, and other foreign countries quite as much. Happily that has now become a closed incident, a past episode.

Return of Indemnity

Again, the United States has exhibited its wish to do full justice to China by a return or waiver of the indemnity awarded to it for injuries and expenses growing out of the Boxer trouble. It has been said that we have done only what we ought to do. This may be so, but a nice sense of international obligation is not so universal that it may not justly increase the friendly feeling between the parties to the transaction.

Reform of American Consular Service

With the full approval of President Roosevelt, Mr. Root secured the legislation needed to improve our Consular service and to place it on a merit basis. I do not think it too much to say that the Consular representatives in China within the last decade have not been up to the standard which the importance of the business interests of the United States in China demanded. Aware of this, the administration at Washington has within the last three years given special attention to the selection of Consuls in China. This was made evident in the selection of both Mr. Rodgers and Mr. Denby as Consuls-General at Shanghai. It is a new sensation for an American to come to a Chinese city and find as his Consular representative one who knows the Chinese language and who understands the Chinese Empire as few Chinese understand it. I congratulate you citizens of the United States on having such a representative of your interests in this great commercial community as Mr. Denby.

Establishment of an American Court.
—Approval of Its Work

Finally, another great step has been taken by the Government of the United States to improve its relations to China. Many years ago the Chinese Empire granted the right to citizens of the United States to reside in so-called concessions within the borders of the Chinese Empire, and there enjoy the security of living under the government and administration of law by officers of the United States. This extra-territoriality was chiefly important in securing an administration of justice in accordance with the principles and laws obtaining in the United States. It imposed an imperative obligation upon the United States to see to it that the justice thus administered by the officers whom it vested with judicial powers should be of the highest and most elevating character. I regret to say that this obligation for many years did not receive the attention and care that it ought to have had; but in the last Congress, at the instance of Secretary Root, under the guidance of Mr. Denby, then the Chief Clerk of the State Department, and now your Consul-General at Shanghai, with the able assistance of Mr. Denby's brother, a Member of Congress from Michigan, and of Senator Spooner of Wisconsin, a law was passed which properly recognizes the dignity and importance of the power conferred by the Chinese treaty upon the Government of the United States to administer justice in respect of citizens of the United States commorant in China by creation of a U.S. Circuit Court for China. Our Government was fortunate in the selection of a gentleman as the first judge of that Court who had four years' experience in the Orient as Attorney-General of the Philippines, and who came to Shanghai with an intimate knowledge of the method of uniting, in one administration, the principles of the common law of the United States with the traditions and conditions of a foreign country. His policy in raising high the standard of admission to the bar and in promoting vigorous prosecutions of American violators of law and the consequent elimination from this community of undesirable characters who have brought disgrace upon the name of Americans in the cities of China, can not but commend itself to everyone interested in the good name of the United States among the Chinese people and with our brethren of other countries who live in China. It involves no small amount of courage and a great deal of common sense to deal with evils of this character and to rid the community of them. Interests which have fattened on abuses can not be readily disturbed without making a fight for their lives, and one who undertakes the work of cleansing and purifying must expect to meet resistance in libel and slander and the stirring up of official opposition based on misinformation and evil report. I am glad to think that the Circuit Court of China has passed through its trial and that the satisfaction which its policy has brought to the American and foreign communities in China and to the Chinese people will not be unknown to the Administration at Washington, at whose instance this Court was first established.

Need of More Complete Body of Laws for Americans in China

I have read Judge Wilfley's opinions both in civil and in criminal matters. He has worked hard and well. He has made it plain that some additional legislation by Congress is necessary to lay down a few more general principles of law which are to govern in the extra-territorial jurisdiction of the Court in China. I sincerely hope and believe that the establishment of this Court will make much for the carrying out of exact justice in the controversies that arise in the business between Chinese and Americans. There is nothing for which the Oriental has a higher admiration than for exact justice, possibly because he is familiar with the enormous difficulty there is in attaining such an ideal. If this Court shall lead the Chinese to believe, as it ought to do, and will do, that the rights of a Chinaman are exactly as secure when considered by this tribunal, as the rights of an American, and that there is no looking down upon a Chinese because he is a Chinese and no disregard of his business rights because he is an Oriental, it will make greatly for the better relations between the two countries.

Federal Buildings for Shanghai

And now what else is needed? It goes without saying. What you need is a great government building here, to be built by the expenditure of a very large sum of money, so that our Court and Consulate shall be housed in a dignified manner. Our Government should give this substantial evidence of its appreciation of the importance of its business and political relation to the great Chinese Empire. In the Orient, more than anywhere else in the world, the effect upon the eye is important, and it must be very difficult for Chinese to suppose that the Government of the United States attributes proper importance to its trade with China when it houses its Consulate and its judges in such miserably poor and insufficient quarters as they now occupy. All over the United States, Congress has provided most magnificent courtrooms for the administration of Federal justice. Will it, now that it has created a Court whose jurisdiction is co-extensive with the Chinese Empire, be less generous in the erection of a building which shall typify its estimate of the importance of its relation to Chinese trade and the Chinese people?

4

Japan and Her Relations
with the United States

*Delivered at a Banquet Tendered by the Chamber
of Commerce, Tokyo, September 30, 1907*

Baron Shibusawa, Mr. Mayor and Gentlemen of the Municipality and Chamber of Commerce and Other Distinguished Citizens of Tokyo: I beg to extend to you my heartfelt thanks and acknowledgment for this magificent evidence of your hospitality and good will. It is a little more than two years ago since a large party, of whom I was one, was the recipient of a similar courtesy and attention in this very hotel at the hands of the then Prime Minister Count Katsura. So many were we then that I ventured to compare our coming to the descent of a cloud of locusts upon this devoted land. But you stood the onslaught nobly and your treatment of us is a bright memory never to be effaced.

At that time you were engaged in a titanic straggle with another great nation, but the first traces of the dawn of peace were appearing in the east. We Americans shall always feel proud of the part that Theodore Roosevelt, with the prestige of the headship of our people, was able to play in hastening the end of the war. Peace has come under circumstances honorable to both parties, and Japan, having proved her greatness in war as in peace, has taken her stand in the first rank of the family of Nations. You have concluded new treaties of amity and commerce with your former antagonist and the wounds of war are healed.

The growth of Japan in the last fifty years from a hermit country to her present position is the marvel of the world. In every step of that development, even at the very beginning, we Americans are proud to record the fact that Japan has always had the cordial sympathy and at times the effective aid of the United States. The names of Commodore Perry, of Townsend Harris, of John A. Bingham, of General Grant and of Theodore Roosevelt will be inseparably connected with the history of the advance of Japan to the front rank among the world powers.

But now for a moment, and a moment only, a little cloud has come over the sunshine of a fast friendship of fifty years. A slight shock has been felt in the structure of amity and good will that has withstood the test of half a century. How has it come about? Well, in the first place it took a tremendous manifestation of nature to bring it about. Only the greatest earthquake of the century could have caused even the slightest tremor between such friends. I do not intend to consider the details of the events in San Francisco. I cannot trespass on the jurisdiction of the Department of State, of my colleague Mr. Root, or my friend Mr. O'Brien, to discuss them. But this I can say, that there is nothing of injustice in these events that cannot be honorably and fully arranged by ordinary diplomatic methods between the two governments, conducted as they both are by statesmen of honor, sanity and justice, and representing as they do two peoples bound together by half a century of warm friendship.

It is said that there is one word that is never allowed to creep into the diplomatic correspondence Between nations, however hostile, and that word is "war." But I am not a diplomat and am not bound by diplomatic usage. I can talk of war. I am not one of those who hold that war is so frightful that nothing justifies a resort to it. We have not yet reached the millennium, and there are international grievances that can be redressed and just international purposes that can be accomplished in no other way. But, as one of our great generals has said, "War is hell," and nothing but a great and unavoidable cause can justify it.

War between Japan and the United States would be a crime against modern civilization. It would be as wicked as it would be insane. Neither the people of Japan nor the people of the United States desire war. The governments of the two countries would strain every point to avoid such an awful catastrophe.

What has Japan to gain by it? What has the United States to gain by it? Japan has reached a point in her history when she is looking forward with confident hope to great commercial conquests. She is shaking off the effects of war and is straining every nerve for victories of peace. With the marvelous industry, intelligence and courage of her people there is nothing in trade, commerce and popular contentment and enlightenment to which she may not attain. Why should she wish a war that would stop all this? She has undertaken with a legitimate interest in so close a neighbor to reform and rejuvenate an ancient kingdom that has been governed or mis-governed by fifteenth-century methods. His Majesty, the Emperor, has shown his appreciation of the difficulty of the task by sending to Korea Japan's greatest statesman, who has exhibited his patriotism by accepting the heavy burden, when, by his years and his arduous labors for his country in the past, he has earned a right to rest. No matter what reports may come, no matter what criticism may be uttered, the world will have confidence that Prince Ito and the Japanese Government are pursuing a policy in Korea that will make for justice and civilization and the welfare of a back-ward people. We are living in an age when the intervention of a stronger nation in the affairs of a people unable to maintain a government of law and order to assist the latter to better government becomes a national duty and works for the progress of the world. Why should Japan wish a war that must stop or seriously delay the execution of her plans of reform in Korea? Why should the United States wish war? War would change her in a year or more into a military nation and her great resources would be wasted in a vast equipment that would serve no good purpose but to tempt her into warlike policies. In the last decade she has shown a material progress greater than the world has ever before seen. Today she is struggling with the abuses which accompany such material development and is engaged in an effort by process of law to retain the good for her people and to suppress the evil. Why should she risk war in which all the evils of society flourish and all the vultures fatten? She is engaged in establishing a government of law and order and prosperity in the Philippine Islands and in fitting the people of those Islands by general education, and by actual practice in partial self-government, to govern themselves. It is a task full of difficulty and one of which many Americans would be glad to be rid. It has been suggested that we might relieve ourselves of this burden by a sale of the Islands to Japan or some other country. The suggestion is absurd. Japan does not wish the Philippines. She has problems of a similar nature nearer home. But, more than this, the United States could not sell the Islands to another power without the grossest violation of its obligation to the Philippine people. It must maintain a government of law and order and the protection of life, liberty and property itself or fit the people of the Islands to do so and turn the government over to them. No other course in honor is open to it.

Under all these circumstances then, could anything be more wicked and more infamous than the suggestion of war between nations who have enjoyed such a time-honored friendship and who have nothing to fight for? "If this be true," someone asks, "why such reports and rumors of war?" The capacity of certain members of the modern press, by headlines and sensational dispatches, to give rise to unfounded reports has grown with the improvement in communication between distant parts of the world. The desire to sell their papers, the desire for political reasons to embarrass an existing government and their even less justifiable motives have led to misstatements, misconstructions, unfounded guesses all worked into terrifying headlines that have no foundation whatever. In each country, doubtless, there are irresponsible persons whom war would aid and make prominent, who try to give seriousness to such a discussion, but when one considers the real feelings of the two peoples as a whole, when one considers the situation from the standpoint of sanity and real patriotism in each country, it is difficult to characterize in polite or moderate language the conduct of those who are attempting to promote misunderstanding and ill-feeling between the two countries.

It gives me pleasure to assure the people of Japan that the good will of the American people toward Japan is as warm and cordial as ever it was and the suggestion of a breach of the amicable relations between them finds no confirmation in the public opinion of the United States. It is exceedingly gratifying for me to have as my companion in my visit to these shores, Mr. O'Brien, the Ambassador to Japan from the United States. We have been friends for years. I am sure you will find in Mr. O'Brien all that could be desired in one whose chief official duty it will be to preserve the friendship between our two countries.

I have already referred to the enthusiastic welcome which was accorded our party of American Congressmen two years ago by the people of Japan. So great was the kindness of his Majesty the Emperor and the officers of the Government that we were overcome with our welcome. Coming now to this country for the fourth time, I am an old story and am not entitled to any other welcome than that to be accorded an old friend who comes often. The distinction of being the Emperor's guest another time, I do not deserve and should feel it my duty to decline, enjoyable as the honor is, but for the fact that I know that his Imperial Majesty graciously adopts this course, not as a personal matter, but to signify to the American people and government the continuance of his friendship for the United States. It gives me the greatest pleasure and is a great honor for me to be able to bring a reciprocal message of good will from our President and our people.

5

An Appreciation of General Grant

New York City, Memorial Day, May 30, 1908

Foreword

My father, Alphonso Taft, was a member of General Grant's cabinet at the end of his second term. They were very warm friends. They were both men of simple, straightforward nature and became very fond of each other. I was brought up with an intense reverence for the memory of General Grant, and a personal feeling of gratitude to him for his kindness to my father. When I was invited to deliver an address at his Tomb on Riverside Drive on Memorial Day, therefore, I felt it my duty to accept. In comparing his life with that of Lincoln, for I had recently been engaged in the study of the latter, it seemed to me that the development of Grant's marvelous qualities after the war began, was even more remarkable than that which took place in the life of Lincoln, and that it would emphasize and make more wonderful the greatness of Grant's character to describe the shadow and utter discouragement that rested on his life before the war. In doing this I stated the facts as I understood them. This evoked in one or two newspapers, and from some individuals of prominence, a severe criticism of what I had said in respect to Grant's early life. By way of explanation I gave the following statement to the Associated Press:

"I am very much distressed that anything I have said should be construed to be an attack upon General Grant's memory. I yield to no man in my admiration for General Grant, in my high estimate of his remarkable qualities and character, and of the great debt that the Nation owes him. In my memorial address I attributed his resignation from the army in 1854 to his weakness for strong drink, because from Mr. Garland's life of General Grant and the evidences he cites, and from other histories, I supposed it was undoubtedly true.

Great Victory of His Life

"I referred to the matter only because it seemed to me that it was one of the great victories of his life that he subsequently overcame the weakness. The wonder of his life was that with all the discouragements that he encountered before the Civil War, including this, he became the Nation's chief instrument in suppressing the Rebellion. I venture to say that no impartial man can read my Memorial Day address and say I do not give General Grant a place in history as high as that given him by any of his historians or his admirers.

"The lives of our great men belong to the country. If facts are told showing that they had weaknesses which they overcame, the force of their successful example is greater to lift the youth of the country up to emulate them than if they are painted as perfect without temptation and without weaknesses."

Address

The custom of decorating the graves of those who have died in war for their country is a beautiful and useful one. It brings us to a contemplation of those crises in our history in which our countrymen, numbered by the hundreds of thousands, from a sense of duty solely, parted with all that the Nation might live. "Greater love hath no man than this that he lay down his life for his friends." I do not know any place which thrills one's bosom with such patriotic ecstasy as the sepulchre of the unknown dead in Arlington Cemetery. The thought of the heroism and sacrifice of those who, without a murmur and without even hope of personal credit or glory, gave up all to maintain a sacred cause, makes all motive of personal advancement or ambition seem small and sordid. It was the distinguishing characteristic of our Civil War that, from generals to the humblest privates, the army was actuated by a real love of the cause. There are those who think the war was unnecessary—that it might have been avoided. I can not agree with them. The situation was one for which only such a convulsion as war, dreadful as it was, could afford a complete remedy. This day, which brings back to us the awful losses that the war entailed and renews the fond memories of those known and unknown heroes whose devotion to duty is an ever living assurance of the patriotism of this people, should for a time take us out of the atmosphere of self-seeking, of money-making, of pleasure-hunting, and of peaceful sloth, that we may value again the many instances it revives of mental and physical courage, self-denial, self-restraint, and self-sacrifice. The day, with its reminiscences, assures us that the hearts of our people today, eager as they seem now in the search for wealth and comfort, would furnish a response to the Nation's call as full, as willing, and as mighty as was the response when the struggle for the Nation's existence began in '61. The Civil War is the great epic of our history, and though fully forty-three years have passed since peace was declared, a grateful Nation is still conferring rewards on the brave participants of the struggle, and honoring the memory of its dead. The enormous effort of the whole people as a Nation, and the burdens they gladly assumed to maintain the national integrity, and to cut out the cancer of slavery that was eating away our national life, do not grow any less, from an historical standpoint, as the decades pass. In the making of history in a republic, political controversy colors the contemporary view, so that a considerable time must elapse before the credit, or lack of it, properly to be ascribed to a free people for carrying out any policy, can be measured. The greatness of our Nation, as shown in the struggle of the Civil War, however, is now everywhere recognized, and in the perspective of forty years, there is none to decry or belittle it.

We are a humor-loving people. We dislike shams. Our sense of the ridiculous is very keen, almost too keen, and in the mercantile and material spirit which has been rife, we are prone to make light of exhortations to patriotism, and the forms and symbols through which patriotism finds expression. I think we have gone too far in this direction. Patriotism is a real virtue, and the forms and symbols which suggest it, and by which we recognize its existence and our respect for it, are proper reminders of a serious duty, and keep us in touch with it as an elevating motive. The disposition to dispense with all form which characterized our Puritan ancestors, has, I think, been greatly modified, and reasonable persons now recognize the advantage of ceremony—not only in religious worship, but also in the discharge of many other functions analogous to religious worship in their sacred character.

Take the administration of justice. It is well that judges should be clothed in robes, not only, that those who witness the administration of justice should be properly advised that the function performed is one different from, and higher, than that which a man discharges as a citizen in the ordinary walks of life; but also, in order to impress the judge himself with the constant consciousness that he is a high-priest in the temple of justice and is surrounded with obligations of a sacred character that he cannot escape and that require his utmost care, attention and self-suppression.

So, too, when the national anthem is played, every true-hearted American should make known his sense of the presence of the vital essence of nationality in the notes of the Star Spangled Banner by rising and removing his hat.

Mere forms these may be, but they are the evidence of the existence of a love of country, and the more frequently we are conscious of the presence in us of such a feeling, the more certain we can be that our acts of courage and self-sacrifice will correspond to it when occasion arises.

Hence, the advantage of the celebration of a day like this, or of the Fourth of July, or of Washington's Birthday—lest we forget the obligations that are upon us as citizens of our common country—lest we forget the gratitude we should feel to our ancestors who founded the Nation, and to their descendants who saved it, in the Civil War, from dissolution and destruction.

It always gives force and emphasis to our interest in memorials of this character if we have, in our minds, the concrete conception of the persons who made the sacrifices that we celebrate; if we have relatives who gave up their lives and whose graves we can reconsecrate, each returning Decoration Day. And to those of us who do not have this inspiring association of kinship for some hero of the war, it gives a personal touch, and the necessary concrete element, to take up and review the life of one of the leaders of the struggle and learn from the vicissitudes of his career the makings of greatness and the tests of patriotic devotion.

It is appropriate, therefore, for us to gather at this magnificent structure dedicated to the memory of one whose name in the history of the foundation and maintenance of this Nation's life will always be associated with those of Washington and Lincoln.

We have in the beautiful white shaft which rises high on the banks of the Potomac, and which comes unbidden in its silent purity into every landscape of the Nation's Capital, the country's expression of its gratitude to Washington. There is as yet no adequate national expression of the popular feeling of love and reverence for the martyred Lincoln. But this magnificent sepulchre on the banks of the beautiful Hudson in the greatest center of population of the new world, is an appropriate expression of the debt which the Nation owes to Grant—the greatest military hero of the Civil War.

At this place, in this presence, and before an Association of his comrades that bears Grant's name, it is fitting to stimulate our patriotism by a brief reference to his remarkable life, character and public service.

When we consider the galaxy of great statesmen and patriots that waited upon the conception and birth of our Nation and made them possible, it is very difficult to avoid a conviction that there was Providential interference to secure to the life of our Nation a successful growth. Consider the wonderful adaptability of the character of Washington to the crises that were presented from time to time in the Revolutionary War, and then after the war was over, to the still greater crisis in the life of the Nation when he was called upon to use his power of composing difficulties in the Constitutional Convention, whose work made the thirteen quarreling states a united country. Consider the abilities of Hamilton and Jefferson, and Madison and Marshall, that were all of them necessary to give strength and substance to the new Nation. So, too, is it difficult not to yield to the conviction that the same Providence presided over the fate of this country

124

when the terrible struggle caused by the cancer of slavery made necessary such a convulsion as that of the War of the Rebellion, and was manifested in the presence of Lincoln and Grant to meet the exigencies of that crisis.

I shall not stop today to dwell upon the grandeur and pathos of the character of Lincoln, or to point out how wonderful it was that from such squalid beginnings there could be developed the traits and qualities needed in our martyred President to save the country. The character of Grant as developed by the war and as necessary to the result, was as remarkable in its way, considering his previous history, as was that of Lincoln. It is true that Grant received an education at West Point; but certainly nothing was developed there in him to indicate his fitness or ability to meet great responsibilities. He did well in the Mexican War, as did other lieutenants. He manifested, as regimental quartermaster, energy and familiarity with his duties. But in 1854 he resigned from the Army because he had to. He had yielded to the weakness of a taste for strong drink, and rather than be court-martialed he left the Army. He returned from Vancouver on the Pacific Coast to his family at St. Louis without money, without property—a disheartened man. He accepted from his father-in-law a loan of seventy-five acres of land upon which he constructed a house for his family to live in, and here he carried on farming operations. His chief business seemed to be that of selling wood, of cutting it and piling it in the backyards of the well-to-do people of St. Louis. After six years of this life, he gave up farming because of ill health, and went into the real estate business for a year. He failed in this. His associate dissolved the partnership. Then, at last, his father offered him $600 a year as a clerk in his leather store at Galena, Illinois, and thence he moved from St. Louis. He worked here for a year also. During these seven years, though everything looked dark, he overcame in a great measure his weakness for strong drink. But he was so constituted, so retiring, so lacking in "push" for himself, that it seemed impossible for him to earn a livelihood, even when he had given hostages to Fortune in the shape of a wife and four children.

Then the Civil War came on. Grant had never been a dreamer of possible military glory. He had gone to West Point because it offered him an opportunity for an education. He did not like life at West Point, and while he seemed in the Mexican War to be well adapted to the command of men, to be well adapted to the duty of quartermaster, he never had that vaulting military ambition that was present in the character of Napoleon and other great military leaders. He tendered his services at the beginning of the war solely from a sense of duty and obligation for his education. His having been a student at West Point and a regular army officer necessarily brought him to the front when military training and experience were in such great demand. He modestly suggested in his letter to the Adjutant-General at Washington that he believed he was fitted to command a regiment. He never gave evidence of military ambition. He visited Cincinnati seeking to become a staff officer of McClellan, but in vain. And then, by great good luck, he was made the Colonel of the Twenty-first Illinois, by Governor Yates.

What a marvelous change came into his life after this! From the time he took command of that regiment until the surrender at Appomattox, his life was one continual, well-directed, well-planned effort to suppress the rebellion. From that time on, his constant quest was to find and fight the enemy. Beginning with the Battle of Belmont, he was always in the field and always seeking the Confederate forces. Though in the west, he suffered, as did the Eastern generals, from the interference of the War Department, and the paper strategists like Halleck; and the freedom of his movements was curtailed and his constant activity restrained by timidity and jealousy of his superior officers. But in spite of all this he pressed on, and by the victories he won he compelled the War Department to give him a freer hand. Fort Henry, Fort Donelson and Shiloh were victories that shone like stars in the darkness of the defeats of other Union commanders, and although relieved from all command for a short period, he finally was put in command of the army charged with the duty of taking Vicksburg— and he took it. Then followed the great battle of Chattanooga and Missionary Ridge, after which he was called to Washington, made Lieutenant-General and Commander of the entire army of the United States. Then for the first time, he commanded against Lee, and for a year he measured swords with that great military leader of the South, who ultimately succumbed and surrendered to him the Army of Northern Virginia, at Appomattox.

Of course, it is not to be questioned that Grant's abilities to command developed with his increasing experience. It is not to be questioned that his success depended, too, upon the resources of the North that furnished him men and equipment. But in war as in other things in life, as in all history, merit is determined by the event, and it was Grant who led the armies and infused his personal spirit in their leadership. It was Grant that finally subdued the rebellion. It was at one time customary to criticise Grant's campaigning and to intimate that his knowledge of military strategy was not such as to justify a comparison of him with Lee and other generals. Grant had a very broad conception of the work which the North had before it in subduing the South. He had an opportunity in his life to know the Southern people and to discriminate in respect to them so as to understand that while they *talked* a great deal, they could also *do* a great deal. He believed that the only way of subduing the rebellion was by fighting the armies of the rebellion, and that after all, the contest between the two parts of this Nation was a contest of resources of men and of wealth. And in the end, it proved to be so. His judgment was vindicated.

It is said that Grant was not a man of military genius. It is difficult to define what genius is. Some describe it as the capacity for taking infinite pains. If so, Grant was a genius. Halleck was a great authority on military science and grand strategy, and he never planned a campaign unless, like a lawyer with his precedents, he could turn to the page of the military textbook and justify his plan by a reference to a battle of Cæsar, Napoleon or Frederick. Had he been able to anticipate Grant's plan for the taking of Vicksburg, he would certainly have prevented it. And yet, in comparing the strategic ability of Grant with that of other generals, it can be truly said that there is no campaign in the Civil War that showed more originality, greater celerity of movement, better calculation of opposing forces, and more effective results, than the one beginning with the capture of Grand Gulf, continued by the battles of Jackson, Champion Hills and the Big Black, and ending with the surrender of Vicksburg. Equally well wrought out, though not so difficult of execution, was the battle of Chattanooga, Missionary Ridge and Lookout Mountain.

We are told by those who know, that Grant was exceedingly familiar with all the campaigns of great military leaders, that his memory was retentive and his interest in the science was great. But he had sufficient common sense, he had a sufficient real grasp of military problems, he had sufficient understanding of the difference in conditions under which previous campaigns had been fought and those which he had to fight, to exercise original thought and to free himself from the bonds of military precedent, as at Vicksburg.

Grant was a man of such a sensitive nature that he could not bear to see even animals subjected to pain. And yet his conception of war and its necessities was so clear that the dreadful losses sustained by him in the Wilderness, at Spottsylvania, and at Cold Harbor, and in the other campaigns against Lee, did not turn him from his purpose or lead him to change his plan, which he had deliberately formed, of wearing Lee out and by constant hammering, of ending the army of Northern Virginia. His purpose was, at the cost of losses which the Northern army was able to stand, to inflict losses upon the Southern army which, in the end, meant its destruction. A calculation of the losses which the army of the Potomac sustained during the first three years of the war shows them to have been far greater than those sustained by Grant during his campaigns of '64 and '65 against Lee; and it is certainly not too much to say that had Grant's military career as a general begun in the east as it did begin in the west, the war would not have been lengthened out to a full four years.

The tenacity with which Grant conducted a campaign, the speed with which he followed up a victory, the promptness with which he was on hand the next morning with a force ready to fight after a drawn battle, if put into practice in the army of the Potomac during the first three years of the war would certainly have brought about an earlier termination.

Grant's idea of a war was a fight and a continuous series of battles, and his theory of winning victories was, that the side which was first ready the morning after a battle to resume it, would win in the end.

The greatness of the man was seen in his willingness to assume responsibilities, and his power of standing the strain when defeat and disaster seemed to threaten the success of his plans and to indicate their weakness. It was then, having determined on what his plan should be, he stuck to it and pushed it through in the face of all opposition and vindicated his judgment by ultimate success. He was entirely willing to receive advice, but his decision was his own.

Another quality which he had as a great military commander was the power of selecting competent subordinates and of instilling into them confidence in him and his purpose, which almost insured success. The men he especially selected were Sherman, Sheridan, McPherson, Rawlins and Logan, and how well they justified his choice! When he came east, he suffered from an absence of that mutual understanding between commander-in-chief and subordinate commanders that had been of such value to him in his earlier campaigns.

The history of Grant's relation to those of his subordinates to whom he gave confidence and whom he had himself selected is a fascinating one. The relations which existed between him and Sherman, it is pleasant to dwell upon. The utter absence of jealousy between them and the pleasure which each took in the successes of the other are as delightful as they are rare. Could anything be more exquisite than the story of Sherman's writing a long protest to the War Department against the wisdom of the campaign east of Vicksburg, which easily is the greatest strategic success of the war, and Grant's pigeonholing and returning to Sherman the protest after the campaign was won? Then, in Sherman's letter to Grant, when Grant was appointed to the command of the army, his expressions of admiration and confidence all make us think more of our human kind, because we encounter so frequently the small jealousies between the great which sometimes are permitted to interfere with the successful progress of events, even in the crises of our national life. The love that existed between Grant and Sheridan is another ennobling relation that it is pleasant to contemplate. And the mutual confidence which each reposed in the other, and which was so abundantly justified, furnishes another instance of the course of true friendship between the great in which no yellow spot of jealousy tortures the eye.

One characteristic of Grant is shown in a letter which Lincoln wrote concerning him in which he says, with respect to previous generals, his experience had been such that he always expected after a general had been appointed, to hear from him that a great many things were needed in the army which he knew that Lincoln was not able to give him, and that this was followed by the statement that if he had those things, then he could win the victory. He said Grant differed from the other generals in this respect, that he took what he had and went ahead and with those things he did what he could and what was to be done. He gave an instance: He said he had fifteen thousand cavalrymen at Harper's Ferry, without horses. He had attempted to get horses and could not secure them. Previous generals had said to him that if they could have that fifteen thousand cavalry, they could accomplish great things and win a victory. What Grant said was, "With your authority I will arm these men and make them infantrymen, or I will send them home."

And so it was that through the battles of Belmont, Fort Henry, Fort Donelson, Shiloh, Vicksburg, Chattanooga, the Wilderness, Spottsylvania, Cold Harbor, Five Forks and Appomattox, with all the numerous contests that these names cover and include, Grant was always fighting with the men and the material he had. He realized that omelets could not be made without breaking eggs. He knew that a war could not be carried on without fighting. And he was conscious that the more the fighting to a purpose was constant, the sooner the war would end. He was willing to be called callous, and indifferent to loss of life, painful to his sensitive nature as that charge must have been, if only by the losses which were sustained peace be ultimately gained.

It is difficult to associate the real personality of Grant as it showed itself in the seven years in civil life before the war and as it appeared in the intimacy of family and personal associations at any time, with that of a victorious commander of an army of a million men. He was naturally so modest, so retiring, so sweet-tempered, so pure of speech and thought, so sensitive at the exhibition of pain, either on the part of persons or animals, apparently so lacking in "push," so indisposed to seek prominence, one could not imagine that underneath these traits there was such an iron will and such a power to stand the strain of any responsibility in the pursuit of a plan which he had made up his mind could be worked and made successful. The directness and straightforwardness of his nature gave him a simplicity with which we do not always associate the power of great concentration of thought and will to accomplish a purpose. And it certainly was a marvelous combination of traits of character that in the seven years before the war made Grant so unsuccessful in business, and subsequently made him the tower of strength that he was, as the victorious leader in the greatest war in modern times.

His modesty, his lack of expectation that anyone would think much of him, seems to have given him an undue appreciation of, and an excessive gratitude for favors done him. He seems never to have forgotten a kind word. And a generous attention, received from no matter whom, he sought to repay many fold. A knowledge of this one of his characteristics led men of little scruple to take advantage of it, and of him. He trusted his friends as no man trusted before. And his trust was in a number of instances misplaced. But the faults he had, and the weaknesses he had, were generous. They were those that make us love his memory the more and forget the mistakes that they led him into.

The country owes more to Grant than can be estimated for the great things which were accomplished during his two terms as President. The Geneva arbitration, the veto of the inflation bill, the passage of the resumption bill, were his work. But in all of his long and useful public life, the two greatest scenes were at Appomattox and at Mt. McGregor.

At Appomattox he showed in its finest degree his modesty, and in his earnest desire to secure a peace in which the defeated would suffer as little as possible, he manifested the highest patriotism.

At Mt. McGregor, after his wonderful and successful struggle under the shadow of impending doom to write the memoirs which were to free his name and estate from debt and financial disaster, his death was heroic.

This magnificent Mausoleum on this grand site upon the beautiful river furnishes such a hero a fitting resting place. May it forever remain to inspire his countrymen to patriotic thought and effort!

6

The Army of the United States

Address before the Board of Trade of
Columbus, Ohio, April 2, 1908

I am always glad to visit this central and Capital city of Ohio, where the Governor executes, the Legislature legislates and the steady growth of this enterprising community measures the progress of our great State. The last time I had the honor of addressing an audience in this city was in this very hall in the heated days of August of last year, the memory of which still makes my heart heat in sympathy for those unfortunates who were subjected to a Turkish bath of an hour and three-quarters duration. I promise to inflict upon the present audience no such cruel and unusual punishment.

I have selected for a topic tonight an institution in this country which I think has too little popular consideration and attention in times of peace. I refer to the Army of the United States. The Navy is a favorite of the people, whether they belong to the web-footed class that go down to the sea in ships, or inhabit the Mississippi Valley, or live upon the Rocky Mountain range. There is something about the concrete strength of a great battleship and the simplicity and courage of the sailorman behind the gun representing us in all parts of the world, and coming into contrast with the ships and sailors of other countries, that appeals to the imagination of the American people. They take the bluejackets into their arms with affection, and no appropriation necessary for the increase and perfection of the Navy seems unreasonable. I am glad that this is so, because I should be the last to detract from the importance of maintaining and increasing the Navy, and am a great admirer of the efficiency and spirit of its bluejackets and marines. But what I wish to plead for tonight is that the boys in khaki and blue of the regular army are just as much entitled to the kindly feeling and high interest of the American people as the sailors of the Navy, and that the work they have done and are doing and may have to do in the future is of just as great importance as any that the Navy has done, is doing or will have to do. The function which the Navy performs is perhaps a bit more spectacular than that of the Army, and that of itself explains perhaps the difference in the popular attitude toward the two services.

Take the battle of Manila Bay, and the operations which followed it. The glory which the Navy properly received from its accomplishment upon that May morning far exceeded anything that was accorded to the Army's arduous and delicate work which it carried on in the four years succeeding for the pacification of the Philippine Islands, and bringing them into a condition in which the benevolent policy of McKinley could be carried out successfully.

The detailed history of the instances of courage, privation, patience and patriotic devotion to our national policy in the Islands, exhibited by the officers and enlisted men of the Army, which will do justice to them, can never be written, first, because an adequate record of it does not exist; and, second, because it can only be known to the people of the United States through results, and not through such a triumphant and dramatic picture as that we all like to dwell upon, of the epoch-making naval victory off Cavite.

The naval action is usually affirmative. To be useful it must strike, and this makes its function dramatic and commands the popular attention. The function of the Army of late years has generally been that of accomplishment by patient effort, stretching sometimes over months and years, but always requiring close attention, tenacious courage and self-restraint. Its work has been not only that of attack but more often and for longer that of police administration and pacification. Take its work in San Francisco. Could anything be more commendable than the maintenance of order by the Army through that stricken city, shaken by the earthquake, destroyed by fire and about to be exposed to the awful violence of mob and riot, when, under the inspiration of the two-o'clock courage of Funston, its control passed into the hands of the regular army, and thereafter theft and rapine and violence were banished by the long faithful hours of the regular soldiers on guard?

Take the instance of Cuba. The formidable naval fleet came first and gave to the hands of those seeking peace the effective power to command it; but in a short two weeks, to the Army fell the task of garrisoning the island in such a way as to discourage lawlessness and encourage the friends of order. I ask you, has anything been finer in the history of the Army than the way in which our 5,000 men have settled down in an alien country like Cuba, have secured the maintenance of peace and order without the slightest complaint that any officer or soldier has exhibited any lack of respect for the feelings of the Cubans under the trying circumstances of our occupation, or any lack of tact in carrying out the difficult task assigned to them? But such work, made up of an infinity of little things and proving a constant and uniform self-restraint, appreciation of the situation and commendable military discipline, does not strike the popular imagination and is not apt to call forth the admiration and gratitude of the country whose servants and representatives these soldiers are.

Then too the Navy is removed from contact with the people. It is flying a flag in foreign waters. It rarely if ever has to exercise any authority in domestic troubles. There is an indefinite, elusive but influential impression in the minds of many that there is something in a regular army inconsistent with the purposes of a republic. It derives its force from the uses to which regular or standing armies have been put in maintaining governments over oppressed and helpless people. The election of an emperor by the Prætorian Guard, the suppression of a Parliament by the army under Cromwell and the many other instances in history in which the will of the people has been defeated by the trained soldiery of a tyrant, are used to point the moral that in a government of the people, by the people and for the people, a standing army should be looked upon with suspicion and reduced to the lowest number. It is doubtless true that the enlargement of popular influence in all governments has exercised a beneficent influence to reduce the probability of war. Still there have been many wars in this century, and not a few of them have proceeded from the popular desire without encouragement by Government authority. Making every concession, therefore, which history justifies in favor of the peaceful character and tendency of a Republic, he is a very unwise statesman who urges upon the people a policy reducing the efficiency and size of the Army so as to make the country utterly helpless should emergencies arise which it is entirely reasonable to anticipate.

We need an army for three purposes: first, as essential to any satisfactory system of national defense; second, as an indispensable instrument in carrying out our established international policy; and, third, the suppression of insurrection and civil strife.

In his Farewell Address, Washington advised his countrymen to remember "that timely disbursements to prepare for danger, frequently prevented much greater disbursements to repel it," and also advised them to take "care always to keep themselves, by suitable establishments, in a respectable defensive posture."

John Adams, Washington's successor as President, said that "the national defense is the cardinal duty of a statesman."

Secondly, we have taken the position with respect to the republics established in this country in Central and South America and the West Indies, which is approved by both the great national parties and which has been repeatedly announced as the policy of the government by various Presidents and Secretaries of State. I allude to the Monroe Doctrine. There are differences of opinion as to what this doctrine includes, and as to how and with what limitations it ought to be stated. Speaking generally, however, it is an assertion on the part of the United States to the European and other powers of the world that no interference with the Central and South American and West Indian governments by a European power will be permitted which shall have for its object and result the acquisition by a European power of the territory of such nations for colonization or territorial aggrandizement. This is not a doctrine sustained by any principle of international law; it is a governmental policy which this government believes to be essential for its own interests and well for the interests of the countries whose integrity it protects. Whatever the motive, whatever the purpose, the assertion involved must rest for its sanction, not upon the international law acquiesced in by all civilized nations, but rather upon the power to enforce it of the nation which asserts it. By virtue of this doctrine we in effect and for defensive purposes extend the frontiers of the United States far beyond the actual confines of our territory, to Central America and the islands of the Gulf of Mexico and the Caribbean, to the mouths of the Orinoco and the Amazon, to Magellan and Tierra del Fuego. As we assume the right, so we must undertake the responsibility of measures for the defense of those boundaries whenever, for the purposes of disturbing the integrity of any of the many nations thus included, a foreign force shall invade their borders. How could we maintain such a doctrine if it should ever be questioned in the strenuous race for trade and for colonization that now is rife among the European powers? Could we do it otherwise than by an expeditionary force to the country invaded for the purpose of assisting the local forces in repelling the invader? It is true that our Navy, enlarged as it is, would discharge a most useful function in the defense of the invaded country, but it would make but little headway against hostile forces landed therein, and after that, the only method of asserting our international policy would be by the use of the Army of the United States.

Third. Of course there is no probability of a recurrence of a great Civil War, but should the forces of anarchy and socialism and revolt against organized government manifest themselves, a well-organized militia would be most necessary. The suppression of local disturbances is to the regular army a very unpleasant duty, and it is one to which the President would summon regular troops with great reluctance. An increase in the efficiency of the militia which we may anticipate may well relieve the regular army of any such duty. The moral effect of a regular army, however, to discourage lawlessness is valuable.

The history of this country since the beginning of the Revolutionary War shows that during at least one-fourth of the life of the country, the Government has had a war on its hands in some part of its territory. It is therefore most unwise to prophesy as to what may happen in this respect in the future. The people of this country down to the time of the Spanish War had pursued a policy utterly ignoring the lessons of the past. Through national parsimony and the prejudice against the efficiency of an Army, and the making of proper plans for the organization of national volunteers, and the drill and mobilization of the militia, we have in times past incurred great losses of life and the expenditure of immense treasure, a large part of both of which might have been avoided had the proper and economical measures been adopted for the maintenance of a small but efficient regular army and a suitable force of militia.

This was true of the War of 1812, of the great Civil War, and of the Spanish War.

There is a popular feeling that an army in time of peace is not maintained and administered to be used for war, and that the army exists merely for show, like the mace which is carried before the Speaker of the House of Commons, or the truncheon of a field-marshal, or the scepter of a king. This impression has led a usually practical and hard-headed people like the Americans to the most absurd military policy. An Army is for war. If there were no possibility of war, foreign or domestic, and we could be guaranteed a continuous peace, we should disband the army; but we have not yet arrived at this happy condition. We have not yet reached a point in the progress of civilization when war and the fear of war do not play a large part in determining the policies of governments. The voice of the United States in favor of international justice will be much more weighty if it is known to have a good army and a good navy to enforce its views and defend its rights.

Now it is a fact that time is indispensable to the making of good soldiers and a good army. Our own experience should prevent us from entertaining any illusion as to the inefficiency of a brave but unorganized people to grapple successfully with another nation equally brave but better organized. We have great confidence in ourselves and in our power of quickly adapting circumstances to meet any national emergency. But this should not make us deliberately blind to the most obvious military principles. We should not be misled by the good luck which has attended us in most of our wars. The most insidious argument against the maintenance of an army of present efficiency is that we once had a magnificent army of volunteers of a million men, the flower of which marched down Pennsylvania Avenue in a grand review under Grant and Sherman; and it is asked, "Can we not raise such an army again?" The awful sacrifice of life and money which we had to undergo during the four years in order to train this great army is forgotten, and the country is lulled into the utterly unfounded assurance that a volunteer enlisted today or a militiaman enrolled tomorrow can in a week or month be made an effective soldier. There are no better officers, no better men in any army than we can raise in America. We are a warlike people. Most privates have an independence and self-reliance that fit them to adapt themselves to different situations, and there are no braver men. But they must know how to shoot straight, they must know how to move at the word of command, they must understand all the duties of a soldier which grow more complicated with modern guns and modern methods. They cannot know it intuitively. We have no right as a nation to ask our citizens to expose themselves as enlisted men in battle without reducing the chances of disaster and death by proper military education of the officers and proper military training of the men.

I am glad to say that our experience in the Spanish and Philippine Wars has had a most healthy effect upon Congress and the people at large with reference to the preparation for our national defense. After the Civil War we rapidly reduced our armament, our navy and our army. Our navy was a collection of wooden frigates and gunboats that could not stand for a minute before the newly invented high-power guns, and our coasts, though lined with old-fashioned forts, were utterly defenseless against European navies. Our army was reduced to 25,000 men, smaller in proportion to the population than ever in the history of the country. Slowly but reluctantly in the eighties we took up the projects of a new navy, of new coast defenses, but the army was still continued until the Spanish War at 25,000 men.

In the latter part of Mr. Cleveland's administration, we asserted the Monroe Doctrine with as much emphasis and what might almost be called "truculence," as ever in our history, and asserted it against the greatest naval power of the world. On the very day when Mr. Cleveland's message went into Congress demanding arbitration as to the Venezuelan boundary, there was just one modern gun mounted on our whole Atlantic, Gulf, and Pacific coasts.

Since then, and under the stress of the Spanish War, we have greatly increased our coast defenses, so that now they are very respectable, both on the Atlantic and Pacific coasts, although they are by no means completed. Since then we have constructed a Navy that in point of efficiency is perhaps equal to any except that of Great Britain. Since then we have taken progressive steps toward the organization of a regular army which is today much more efficient than ever in the past, and is much more capable of expansion and efficient addition. But much remains to be done. If I may trespass on your patience a while longer, I should like to invite your attention to the character of the present army, its size, and its capacity for expansion, together with needed measures to increase the possibility of its being made adequate and useful in time of war.

The change in the army, its improvement and adaptation to modern needs are largely due to the ability, energy, deep interest and enthusiasm and well-directed effort of Elihu Root, Secretary of War under McKinley and Theodore Roosevelt. The legislation under which it is now maintained was almost all of it drafted and pressed upon Congress by that distinguished statesman. Such legislation as has been adopted since he laid down his office is only corollary to that which he had recommended and put through, suggested by actual experience under his new system.

The regular army of the United States today is limited in number of enlisted men to 100,000, exclusive of the hospital corps men. There is authority given the President to enlist upwards of 50,000 Infantry, 18,000 Cavalry, 20,000 Coast Artillery, 6,000 Field Artillery, and enlisted men of the Signal Corps, the Engineer Corps, the Ordnance Corps, and the other subsidiary corps, together with 12,000 Philippine scouts, who are a part of the regular army, to make that number about 114,000 men. But this right to increase the number of enlisted men in all the different corps is limited by the superior restriction that altogether they shall not exceed 100,000 men. Of course the power of the President to enlist this number of men is subject to the further limitation that Congress may withhold appropriations to pay more than a certain number, so that while he might temporarily increase the force, his power would practically soon be at an end on the failure of Congress to approve such an increase by withholding the necessary money with which to pay them in the future. The number of men and officers actually authorized by order of the President in the aggregate is in round numbers 76,000 men, while the number of officers and men actually in the army does not reach 60,000. The reason for this difference between the number authorized and those actually in service in the army is the difficulty that we have had in recruiting. The enlisted man today receives the same pay which he received in 1861, to wit, $13 a month. This is not enough to attract him, although of course it does not at all measure the actual compensation which he receives, because he is fed and well clothed and well housed. Still there ought to be an increase over the wages which were received by him thirty years ago.

A still greater defect in the present system of compensation in the army is the failure to pay the non-commissioned officers, the sergeants and corporals, a sufficient salary to make them permanent members of the army. They are in a sense the disciplinary backbone of the army. They are the ones who whip the recruits into service and make good soldiers of them. They are the ones who come much more intimately into contact with the men than do the commissioned officers, and their pay should be made much nearer to that of the commissioned officers than it is today. I am glad to say that a bill is now pending in the House, which has passed the Senate, giving an adequate increase in the pay of the enlisted men of the different branches of the army, which I hope and believe will relieve us greatly in the matter of our recruiting, and enable us to fill up the army to the quota authorized by the President. We are striving in every way to remove from the life of the private soldier those features of it which tend to discourage reënlistment, and with the increased pay, we hope that we may make the life of an enlisted man a comparatively attractive one.

In order properly to discuss the army, we should divide it into two forces, the mobile and the immobile army. The mobile army is that which may be sent into any part of the United States or of the world as an expeditionary force. It consists of the Infantry, the Cavalry, the Field Artillery, the engineers and the signal corps, with a suitable part of the hospital corps; and it is divided into tactical units, regiments, brigades, divisions and army corps. The immobile army is the coast artillery, the duty of which is confined to manning the guns of the coast defenses and operating submarine mines, torpedoes, searchlights and power plants used in connection with the defenses of all fortified harbors of the United States. The authorized force of the coast artillery is, in round numbers, 20,000. Of this 5,000 are necessary to operate the submarine mines, torpedoes, searchlights and power plants. This leaves a little over 14,000 for the manning of all guns now mounted in the fortifications of the entire country.

In order to man these guns with one shift of men, there are required 37,000 enlisted men, so that the maximum number of men authorized today available for manning guns would be about 4,000 less than one-half of a complete manning detail. When our coast defenses are completed, as they are now projected, both in this country and in our insular possessions, and at Panama, the number of men required for one complete manning detail both for the mines, searchlights, power plants and guns will be 55,000. In war this would have to be considerably increased, because one detail would hardly be enough. As it is, under existing circumstances we have only 20,000, where we need 37,000 for a complete detail. It is now proposed and seems to be practicable, to make up the deficit in this manning detail by training a militia coast artillery to man the guns of the coast defenses. The idea has been suggested to the state authorities, and in many of the states along the coast militia companies have been organized for this purpose. It offers an opportunity for service to men who do not wish to go far from their homes, and yet who would be glad to be enrolled in the ranks of the defenders of their country when she is in danger, and are willing to devote the necessary month or six weeks of each year to the training necessary to render them efficient for the purpose. In time of war they might be willing to enlist in the regular coast artillery during the war and thus make up the regular detail which is essential to the effectiveness of our coast defenses. Taking away 20,000 from the authorized strength of the army for the immobile force, it leaves 55,000 as a mobile army under the present quota authorized by the President, or 80,000 for a mobile army if the President were to increase the authority to enlist to 100,000 men. There are 30 regiments of Infantry, 15 regiments of Cavalry, 6 regiments of Field Artillery, two regiments of engineers, and two regiments of the signal corps. This by no means represents the proper proportion for an army in the field. For an army in the field the Cavalry ought not to exceed 10 percent of the total force of which the Infantry will represent more than 80 percent. It will be necessary to amend the law distributing the Cavalry so as to double the number of cavalry regiments and reduce each regiment to six troops, instead of twelve as now constituted, because in no army in the world but ours does the regiment of Cavalry have more than six troops. Most of them have but five.

The drain upon the army by sending 5,000 troops to Cuba and 12,000 troops to the Philippines, is such that there must be an increase in the Infantry regiments. Whether this shall involve an increase in the actual number of Infantry or only divide them into more regiments is a question which it is not necessary at present to discuss. But certainly there ought to be more regiments of Infantry in view of the constant necessity for changing their tours of duty from the United States to the Philippines and from the United States to Cuba.

The separation of the Coast Artillery from the Field Artillery, effected by the law of last year, has been a move in the right direction and a great improvement. There was no logical connection between the duties of those engaged in our coast defences and the manning and use of the great guns of the fortifications and the drill and tactics of the Field Artillery. The latter belong to the mobile army just exactly as the infantry and cavalry do, and they are now placed where they belong.

We are attempting to enlarge posts so that we shall have brigade posts, with the tactical unit of a brigade for maneuvers under general officers and with the brigade discipline and drill which prepare the men and officers for field work in large maneuvers. All this progress is slow but it is being made.

One of the greatest improvements which has been made in our Army is in the graduate education of its officers. West Point is as thorough a school for general military education as there is in the world, and this has been long established. The great improvement, however, in the education of our officers in the last decade has been the institution of graduate schools in the different branches of the service. Officers are now studying in garrison schools, and then are offered the opportunity, if they show themselves fit, of taking a course in the Artillery School at Fortress Monroe, in the Engineers' School at Washington, in the Infantry and Cavalry School at Fort Leavenworth, or in the Cavalry School of Equitation at Fort Riley, according to their respective branches. Then if they succeed by competition in establishing their right to do so they are enabled to take a course at the Staff College at Leavenworth. Selected from all the Army are the most likely young officers for the War College at Washington, where they are engaged in working out problems of grand strategy.

The other great improvement in the Army has been the establishment of a General Staff, consisting of men selected by a board of general officers without consultation with the President or the Secretary of War for their fitness, who act as advisers to the Chief of Staff and to the Secretary of

War, and whose business it is to recommend policies and to make plans for defense and for possible campaigns. The Chief of Staff and the General Staff coördinate all the Bureaus of the Army and preserve a consistent policy without respect to changing Secretaries and the changing personnel of the general officers. The systems of education and of the General Staff have been in operation now for several years, and fully justify the hopes of those who brought about these two reforms.

There is a dearth of officers. We have only about 3,600 officers, and so many are detailed on important duties connected with military schools, with militia, with teaching at West Point, with the graduate schools in the Army, and with the recruiting service and on the General Staff, that a bill has passed the Senate authorizing the increase of officers by something over 600. This will enable us to detail officers to take charge of the militia in every state and to remain permanently on duty with the National Guard, and thus make it possible to make the discipline of the National Guard like that of the regular army.

This brings me to the great improvement which has been made by recent legislation in respect to the militia. By the "Dick Bill," which was introduced in Congress by the then Representative and now Senator Dick, and which passed in 1902, the National Guard became recognized as the organized militia of the state, subject to call by the general government and entitled to arms, ammunition, clothing, supplies and transportation, in case it organized and adopted the discipline of the regular army.

Another bill is now pending which is likely to pass increasing the benefits to be derived by the National Guard, enlarging the time of service and the character of service, under direction of the Federal authorities, and authorizing a continuance of the joint maneuvers between the regulars and the militia which have already proven to be successful and have developed an intense enthusiasm and interest on the part of the state soldiers. In the course of five or six years we may count on having a well-disciplined force of organized militia, subject to call by the President, amounting to 120,000, so that we might be sure of putting in the field on short notice an army of 200,000 men. This would not be enough, and we should have to resort to a volunteer law which has been introduced in Congress, and which I hope will pass, preparing for the organization of volunteers under regular officers and officers of the National Guard, which shall constitute a third or volunteer force of the United States Army.

A bill is now pending in Congress also authorizing the employment upon a small stipend for a drill every two years, of men who have served in the regular army and been discharged, as a reserve corps out of which the regular army could be enlarged at once in case war were declared or threatened. This would enable us to increase the regular army to 150,000 men without great difficulty, and would secure us 250,000 well equipped, well drilled soldiers of the Republic. This plan for a small army, capable of rapid expansion, is perfected but not carried out fully in legislation. I am glad to say, however, that Congress manifests such an interest in the development of the Army and a willingness from time to time to improve the various branches that during the next decade I feel confident that we shall soon have a regular army and a reserve citizen soldiery sufficient to put into the field 250,000 men capable of carrying on war with courage and efficiency. Of course in the support of such an army the Republic is subjected to very heavy expense, because the whole army, both regular, militia and volunteers, are volunteers and must receive compensation sufficient to enable them to live and support somebody beside themselves.

We do not raise the armies by conscription except in the very last resort. As a consequence, our armies are vastly much more expensive than the European armies even in time of peace. Our regular army today of 60,000 men costs us about $72,000,000 a year. France maintains an army of 546,000 men, and it costs her $133,000,000 a year. Germany maintains an army of 646,000 men, and it costs her $144,000,000 a year. In other words, France has an army nine times the size of ours which it costs her less than twice the sum to maintain, while Germany has an army ten times as large as ours which it costs her just about double our sum to maintain. In addition to this we are paying out pensions for our Civil War and Spanish War veterans of $150,000,000. In view of this it is entirely natural for the representatives of the people in Congress to hesitate to increase a military establishment so expensive as compared with other nations. The lesson from the pension fund, however, instead of being, as it is thought to be, a restraint upon expenditure to secure an efficient army, ought, if historically and critically considered, to be a warning against the lack of preparation, for the extent of that pension roll is itself the greatest exponent of the fatuity of a policy of insufficient national defense.

A short-sighted parsimony with respect to an efficient army, which might suppress a rebellion or end a foreign war in a short time, leads to the raising of enormous fresh levies of unskilled troops and the expenditure of great treasure which might have been avoided. After the emergency arises, and when it is too late for economical preparation, then the Legislature opens the Treasury by appropriations and provisions of the greatest liberality to meet the necessities which only time and thorough preparation could properly and economically meet.

I do not think that I can close this address by any words more appropriate than those of Washington while he was President when he said:

"The United States ought not to indulge a persuasion that, contrary to the order of human events, they will forever keep at a distance those painful appeals to arms with which the history of every nation abounds.

"There is rank due to the United States among nations, which will be withheld, if not absolutely lost, by the reputation of weakness.

"If we desire to avoid insult, we must be able to repel it.

"If we desire to secure peace, one of the most powerful instruments of our rising prosperity, it must be known, that we are, at all times, ready for war."

7

The Panama Canal

At the Meeting of the Ohio State Bar Association,
Put-in-Bay, July 11, 1906

Ladies and Gentlemen, Members of the Ohio Bar: It is a great pleasure to renew my acquaintance with members of the profession, and especially members of the profession of my own state.

It was not as easy as it might be for me to fill this engagement, though it was of a year's standing, and I must apologize to the members of the profession for not taking up a legal subject. But if you will take a man as your speaker this afternoon who has forgotten about all the law he knew, you must expect him to select some subject that is rather easier to him than sound law.

While you are lawyers and lawyers' wives, you are also Americans, and you are certainly interested in the great project that the United States has assumed to carry through—the union of the two oceans by a canal across the Isthmus of Panama. The enterprise has been a subject of consideration almost since the Isthmus of Panama and the Pacific were discovered; and I believe one of the first suggestions in the sixteenth century was the construction of a sea-level canal. We had to wait something more than three hundred years before a real attempt could be made to do that which has been in the minds of men so long.

There were three routes suggested. One was the so-called San Blas route, the shortest of all proposed. It is only thirty miles from shore to shore, and a large part of that on the Atlantic side could be located in the bed of the San Blas River, but the difficulty with the route is that right in the middle of it is a mountain fifteen hundred feet high. The advocates of the route proposed a ship tunnel some five miles long, one hundred and fifty feet high, and from one hundred and fifty to two hundred feet in width. If the mountain were granite, if it were solid rock, the proposition would be more feasible than it is. According to our best information, the mountain instead of being granite, instead of being solid so that when pierced it would hold the shape of the projected tunnel without support, is probably of a volcanic and friable nature, such as to require the making of a supporting arch, and an arch of that extent, five miles long, one hundred and fifty feet high and two or three hundred feet wide, is as yet beyond practical engineering accomplishment.

The other route, that is, other than the Panama route, is the Nicaragua route, which has the advantage of the lowest natural level and a natural lake at that level, through which a channel could be dredged. The level of the water in the lake above the sea is one hundred and ten feet. But the route has the disadvantage of greater length, one hundred and thirty-seven miles, and also the disadvantage of a river—the San Juan River—floods in which would have a dangerous tendency to swamp any canal that might be constructed.

The most practical route—and that which Congress has settled upon—is the Panama route. This passes over the continental divide, between the two oceans at Culebra Hill. With the exception of Nicaragua, this is the lowest natural continental divide between Alaska and Patagonia. Originally Culebra Hill, through which the cut is to be made, was three hundred and forty feet high. It has been reduced by the French so that the present level of the lowest part of the cut is about one hundred and forty feet above sea level. The difficulty with this route is the very extended excavation necessary, and even a greater difficulty is the control of the Chagres River.

De Lesseps, after he had completed the Suez Canal, came, fresh with that victory, to build the canal at Panama, and his plan, not settled upon by careful consultation of engineers, but reached in the enthusiasm of an arduous work done, was for a sea-level canal. He attempted it and spent two hundred and forty-seven millions of dollars, but his effort proved to be a failure. His projected canal was seventy-two feet wide and twenty-nine and one-half feet deep—a sea-level canal. You will all remember the disastrous result, the breaking up of the company, the liquidation, the bankruptcy and finally the transfer of the assets to a new French Panama Canal Company that called together a committee of engineers—indeed, called together two committees of engineers—who went into the subject of the proper type of canal with great care and proposed the construction of a lock-canal. The lock-canal proposed was sixty feet above sea level. It was to be a sea-level canal to Bohio, a place thirteen miles from the Atlantic shore where a dam, lake and flight of locks were to be made. The canal was thence to be carried clear across the Isthmus at a level of sixty feet to within four miles of the Pacific, where the sea level was to be reached again by a flight of locks. The French Panama Canal Company continued the work under this plan, but finally that company also ceased energetic work because its money gave out and it continued thereafter only desultory attacks upon the problem.

In 1899 the Isthmian Canal Commission was appointed by the government of the United States to make recommendations, and they considered the matter from 1899 to 1902. They first recommended the Nicaragua Canal, because, after consultation with the French Panama Canal Company, they considered that the price demanded was much too high. Subsequently, however, in January, 1902, the new French Panama Canal Company telegraphed to say that it would sell all that it had there, which had cost upwards of two hundred and fifty millions of dollars, for forty million dollars, including its stock in the Panama Railroad Company, of which it owned sixty-nine seventieths of the entire issue.

On June 28, 1902, Congress passed the Spooner Act, which gave preference to the Panama Canal route over the Nicaragua route, and thereupon Mr. Hay made a treaty with Señor Herran, of Colombia, by which the right of way contemplated in the Spooner Act, for which ten million of dollars was to be paid, was granted across the Isthmus along the line of the canal as projected. I need not rehearse the history of that treaty, the failure of the Colombian Senate to ratify it, the revolution in Panama, the establishment of the new Republic of Panama and the subsequent making of a treaty between the United States and Panama by Mr. Hay and Mr. Buneau-Varilla, and its ratification by the Senate. Panama, by this treaty, conveyed not only a right of way for the construction and maintenance of the canal, as the Colombian treaty provided, but also a zone for governmental purposes of ten miles in width, five miles on each side of the axis of the canal, and forty miles from shore to shore, together with governmental control over the harbors and any additional part of the Isthmus that in addition to the ten miles it may become necessary to take in order to complete the canal. This is a most important gain for the United States in the substitution of the Panama treaty for the Colombian treaty, because governmental control of the canal strip is vital in securing proper sanitation and police regulation.

The Spooner Act does not specify exactly what kind of a canal shall be constructed. It directs the President to construct a canal and the necessary locks and other appurtenances. It provides, however, for the issue of one hundred and thirty-five million dollars of bonds that are to furnish the means by which the canal can be constructed. At the time that act was passed, the then Isthmian Canal Commission had recommended a lock-canal and had reported to Congress that it would cost one hundred and forty-five millions of dollars. This act provides ten millions in cash for preliminary work and one hundred and thirty-five millions in bonds, so that it is evident that Congress had in mind the construction of a lock-canal, according to the plan recommended. The language of the act, however, as I have said, directs the President to construct a canal and therefore, of course, every lawyer knows that, in order that he may execute the mandate, he is impliedly given the power to determine what the type of the canal shall be.

The President appointed, in the spring of 1904, after the ratification of the treaty, an Isthmian Canal Commission under the terms of the act and directed that Commission to convene and consult distinguished engineers who should report upon the type of the canal.

In the transfer there were conveyed the machinery, sixty-nine seventieths of the stock of the railroad and all the land and right of way owned by the Canal Company. There are some machine shops that are valuable. The railroad is valuable and of course indispensable to the construction of the canal. There are twenty-one hundred houses for residences of the employees of the canal, and there are three or four very extensive hospitals, but as all of these had stood in the torrid zone for eight or ten years, with very little done to them, they were in a bad state of repair and needed much work to make them habitable and sanitary. In the first place, we could not invite anybody to go there unless we made it a place in which people from the temperate zone could safely live. The construction of the Panama Railroad and also of the Panama Canal down to the period when we went there had been attended with great loss of life from yellow fever and malaria. The first matter that we had to take up was the question of health on the Isthmus. The gentleman who had been in charge of Havana when the yellow fever was stamped out—Colonel Gorgas—was put in charge at Panama, and he based all his plans for action on the mosquito theory of the transmission of yellow fever. There has been a good deal of fun made of that theory, but Colonel Gorgas, by two years' work, has vindicated the wisdom of his confidence in the theory. It may be that the disease is transmitted by other means than mosquitoes, but certainly it is transmitted by mosquitoes, and when we prevent the mosquitoes from getting at yellow fever patients so that the mosquitoes cannot catch the yellow fever, we save the persons whom they sting from contracting the disease. We have had yellow fever on the Isthmus, but by isolation of yellow fever patients and by fumigation and destroying the particular kind of mosquito that carries the disease, we have really stamped out the disease. The mosquito that transmits yellow fever does not fly very far and likes damp places in old houses. He does not breed in lakes outside, but he breeds in pools of water in dark cellars and in uncleanly houses, and therefore the fumigation of the houses is a very effective way of destroying this transmitter of the disease. It is different with respect to the malarial mosquito. He breeds in pools in the field, and the method of preventing his generation and increase is by draining possible breeding places, and, when this is impossible, by spreading oil over such pools.

The strip is forty miles long and is used for about a half-mile in width, and through that strip four or five thousand employees of the health department are employed daily in draining marshes, in cutting down the vegetation and in spreading oil over the waters that cannot be drained. In this way, much good has been done in reducing the amount of malaria.

We are not quite so well situated with respect to malaria as we are to yellow fever. So far as mosquitoes are concerned, all the natives, at least those who live on the sea coast, are immune from yellow fever. The disease attacks only the men that come from the highlands or the Americans or the Europeans that go there. The cases of yellow fever, even in an epidemic, therefore, are few, as compared with the whole population and offer few opportunities to the transmitting mosquito for taking in the poisonous germs. In respect to malaria, however, the case is very different. About sixty-five or seventy percent of all the natives on the Isthmus and of all the blacks that come from the surrounding islands, are infected with malaria, and of course, we cannot isolate them from mosquitoes that settle on them and take the malarial germ from their victims. It does seem, therefore, an almost impossible, a hopeless task, to prevent the spread of malaria when sixty-five or seventy percent of the people are infected with it at any rate, and yet by Colonel Gorgas' methods, already described, great improvement has been made.

Of course, if we would have health we must have proper houses. These twenty-one hundred houses have to be increased in number because we have in our employment from twenty-two to twenty-five thousand men, and we have to take care of their families, which run up the class of new settlers to nearly double that number. The reconstruction of the houses has involved much time and labor. So, too, we have to give them good water. We had to put in a complete water supply for the city of Panama and the city of Colon, and for the sixteen or seventeen towns between. We have to drain every town by a system of sewers, and then we have to increase the hospital resources so that now we can take care of about one thousand in each.

All these are preparations before the "dirt begins to fly." The American people want everything the next morning, and if they do not get it they are not entirely reasonable in their complaints. But the truth is that the way to carry on a great enterprise like this is to get really ready before you begin. Mr. James J. Hill, one of the greatest railway constructors of the world, told me that he worked two years making preparations before he put a spade into the ground in building the Great Northern Railway. He said to me: "The trouble with you and the President will be that you will be under more or less pressure of public opinion to make appearance of doing the work of actual construction and will be pushed into beginning construction before you are ready." There has been a very great pressure to go on and make the dirt fly. Everybody wants to know, "Well, are you digging the canal?" Well, we are digging dirt, but it is not the work of construction—it is work of preparation. We are just about ready to begin actual construction.

We found on the Isthmus a single-track railroad with an excellent roadbed, but with very little else adapted to the tremendous work of transportation that has to be done. The great problem is the disposition of the material that is taken out of the trench that is dug. We cannot put it anywhere except where it will not flow back into the canal under the influence of heavy rains or will not be in our way when we are building the works of construction, and, therefore, we have to take a great deal of that soil fourteen or fifteen miles either way from where it is dug. We, therefore, have to double-track the railroad; then we have to increase the terminal facilities in order that the equipment and supplies can be landed and carried promptly to the place where they are to be used and set up.

Then, in addition to the terminals, in addition to dredging out the harbor so that the vessels can reach the terminals, we have to construct, especially in the Culebra cut, what are called spur tracks, running from the line of the railroad to the point where the excavation is to be made by steam shovels. The spur tracks run along levels, constructed in such a way into the cuts that the excavated material will always be delivered down hill on one side or the other. The length of the spur tracks of that sort to be constructed at different times is calculated to be about three hundred miles. The levels are being now made. The tracks are being made.

In order to work them in the Culebra cut, we have now on hand about sixty-nine steam shovels. But we cannot put them into operation all at once. We have to work them in gradually. We hope to put as many as one hundred steam shovels into operation under such a plan that the work of each shovel will be continuous, i. e., that as soon as a shovel fills one car, another is at hand to be filled and the steam shovels can be thus occupied twenty-four hours a day. As we go in, the steam shovels we can use will number about forty and will gradually be increased until we reach one hundred; and as the work progresses towards completion and the place of operation sinks lower and lower and becomes narrower and narrower into the bottom, the one hundred shovels will have to be diminished until they will number but thirty or forty.

The Culebra cut is eight miles long, and if a sea-level canal were constructed the depth of the excavation would be one hundred and eighty feet and its width two hundred feet at the bottom and more than three hundred feet at the top.

The eight-hour law applies on the Isthmus because it is government work. Congress has provided that aliens may be worked longer than eight hours, and so also their foremen and their superintendent. The question of labor is a very difficult one. Three of the West Indian blacks are not equal to one of our day laborers in efficiency and amount of daily work. It has been proposed to try Chinamen. The law does not forbid it. The difficulty in working large gangs of Chinamen is that the contractors are inclined to insist on such regulations for the control of the laborers that it is difficult to distinguish the method of supervising them from involuntary servitude. We are hopeful, however, that workable contracts can be made which secure all lawful and proper freedom of action to the individual Chinese laborers. We have been quite successful with about five hundred men brought from the northern provinces of Spain, who worked in Cuba and who are doing good work now on the Isthmus. One man of this class is worth just about three of the West Indian blacks.—I shall not further discuss this subject except to say that the question of the necessary labor in building the canal is a very serious one.

Now the Panama Isthmus, if you have not looked at your geography, will surprise you by running east and west rather than north and south, so that the canal, instead of running east and west, runs from northwest to southeast. It is about forty-two miles from shore to shore. The line of the canal runs up the valley of the Chagres River about twenty-six miles to Obispo and Gamboa, where it leaves the valley of the Chagres and follows the valley of the Obispo, a tributary of the Chagres, for four miles to Culebra Hill, where is the great cut, and thence down on the other side for ten miles to the Pacific Ocean. The Culebra Cut is three-quarters of the way across the Isthmus.

The Chagres River presents the great problem. It is a very winding stream, and a sea-level canal must follow its valley. In the dry season—and there is a very dry season on the Isthmus for three or four months—the Chagres at Gamboa, where the canal line and the river valley unite, discharges about three hundred and fifty cubic feet per second, but in times of flood it has been known to discharge seventy-six thousand cubic feet a second. The rainfall at Culebra is about ninety inches a year, but at Bohio, in the valley of the Chagres, it reaches one hundred and forty-two cubic inches a year. Provisions must be made to prevent such a flow from overwhelming the canal at Gamboa and all the way down for twenty-six miles to the Atlantic seashore. There are, between Gamboa, the place where the Chagres River comes into the prism of the canal as projected and the mouth of the canal on the north side, some seventeen or eighteen streams that now empty into the Chagres, and the water from these streams, which, in times of flood, is about equal to what the Chagres discharges at Gamboa in times of flood, has also to be taken care of. This is the chief reason why previous boards of engineers have recommended that a sea-level canal be not constructed. They have said not that it was impracticable, but that it presented such difficulties in the matter of construction in time and cost that they did not recommend it as feasible.

In the summer of 1905, the President appointed a board of consulting engineers to consider and recommend the proper type of canal. There were thirteen members and there were included in the number eminent English, French, German and Dutch engineers with experience in canal construction, as well as leading American engineers. The Board divided in opinion. All the foreign engineers and three Americans favored a sea-level canal, while five of the American engineers recommended a lock-canal. The Isthmian Canal Commission, to whom the board of engineers reported, transmitted it to the Secretary of War, concurring in the recommendation of the minority in favor of a lock canal. The Secretary of War also favored a lock canal and the President transmitted all the reports to Congress for its action, with a strong statement of the advantages of a lock canal and the disadvantages of a canal at the sea level as proposed.

The sea-level canal, as projected by this majority of the consulting engineers, begins on the Atlantic side, about a mile to the north of Colon, in the Bay of Limon, through which the entrance to the canal must be made.

Indeed, both types of canal, in order to protect against the constant northerly waves and winds, provide a long breakwater, which runs from this point of beginning for four miles to the shore of Limon Bay, and both plans contemplate a channel dug forty feet in the one case, forty-two in the other and five hundred feet wide from the mouth of this breakwater and parallel to it to the shore; then the line of the sea-level canal follows in a general way the Chagres River up to a point where the Chagres River comes down from the mountains at Gamboa, twenty-six miles from the Atlantic shore. At Gamboa, in order to take care of the Chagres River where it would enter directly the prism of the canal, there is to be constructed a dam on rock one hundred and thirty feet above the level of the Chagres River, so that the level of the water held by the dam will be one hundred and seventy feet above the water in the projected sea-level canal. This Gamboa dam forms a lake by flooding the water clear back up the upper valley of the Chagres some ten or fifteen miles. In connection with the dam, there is to be a spillway, which, in times of flood, it is proposed to use to let out fifteen thousand cubic feet of water a second into the prism of the canal. The water is to be let down one hundred and seventy feet on steps, in order to break the fall, before it is ultimately let into the prism of the canal. On the other bank of the Chagres, and below Gamboa, there are three other dams projected in the sea-level plan; one dam twenty-two hundred feet long, made of earth, and seventy-five feet high, of sufficient height to back the water over the height of land from which the branch stream comes and carry it down into another valley. Then there is another dam eight hundred feet long and seventy feet high, and another dam four hundred and ninety feet long and twenty-five feet high; so that you will see in the sea-level canal we are not without dams; and among those that we would have would be the highest dam in the world—the Gamboa Dam.

The width of the projected sea-level canal is one hundred and fifty feet across the bottom for twenty-one miles of the canal between shore and shore. It is one hundred and fifty feet wide for about twenty-one miles and two hundred feet wide for about twenty-one miles.

Where the bottom is two hundred feet it is in rock, and there they make the width about two hundred and eight feet across the top. The bottom width in earth is only one hundred and fifty feet, but the surface width, due to the greater slope of the banks, is greater than the surface width of the canal in rock. When the Pacific Ocean, or, rather, the shore-line of the Bay of Panama is reached, the canal widens into a channel three hundred feet wide that runs out to what is called the forty-feet contour of the bay.

The current, in times of highest flood from the discharge of the fifteen thousand cubic feet a second from the Chagres River, and the discharge of water from the fifteen streams that are to be allowed to empty directly into the prism of the canal, would be at Bohio, halfway down, about two miles and sixty-four hundredths an hour, a current which, in the Suez Canal, has been found to be one in which large steamers steer badly. The sea-level canal is not to be widened at curves and has no wider stretches for passing places or stations. The Suez Canal is only one hundred and eight feet across the bottom, but at passing places it is one hundred and forty-seven feet, and at curves it is one hundred and thirty-seven feet, so that for practical purposes the Suez Canal is of very little less width than the proposed sea-level canal at points where the width of the canal becomes important. In the Suez Canal steamers are not allowed to pass except by having one steamer tie up to the bank and the other go by very slowly. That is what would have to be done in this sea-level canal if it were constructed. The curvature of the sea-level canal, from Gamboa Dam to Gatun, within three miles of the shore, a distance of twenty miles or more, would be four and one-half times what the curvature is in the Suez Canal, and the current is just about as great at times of flood as it is in the Suez Canal at certain stages of the tide. There are no streams that enter into the Suez Canal at all. There is one fresh-water canal. The Suez Canal, as you know, is through a desert and there is no rainfall. The consequence is, that the conditions surrounding the Suez Canal and its location are very different from those which would surround the sea-level canal as here projected. A rainfall of one hundred and forty-two inches, with sixteen streams entering into the canal, carried right into the same prism of the canal, would be very certain to produce cross-currents where the streams enter, in addition to the direct current varying from two miles to two miles and sixty-four one-hundredths an hour during times of flood. A vessel as large as the largest now under construction, which is seven hundred and eighty-eight feet long, eighty-eight feet beam and thirty-eight feet draught, would have very great difficulty in getting through a canal one hundred and fifty feet wide in a current from two to two and a half miles an hour, with a curvature of four and a half times that in the Suez Canal, and I think that those considerations were probably what led Congress, the House and the Senate, to prefer the lock canal, which has now been decided upon and which I am, with your permission, about to describe.

The lock canal is not a canal in the proper sense. It is a series of lakes. It begins as the sea-level canal began, about a mile away from Colon, with the breakwater four miles long, carried clear to the shore of Limon Bay, with a channel five hundred feet wide by forty-two feet deep, until the shore is reached; thence a five-hundred-foot channel of the depth of forty-five feet is continued to Gatun, four miles further. At Gatun there is to be a dam seven thousand and seven hundred feet in length, one hundred and thirty-five feet in height, half a mile thick at the bottom, three hundred and seventy-four feet thick at the water level, which is eighty-five feet above sea level. The dam rises fifty feet above the water level to its crest, which is one hundred feet across. The dam is to be constructed of earth. We have more earth from excavation than we need. It is hard to dispose of it; therefore, it is convenient to dispose of some of it that otherwise we might have to carry out to sea in the construction of this immense dam. The dam is to be constructed by the method known as sluicing, that is, the material mixed with water is to be pumped in and the water drawn off. This method secures greater solidity of material, for when the water is drawn off no crevices are left. At the end of this dam, and in a hill with a soft but solid rock foundation, there is to be constructed a flight of locks. These locks are in three steps for the purpose of raising the vessels that come, eighty-five feet from sea level to the level of the water behind the dam. The locks were projected by the minority of the consulting board about nine hundred feet long, usable length, forty feet over the miter sills, that the miter gates rest on, and ninety-five feet in width, but the President is inclined to enlarge those locks to make them one thousand feet long and one hundred feet in width and forty feet in depth, in order to meet the requirements of vessels one thousand feet long, which may be constructed.

These locks, as I say, are in steps. The walls of the locks are to be made of reinforced concrete. The outside walls are thirty-six feet in thickness. The locks are to be in duplicate. The middle walls between the locks are forty feet in thickness. The lock structure will be upwards of thirty-six hundred feet in length and three hundred and thirty feet in width. The locks are built into a hill which lies just to the south of the dam, so built that the earth covers the walls of the locks to the top. The locks are to have double gates so that always against the water above there will be two protections. When a vessel enters, if it were to drive through the gates it would have to overcome the weight of four gates four hundred and fifty tons each of weight and a cushion of water about eighty feet thick and thirty feet high. These locks as a feature of the plan have been criticised on the ground of the danger of accidents in their operation. I shall return to that again and point out what the danger is and how great it is, in view of experience that has been had at the Soo Canal. I might say that the lift of each of these locks is twenty-eight and two-thirds feet. The lift of the lock at the Soo Canal is twenty-one feet.

The effect of the construction of the dam at Gatun is to create a lake that from here around to this point [indicating] is about thirty miles long. It creates a lake in which the navigation for the purpose of the canal is twenty-three miles in extent. At the dam the depth of the water is seventy-five feet. As we proceed into the narrower portion, the depth reduces to forty-five feet and excavations will have to be made in order that that depth may be attained. All this white [indicating on the map] that you see means a depth of forty-five feet or more, so that from this point around by the channel for fifteen miles it is really lake navigation, and there will be plenty of space for anchoring or anything else that a vessel would choose to do in a lake.

The great advantage of the lake, in addition to the wide and free navigation it affords, is that it offers a safe and easy method of providing for the influx of the water from the Chagres River and these fifteen or eighteen streams that lie between the Gamboa Dam in times of flood and at other times. The lake is so extensive—it is one hundred and eighteen square miles in superficial area—that it can take in all the water that in floods will come from the Chagres and its tributaries and not feel it in the slightest. In the middle of the Gatunda, there is a hill in which a sluiceway is projected, through which the flow of water from the lake to the sea can be regulated, and the level kept at eighty-five feet.

These streams are taken into the lake on the shore of the lake and at points so far from the channel for steamers that there is no danger of a deposit of silt or the mud which might fill up the channel and require constant dredging at a great cost. In the sea-level plan, it would be impossible to avoid the necessity for persistent dredging and the great expense due to it.

Here [pointing to the map] you observe these streams come in at points all the way from five to eight, and, in some cases, ten miles away from the channel, so that the heavy material in the water that is brought in falls on the shore and does not reach to the channel.

The lock canal has a channel five hundred feet or more in width for two-thirds of the whole length and forty-five feet deep. Only one-seventh of it is two hundred feet wide and that four and seven-tenths miles through the Culebra Cut. After it passes through the cut at Culebra, four and seven-tenths miles, it widens into three hundred feet until we reach a lock at Pedro Miguel, of thirty feet fall. This is to let vessels down into another lake with a level of fifty-five feet above the sea, constructed by the erection of three dams on the Pacific Ocean, and to be known as Sosa Lake. This lake also has a depth of forty-five feet and offers lake navigation of five miles from Pedro Miguel to the shore of Panama Bay. On the shore at the mouth of the Rio Grande River is Sosa Hill, and at each side of it are the necessary dams. In Sosa Hill itself duplicate flights of two locks are to be constructed by which vessels are to be let down to sea level into a channel three hundred feet wide and forty feet deep, running out to the contour line of forty-foot depth in Panama Bay.

I omitted to say in my description of the sea-level canal that there is to be a tidal lock on the Pacific side. The tide on the north or Atlantic side rises and falls but two feet. The extreme tide variation on the other side is twenty-three feet. In order to avoid the current that would of course be produced by this difference in tidal levels, it would be necessary to have a tidal lock, having a total lift of twenty-three feet. It has been supposed that that tidal lock might be left open half the time, but experience with the tidal lock at the Kiel Canal has shown that the channel through the lock has to be narrowed to such a point that when the lock is open at both ends, the current is increased so as to become dangerous to navigation. It is necessary, therefore, to keep the tidal lock at Kiel closed all the time, and so would it be with a tidal lock in the sea-level canal at Panama.

Returning for a moment to the lock canal and Sosa Lake, at the Pacific terminus, it is a question of doubt whether that lake will be constructed. One objection is that it brings the locks, with all their machinery, immediately down to the shore and makes them an easy mark for an enemy's guns. That is not true of the lock plan on the Atlantic side, because the Gatun locks are four miles away from the shore, and no vessel could come in within three or four miles of shore of Limon Bay. Again, it is doubtful whether the effect of a fresh water lake immediately in the neighborhood of Panama, which is so near, would be beneficial to the health of that city. It has been proposed, and I think Mr. Stevens, the chief engineer, is in favor of the proposition, to make a sea-level canal from the Pacific shore up to Miraflores or Pedro Miguel, where good foundations may be had, and there construct a dam and a flight of locks as at Gatun, and thus have the series of three locks on one side at one place and the three locks on the other at one place. That, I think, would economize the management of the locks and certainly would enable the persons in charge to guard more carefully, with less trouble, two centers of possible danger and injury rather than three.

Now I should like to go back for a moment to the Gatun dam, which is the keystone, if I may use that expression, of the whole lock canal. There are high hills at Gatun on each side of the Chagres River seven thousand and seven hundred feet apart, very near to this shore, as you will see, and those hills, therefore, make the placing of the dam here of very great advantage, because by damming these you flood a large territory and make a great lake. I ought to say that the plan recommended by the Isthmian Canal Commission in 1899 and that favored by previous commissions acting under French auspices, contemplated the dam at Bohio some thirteen or fourteen miles up the Chagres River, and a sea-level canal up to that point. But the foundation at Bohio was found to be not as satisfactory as at Gatun, and another difficulty was that with the dam at Bohio, the lake formed was much smaller, the lake navigation was less extensive and did not make as satisfactory provision for taking in the flood waters of the Chagres and its tributary streams. Most of the experts supporting the sea-level canal project admitted that the Gatun dam was stable. Mr. Hunter was the engineer of the Manchester Ship Canal and was on the French Committee Technique which reported in 1898 on the plan and reported against the sea-level canal, but in his later investigations he had seen a new light, and when he came to vote this time he voted in favor of the sea-level. Mr. Burr was in favor of the sea-level. He had been on the Isthmian Canal Commission of 1899 and he had voted then in favor of the lock canal with a height of eighty-five feet, but he also changed his mind and voted in favor of the sea-level canal, and those two by changing carried the majority of the consulting engineers in favor of the sea-level as against the lock canal.

Mr. Burr attacked the stability of the Gatun dam. Mr. Hunter did not and neither did Mr. Parsons, the other American engineer favoring the sea-level canal. Mr. Burr's attack was based on this ground. He said that the foundation of the dam was not proper to make the dam of a stable construction. The dam is to be seven thousand and seven hundred feet in length. Under five thousand feet of this length there is a foundation of twenty feet below the surface of the ground of what is called "indurated clay." It is really a soft rock like soapstone. It is a rock which, when exposed, does not yield to the water. There has been at Colon for thirteen or fourteen years an excavated dry dock of this material, the sides of which now are just as plumb and just as smooth as they were when it was constructed. But in the length of seven thousand and seven hundred feet, there are two depressions in this rock foundation that we have described, one eighteen hundred feet and the other nine hundred feet in length, which were probably the beds of old streams of the Chagres. In these depressions are clay and sand mixed—an impermeable material—running down to the rock from one hundred and fifty to two hundred feet. At the lowest part of the depressions two hundred feet at one point and two hundred and five feet at another is found a material of coarse gravel and sand, which is water bearing, so that when a pipe is sunk down into it two hundred odd feet the water comes up and has overflowed the pipe, I think in one case an inch and a half and in another case possibly two inches. Now that is thought by Mr. Burr to indicate that the foundation for the dam is not of the proper material, and that it will be unstable. It is said that the fact that underneath that is water flowing is an indication that there is some connection with the river and that the water of the river must necessarily communicate with it. It is demonstrable that the water cannot communicate with the river, at least not near the dam, for the river is at sea level as far as Bohio, seven miles above, and this water comes out of the pipes some eight or ten feet above the level of the river. The water, therefore, probably comes from pockets in the neighboring hills.

To begin with, the construction of earth dams has been a science in which marked improvement has been made during the last ten or fifteen years. The question of filtration of water has been studied with great care. Mr. Stearns, of Boston, who planned the Gatun dam, is, I suppose, the greatest living authority on that subject. All earth dams which have been properly constructed have proven generally to be rather better than masonry dams—certainly better than masonry dams constructed with earth and a core of masonry, because the union of the masonry with the core is not generally as successful as it should be.

There are three ways of destroying a dam. The water may flow over the top of the dam and carry it away by working down into it as at Johnstown; then it may percolate through the material of the dam in such a way as to carry away the material of the dam, the face of the dam falling over; and then it may, although there are very few instances of it, percolate under the dam with so much force as to carry away the material under the dam and up in front of the dam so that the dam falls into the cavern thus made, but it requires great pressure to do that.

Now for the benefit of those who do not know what I did not know until I looked into the subject, the science of hydrostatics shows that the pressure against a dam of this character is in proportion to the height of the water, without regard to the volume of water, and whether you have a lake of thirty miles extent or a lake that only extends back a half a mile from the dam, the pressure is exactly the same, if the height of the water against the dam is the same. Now there is no danger at all—everybody admits that—of breaking over the top of this dam, which, according to the plan of construction, is fifty feet above the level of the water. There is no danger of breaking through the dam, which is a half-mile thick at the bottom and three hundred and seventy-four feet thick at the level of the water, because it is practically possible to construct a dam with clay by sluicing so to make it absolutely impermeable. Then the question comes: Is there any danger from the percolation underneath the dam? As I have said, there is an impermeable blanket there one hundred and fifty to one hundred and sixty feet thick between the bottom of the lake and any water-bearing material in the ground underneath. How, then, can water from the lake penetrate under the bottom of the dam and not only percolate there but percolate with such strength as to carry away the material through which it percolates for a distance of half a mile? You have all seen a spring that comes up at the bottom of the mountains—when it first breaks out, a little sand comes with it, but afterwards there is no material. The water is clear and pure. So here even if water could escape, it would not have force enough to carry material upward under the toe of the dam. Mr. Stearns, by experiment, shows that even if the foundation in these depressions were only average coarse sand, through which water would flow, instead of impermeable clay and sand as it is, there would not flow from the surface of these depressions more than ten cubic feet a second across the whole twenty-seven hundred feet. That is a negligible quantity with no possible destructive force.

I should say something with reference to the tonnage of the lock canal. Filling these lock cavities takes a good deal of water, and you have to have enough water in the lake so that you will not draw off in the dry season enough to reduce the depth of the lake water below what you need for navigation of vessels. After thirty-six or thirty-seven million tons of shipping have been passed through in a year—that is, at that rate per year—the water would be drawn so low by lockage during the dry season that there would have to be a reservoir constructed at Alajuela to keep water in reserve which could be used to maintain the lake at proper level. Such a reservoir can be constructed for two millions of dollars, and then the total tonnage which could pass the canal in a year would be about eighty million tons. When you consider that the Suez Canal began with about five million tons of shipping and has increased to about fourteen million tons a year, you will see, if you calculate it, that at the same rate of increase the tonnage would be about fifty million tons for this canal in the year 2000. I think we can readily postpone anxiety, therefore, as to its capacity for consideration of our great-grandchildren.

The weight of this dam is sixty-three times the pressure against its face. The dam is larger than any dam in the world and larger in the proportion of resistance to the water than any dam in the world, and I should like for a moment to invite your attention to a map, showing the various earth dams now constructed and in use. This is the highest earth dam in the world [indicating]. It is in California on the east side of San Francisco Bay, and is called the San Leandro dam. The water here is ninety-five feet high. This dam hasn't such a height of earth as the Gatun dam, but the water level is higher and the water level among engineers is regarded as the height of the dam. You will observe the difference in the extent of the material used to hold back the water of Lake Gatun, as it is called, and San Leandro. Gatun dam is much larger. There is something quite interesting about the San Leandro dam. That was about five miles east of San Francisco Bay, where they had an earthquake. It is, as I have said, the highest earth dam in the world, but it was not injured in the slightest and lost no water. The Pelarcitos dam in California has a water level of eighty-five feet, just the height of this Gatun dam. It is situated on the peninsula on which San Francisco is located. The earthquake slid one great layer of earth and rock over another and cut off the water pipes leading from this dam to San Francisco. The movement followed the line of an old geological fault. The fault came through this end of the Pelarcitos dam [indicating]; and yet, although the fault went right through the dam, there was not a drop of water lost. It shook the dam but the cracks were closed up by the weight of the material of the dam. I ought to add that the fear of danger from earthquakes to our canal works founded on the San Francisco earthquake, is shown by the effects of that earthquake not to be justified. Not only did this Pelarcitos dam—an all-earth dam—withstand the direct movements of the earthquake, but there was a dam just half a mile away from the line of fault, called the Crystal Springs dam, made of concrete masonry. It was something like one hundred and twenty-five feet high. The whole dam was pushed and thrust by the earthquake in such a way that when a man went to examine it it was perfectly possible to see how it had been moved. Yet it stands there today and holds the water of San Francisco. In other words, the earthquake has shown that what an earthquake does is to shake down the buildings and the walls and the structures that are not properly constructed, but that when they are constructed as they should be generally, they are immune from destruction. On the Isthmus of Panama they occasionally have earthquakes, but there is to be seen in an old convent on the Isthmus a very flat arch that has stood for three hundred years. Colonel Hecker, who is present, told me that it was the wonder of engineers, and if there had been an earthquake of great force on the Isthmus of Panama, it is impossible to see how it could have stood, and yet it is there as living evidence of the fact that if we are going to count on earthquakes destroying the Panama Canal, we are merely allowing dreams to affect us, which ought not to influence practical men.

Now, as to the danger from the locks. In the Soo Canal and approaching channels three times more tonnage streams through the forty miles of the passage and the locks in nine months than passes through the Suez Canal in twelve months. Yet, in fifty years of operation at the Soo Canal, they have never had a dangerous or a destructive accident. The experts favoring a sea-level canal were greatly troubled lest the gates of the top locks might be destroyed by a vessel which failed to stop when it should and the water would flow out from the top. If the water began thus to flow, they insisted that there would be no way to stop it; that the water would flow out of the lake destroying everything before it and would drain the lake, which it would take a year to fill again. Mr. Hunter, of the Manchester Canal, was sure there was some danger of that sort and he detailed several accidents of the kind occurring at the Manchester Canal. Mr. Noble, the dean of American engineers, who was for years in charge of the Soo Canal, and Mr. Ripley, who has been for twelve years in charge of that canal, testified that such accidents are most unlikely, especially with the double gates which they do not have either at the Soo or at the Manchester Canal. They say the accidents on the Manchester Canal occurred for lack of proper precautions, that snubbing the vessels in by lines so that they are not under the control of the engines but under the control of skilled employees on shore is the proper method and will insure slow and safe movement.

To recur again to the comparison between the two types of canal, I ought first to say that while with small steamers the passage through the sea-level canal would be shorter than through the lock canal, it is not so with larger vessels after the business increases to say twenty vessels a day. Then the time of passage will be about the same in the two types of canal, or about ten hours. If the vessels increase in number and size, the passage through the lock canal will be less than in the sea level. This is due to the necessity for slow movement in the narrow channel of the sea-level canal and for tying up one vessel when two pass and to the speed of navigation possible in the lakes of the lock canal which more than compensates for the delay of two hours and twenty minutes in going up the locks and the same time going down.

The time of construction for the lock canal I hope will not exceed seven years. Generously our engineers have added a year and made it eight. The time of the sea-level canal would be from fourteen to sixteen years and the chief engineer thinks twenty. The cost of the canal will probably be about one hundred and fifty millions. The cost of the sea-level canal would probably be about three hundred millions. Thus the lock canal is a better canal than the sea-level canal—of the size and type proposed—and can be constructed at half the cost and in half the time.

8

A Republican Congress and Administration,
and Their Work from 1904 to 1906

Boise City, Idaho, November 3, 1906

Ladies and Gentlemen: It is a great privilege to visit your beautiful City of
Boise. It is a great pleasure to meet this intelligent audience. It is a great
honor to meet you. I especially appreciate the coming of the fifty veterans
who have marched from the Soldiers' Home, showing that they still retain
a deep interest in the history of that country which they did so much to
save. But I never meet an audience like this, with your interested, upturned
faces, without the deep regret that I can not occupy your attention in the
way in which you evidently expect, because I fear that the result of my
remarks before I get through will be rather soporific in its tendency. But I
must discuss the issues of the campaign in my own way, and as some of
the issues involve a discussion of rather abstruse points of law, I must ask
your attention and your patience while I go on to discharge my duty and
ask you as an audience to discharge yours.

It is now two years ago, or nearly so, since the electorate of the United
States decided, by an overwhelming vote, that Theodore Roosevelt should
be President, and that there should be a Republican House and a Republican Senate. During those two years the Republican House and Republican

Senate have had one long session, and the question now in determining as to the return of successors to those two Houses is, whether they have done anything or failed to do anything which should disentitle them to the confidence which you so overwhelmingly expressed in November, 1904, and that requires an examination of what they have done.

One of the great features, one of the great historical facts, of the last five years has been the enormous increase in the wealth of this country and in its prosperity; and in that increase in wealth have developed certain evils, to remedy which has been the study of many men and many statesmen. Now, one of the easiest habits to fall into in discussing a situation, especially if you are in the opposition party, is to denounce everything, to hunt adjectives of a very intense quality and use them in describing conditions.

One of the texts which have furnished the most opportunity to the Democratic orators is the subject of trusts. Trusts have developed into an evil, but I think it would help us, and might help the Democratic orators, to whom I refer, if they would define exactly what they mean by trusts, and explain what the evils are of which they are guilty, with a view to possibly reaching a conclusion as to how they ought to be remedied. But before we come to the question of trusts, or rather defining them, we may say that they are enormous aggregations of wealth used as capital, but so used as to deprive the public of the benefit of the use of that capital to which they are entitled. We must all recognize that wealth used as capital is the basis of modern civilization, that the right of property is the most valuable right in building up our society, next to the right of personal liberty. The right of property develops in men, and developed in men in the Dark Ages, those virtues of self-restraint and providence upon which we build all the other virtues. The use of wealth, therefore, as capital, that is, to reproduce itself, is a virtue. That is what we have it for. The corporation— the artificial entity known to the law as the corporation—is the most important instrument in modern times in perfecting and helping on the use of wealth as capital to reproduce wealth, because it offers the opportunity to amass the savings of many into one fund—one great fund—with which railroads and other great commercial enterprises can be carried on; and the incident of the transfer of shares of stock is what enables so many millions of people to have an interest in these immense corporations which they have helped to build up by contributing their modest savings. Any man who would discourage corporate enterprises, who would discourage the saving of wealth in that way to be used in increasing the prosperity of this country, would be doing a greater harm to the poor man, to the wage-earner and to the small dealer than he would to the manager and the president of the great corporations. We must keep that in mind. Any man who would interfere with the prosperity of our country, considering what it is, would be an arch-conspirator against the people.

Let us consider what an enormous development this country has had in the past five years. The manufacturing plants alone have increased in value from nine billion dollars in 1900 to thirteen billions, or forty percent in five years. The products of those plants have increased from eleven and a half billions to fifteen billions, or thirty percent, showing that the capitalist in 1905 was not receiving as much for his money as he was in 1900. On the other hand, the wage-earners employed in those factories in 1905 increased sixteen percent over the wage-earners of 1900, but in the wages paid there was an increase of thirty percent, showing that the wage-earners in 1905 were receiving fifteen percent more per man on the average than they were in 1900. With that kind of prosperity before us, we must be sure that the men who attempt to remedy the evils that have grown out of the organization of capital must be conscious of the necessity for preserving the use of capital, which is indispensable to our well-being. It will not do to destroy our whole structure just to suppress the evils which have arisen in its organization.

What are the evils of trusts? For the sake of simplicity, we may divide the trusts into two kinds. One is formed by a contract, or loose arrangement, binding together a number of independent firms or corporations. They agree to divide the territory for their customers, or they agree in some other way that they will maintain the prices of the goods which they sell at a particular height. By so doing they eliminate competition, and while by the use of the corporation and the use of capital they reduce the cost of production, they still maintain the prices, and thus appropriate to themselves all the benefit of the reduction in the cost of production and deny it to the public.

The second development is that all these firms or corporations are finally combined in one great corporation that may embrace eighty or ninety percent of the producing capacity of the country for that particular commodity, and because they absorb so much of the producing capacity, they are able to deal with middlemen and retail dealers in this wise. They say to them: "Here, you must sign a contract with us by which you shall not sell below a certain price, and by which you shall deal with us exclusively, because if you don't comply with such a contract, if you don't sign such a contract, when the demand for our goods is active, and when you want more than you can get from these independent firms who are furnishing them, we will decline to sell you these goods except at a much higher price." In that way they coerce the retail dealers and the middlemen into dealing with them exclusively, and in that way they drive out competition. This subject had consideration some twenty years ago or more. In the second Congress of Mr. Cleveland's first administration—a Democratic Congress—they took a great deal of evidence on the subject. They said trusts were increasing, and that they ought in some way to be restrained, but the committee thought and thought and finally said that they gave up the problem and turned it over to the next Congress, which was then known to be Republican. That was in 1889. In 1890 the Republican Congress came in, and passed the Sherman anti-trust act. You must bear in mind that Congress can not deal in trade inside of a state, but in interstate trade, that is, trade across state lines, and that limitation sometimes interfered very much with the efficiency of Congressional legislation on this subject; but Congress passed this act, which in its first section denounced as a crime and provided for restraint by injunction, any combination in restraint of interstate trade. The second section denounced and provided for restraint by injunction a monopoly of interstate trade. There were other sections, but substantially that was the act. It was not as full in detail as it might have been. It needed a great deal of generous construction to make it operative and so it was brought into the courts. The first case brought up was the sugar trust case. There the government attempted to enjoin the absorption of a lot of sugar-refining companies so that the plants would include about ninety percent of the producing capacity of the country, but the court said that that was not interstate trade; that those were only factories in different states, and the mere fact that the refined sugar which was to be made by those factories might subsequently go into interstate trade, and thus the union would enable them to control that business, did not make the products of the factories interstate trade, and so the bill was dismissed. Mr. Olney, the attorney-general of Mr. Cleveland, was so discouraged by that that he thought it was necessary to relegate the whole matter to state courts and to state legislation. But Mr. Harmon, who succeeded him, under Mr. Cleveland, went into court and obtained two decisions against railroads which were interstate. Then there came a decision in the Addyston Pipe case. In that case there were eight or nine different corporations manufacturing cast-iron pipe in different states, and they divided up the territory. They not only divided up the territory in which they should sell their pipe, but they also had an agreement by which, when bids were invited by any town for the sale of cast-iron water pipe, they had a little meeting—a little auction in advance of the bidding—and they decided among themselves, by bidding among themselves, which one should have the contract, and then having decided which one should have the contract, they arranged the matter so that the competition should appear to be very active. The stenographer of the head of that concern turned state's evidence and gave the whole matter away to the courts. The result was that they were enjoined and the Supreme Court sustained it, on the ground that the trade in cast-iron pipe was across state lines, was interstate trade, and that there was a combination in restraint of interstate trade.

The most important decision, however, was one obtained in Mr. Roosevelt's first administration, called the Northern Securities Case. There a corporation was organized in New Jersey to hold the stock of the Great Northern and the Northern Pacific Roads, with a view to a common management. They were competing railroads in interstate trade, and the question was whether that New Jersey corporation was a combination in restraint of interstate trade. The Supreme Court held that it was, by a divided court, and that prevented what might well have gone on, had the decision been otherwise, the union of all the railroads in this country under one head. It did not make Mr. Roosevelt popular in Wall Street. The number of trust suits brought in Mr. Harrison's time was six. The number of trust suits brought in Mr. Cleveland's time was seven; the number of trust suits brought in President McKinley's time, during the Spanish War, was but three. The number of trust suits, that is, suits under the anti-trust law, original proceedings, under Mr. Roosevelt, has been sixteen. The results are that the Northern Securities Trust was dissolved, the paper trust has been dissolved, the cast-iron pipe trust has been dissolved, and there are others now in the course of litigation. In pursuing this statute it became necessary for Congress to pass a number of auxiliary statutes. One was the creation of the Bureau of Corporations under Mr. Garfield. He has investigated a great number of the corporations and a great number of the trusts, and has found, to use the expression of Attorney-General Moody, that the greatest instrumentality in the maintenance of trusts is discriminating rates upon railroads. When a trust has enormous freight to give to a railroad, it says to the railroad: "If you do not give me discriminating rates, secret rebates, against my competitor, I will give my freight to another railroad." The railroad yields, sometimes willingly, and sometimes unwillingly, but it generally yields. That brought to Mr. Roosevelt's attention the necessity for a change in the interstate commerce law, a change which should put into the Interstate Commerce Commission greater power than it ever had before. But it was really only an advisory board. It could tell the railroad company what was an unreasonable rate but it could not tell the railroad company what was a reasonable rate. It might make an order against the railroad company, but the railroad company was not obliged to obey it. So the whole matter had to be brought into court and the whole case gone over again.

The rate bill contained two provisions, insisted on by Mr. Roosevelt, namely, that the Commission might fix a reasonable maximum rate, and also that its orders should go into effect and be obeyed by the railroad company. That rate bill passed the House and the Senate, and was signed in June, and by its terms was to go into effect the first of September. What was the result? Between June and September there were more notices filed by the railroad companies to reduce rates than had been filed in the twenty years previous under the interstate commerce law. On the 29th of August, two days before the act went into effect, there were filed in the Interstate Commerce Commission office five thousand notices to reduce rates by the railroad companies—voluntary notices. The Standard Oil Company was indicted in I don't know how many suits for rebates reported by Mr. Garfield, and before those suits came to trial the Standard Oil Company had rearranged their rates. In New England, for instance, they had so arranged their rates that no independent producer of oil could go into that country at all. They changed that in view of their indictments, and today the independent oil producers are going into the New England territory, and the price of oil has fallen.

The tobacco trust has been indicted as a trust under the anti-trust law. It had proceeded on the theory which I suggested some time ago. It went to its middle men and to the retail dealers and said: "Here, you must deal with us exclusively. You must charge our prices or we will not let you have any licorice," licorice being the basis of most manufactured tobacco. When under this indictment they were charged with violating the anti-trust law, they announced by advertisement that they had withdrawn their discriminating rates that had been insisted upon in the contracts, and would sell to the independent companies at the same price at which they would sell to the trust companies.

The New York Central Railroad has been indicted and convicted of granting rebates to the sugar trust, in order that that might compete with the beet-sugar factories in Michigan.

Now, I mention these various incidents happening within the last two years, or eighteen months, merely to show you that by the activity of Theodore Roosevelt, by his determination to have these laws enforced, by his determination to ask Congress that if these laws can not be enforced to have laws which can be enforced, the fear of the Lord and the fear of the law has been put into the hearts of the managers of railroad companies and the managers of trusts.

Under Mr. Harrison's administration there were seventeen original proceedings brought under the interstate commerce law; under Mr. Cleveland thirty-two; under Mr. McKinley thirteen; and under Mr. Roosevelt about seventy-five. The truth is that it has been demonstrated in the last year that it is possible, through the instrumentality of the courts and through statutes properly directed, to suppress these evils, if time is taken and energy and vigor put into the prosecution.

But our Democratic friends say we must destroy the trusts, we must not regulate them—we must not simply suppress the evils that occur in their operation. That sounds well rhetorically, but when you come to examine it, you will find that it is a very serious question. Why should those great business enterprises be destroyed? Why should you take out of the general prosperity of the country that which has furnished the pay-rolls and an enormous wage fund which has brought about the prosperity that we are now enjoying? What we ought to do is to regulate them in order to suppress the evils of their operation, but to allow them to go on and contribute to the general welfare of this country.

But the Democrats say the way to destroy the trusts is to revise the tariff, with a view to taking out of the tariff protection those things which the trusts manufacture. That sounds attractive, but when you examine the schedules that go to make up this protective tariff of ours, you will find that it is absolutely impossible to segregate any one commodity from this schedule, made up with the greatest care, the items in which are interdependent on each other. If you take out one item you will find that you break down the whole system, and you will find that you will not only injure the trusts, but you will injure a great many innocent manufacturers who are not a trust and who are doing a legitimate business. In other words, it is a mathematical proposition that can not be worked out in that way. It is true that if you were to abolish the protective tariff system altogether, and have free trade, it would be less easy for anybody to absorb an entire business in a trust, because he would then have to absorb the producing capacity of foreign countries. In other words, the protective tariff obstructs foreign competition and in so far as it does that it enables trusts the more easily to form. But then the question which you have to answer is this: Do you desire to destroy your protective tariff system entirely merely to destroy the trusts, or is it not better to destroy these evils of trusts by direct legislation and by compelling them to obey the law, and still continue the protective tariff system that such a great majority of this country have determined shall be the basis of our commercial structure? We know what a change of the tariff means. We knew it in Mr. Cleveland's time, when the Wilson-Gorman Bill passed. We know the disaster which followed, and which necessarily follows with a change of the rates of duty upon the articles that enter into our consumption. The tariff is something upon which business depends. If you change it you are certain to disturb the calculations of business men and to bring about financial disaster. Therefore, it seems to me that the method pursued by Mr. Roosevelt is much more logical, much safer and much less dangerous.

Reference was made by the Chairman to the meat inspection law. That was a law against which at the time a good deal of criticism was directed.

The investigations which were made—the reason for recommending the passage of the law—revealed a condition in respect to the taking care of our meat in the Chicago market that certainly was most revolting, but by the passage of the law, by the securing of the most thorough inspection by the inspectors of Uncle Sam, the whole business has now been put upon a sound basis, so that when in Ohio or in Washington we get beef, either in the can or in the carcass, which comes across state lines and bears the imprimatur of Uncle Sam's inspectors, we know it is edible and is certified to by men who are capable of knowing. And now what they are trying to do is to put the business on a perfectly sound basis, and though for a time it may have injured that trade, it has given to all those interested in stock-raising a business now that they can be certain will be permanent.

So too the pure food law. That was passed at the instance and by the pressure of your Senator Heyburn. That provides for keeping out adulterants from medicines and from other things used as beverages and foods. They too now bear the mark of the inspector of the United States, and therefore carry on their face a certificate of their healthfulness. So too the denatured alcohol bill. That was a bill providing that alcohol, which was to be used in the arts, to be used for lighting and heating, and alcohol can be used most cheaply for that purpose, should not pay the enormous tax that alcohol has to pay when it goes down men's throats. In order to prevent its not paying a tax and then going down men's throats, they have to mix something with it that no man can drink.

These four acts are most important in promoting the welfare of the people, and they are especially significant in this that they were all opposed most bitterly in their passage by the most powerful private interests of this country—the rate bill by all the railroads, the meat inspection bill by the packers of Chicago, Omaha and Kansas City, the denatured alcohol bill by the Standard Oil Company, and the pure food law by a great many quacks; and in spite of that opposition, in spite of the bitterness with which the laws were attacked by all of them, they went through both the House and the Senate, and were signed by the President in one session.

Then there was the act fixing the type of the Panama Canal; the statehood act which provided that Oklahoma and Indian Territory should come in as a state, and that New Mexico and Arizona should either come in as one state, or wait until they were large enough to come in as two states; the consular act which put the consular system on a proper basis, on a merit system, and took it out of politics.

But as to the four acts that I first mentioned, I wish to emphasize the fact that they were bitterly opposed by private interests, by what Mr. Bryan calls the predatory wealth of the country. I wish to do that because I wish to call your attention to the fact that this Congress was the greatest Congress since the war because of the importance of the legislation which it passed. And yet Mr. Bryan and other Democratic statesmen have the audacity to ask the people of this country, after praising Mr. Roosevelt's policies, to send back a Democratic House to uphold his hands, and a Democratic Senate to uphold his hands, because a Republican Senate and a Republican House can not be trusted. And yet the record is as I have stated, that these great acts, in the face of the opposition of predatory wealth, if you choose to call it such, went through both the Senate and the House. They went through the Senate, which it has been charged is the home of special interests. The rate bill which was to die in that body came out of it a better act, a more drastic act and a more comprehensive act—a more efficient act than it was when it passed the House.

Now Mr. Bryan says to send back to the President, apparently as a Christmas present, a Democratic House. What does he mean by that? What is a Democrat today? Is he the follower of William Randolph Hearst of New York? Mr. William Randolph Hearst says he is a protectionist. Is he a follower of Alton B. Parker, the candidate whom the Democrats voted for at the last election? Mr. William Randolph Hearst says that Mr. Parker is a political cockroach. Is it Mr. Bryan? Mr. Bryan is in favor of government ownership of railroads. He wishes us to issue fifteen billion dollars worth of bonds to buy all the railroads and run them by the government. Think of the immense power which anybody in the Presidency would wield with all the railroad men of this country at his beck and call. But is a Democrat in favor of that? If he is, then it means the denunciation of Senator Bailey of Texas, and John Sharp Williams, the leader of the Democratic House, who say that they will have none of government ownership. Then there is another gentleman in Massachusetts who has come forward. He has wiped out the old Democrats, and he bears the significant name of John Buttin Moran. There is another man in California on the Democratic ticket who is going about California denouncing William Randolph

Hearst, who is running on the Democratic ticket in New York. When Bryan says, "Send back a Democratic House," just tell me what the quality of the membership of that House under this chaotic state in the Democratic Party is to be. It is a subject of great regret that the Democratic Party has fallen into this condition. It ought to be to every lover of this country, because we are a popular government that must depend for our safety and the carrying on of the government on the maintenance of two great parties having solidarity, having a definite purpose, and each having the patriotic purpose to conserve in the government that which is best—both parties having a sense of responsibility, so that in a Presidential contest when we may differ as to economic policies, the members of each party may be confident that if the other party comes into power the government will still be conducted with patriotism and with a view to the benefit of the whole people. But when you find a party that has permitted itself to be carried to extremes, without any sense of responsibility on the part of the would-be leaders, I am sorry to say that it does not come up to the standard of the great historic Democratic Party that we knew, with its conservative element to keep it straight and to keep it out of the quagmire of demagoguism, and we have to depend, I am sorry to say, upon the Republican Party alone.

Two years ago Theodore Roosevelt was a candidate for the Presidency. What I am about to say is apropos of Mr. Bryan's admission now that the policies of Mr. Roosevelt are such that they ought to be upheld by somebody. Of course we differ as to who ought to uphold them, but he thinks they ought to be upheld by somebody. Two years ago Mr. Roosevelt was a candidate, and the song that was sung in one note by the Democratic orators from the Atlantic to the Pacific Ocean was the unfitness of Theodore Roosevelt to act as President of the United States. They said that he was a swashbuckler; that he was going about with his sword ready to cut somebody's head off; that he was looking for a fight; that he was dragging his coat-tails on the floor in order that somebody might step on them; that he had a chip on his shoulder, looking around in order that he might show the great power of this country, and what he could do if he were President, and therefore that he was not to be trusted in conducting the foreign affairs of this country. I do not exaggerate. I have heard those statements and read them in the Democratic papers time and time again. They said he was a usurper, a violator of the Constitution; that he would carry this country to perdition if you elected him to the Presidency and gave him free scope. What has happened in those two years? We haven't quite got to the perdition that they predicted, though President Roosevelt is maintaining the army and navy so that we are not pusillanimous; so that we are able to look other nations in the face and not take from them insult of any kind; yet, on the other hand, he has pursued such a policy as, with the prestige which the nation has and with the prestige which he has acquired as the head of this government before the nations of the world, to put an end to one of the greatest of modern wars, the bloody war between Japan and Russia by the signing of peace at Portsmouth. He was able, not less than six months ago, to bring Guatemala and San Salvador, two republics of South America that were engaged in a most bloody contest—to bring their representatives on the deck of an American warship, and there have them sign a protocol of peace. He was able, by the mere force of his character, by his prestige as President, as the peace-loving President, to bring about a truce, by a letter which he sent to the Cubans, and to send back peaceably to their farms the men who were in arms. He sent Secretary Root to South America to convince the republics of that continent that we are not land-grabbers; that we are not seeking to exploit them for our benefit; that we are merely trying to secure fraternal relations with them and merely saying to them, "We shall stand by you to see that you do not suffer in your independence from the possible aggression of European powers." In Santo Domingo in the West Indies he found a dissolution of the bonds of society; they had had an election and then a revolution, and then an election and then a revolution, until they had worn everything out; and they said, "Can not you come in and help us?" The President concluded a treaty, subject to confirmation by the Senate, by which we became the receiver of that island in a sense and collected its customs; but the Senate, or rather the Democratic part of the Senate which prevented the Republicans from having a full two-thirds vote necessary to the confirmation, was afraid that four or five of their members might vote for it, so they caucused to prevent the sanction of the treaty, and it is therefore still hung up in the Senate. Meantime, the President, at the instance of the President of the Santo Domingo Republic, has sent to that island perhaps a dozen American collectors of customs, under an arrangement by which they pay over 55 percent to run the government, and deposit the remaining 45 percent in a New York bank to meet their obligations to European countries, which were very heavy—heavier indeed than they ought to have been. The 45 percent has heaped up a million and a half dollars gold in a New York bank where it has induced the bankers of New York to arrange for a refunding of the debt, and soon it is hoped that with the passage of the treaty that country will be put upon its legs again. Meantime they have had another revolution, and through the intervention of our navy and our collectors of customs that revolution too has come to an end. The result is that this swashbuckler, this gentleman that was going to carry us to perdition, instead of being what was prophesied by our Democratic prophets has turned out to be the most successful peacemaker that ever sat in the Presidential chair.

Now one word as to our colonial policy. We got into the Philippines against our will. That is, Dewey won a victory there and after he had won that victory we could not get out because we had a dilemma before us of three horns. The first one was, Should we turn the islands back to Spain? When we had invoked the aid of the Filipinos to assist us in turning the Spaniards out, it would not have been fair for us to turn the Filipinos back to the tender mercies of Spain, with whom we had fought with the Filipinos on our side. The next horn on the dilemma was, Should we turn these islands over to the Filipinos? While we were there the Filipinos had a government under Aguinaldo of five or six months,—perhaps a little longer,—and there never was in the history of those islands, in the palmiest days of Spanish tyranny, such corruption, such tyranny, such a want altogether of a decent government, as there was under Aguinaldo, demonstrating to those who were there that it was absolutely impossible to turn the islands over to that government, or to those people at that time. The other horn of the dilemma was that we should take the islands ourselves; that we should do for the Filipinos as we would if they were our children, exercising a sacred trust for them; that we should treat the islands as for them alone, and should educate them and gradually train them up by practice in self-government until possibly at the end of that time they could stand alone, and that is the theory that we are attempting to carry out. We have instituted a system of education there, by which today there are in the public schools a half million of Filipino children, reading, writing and reciting in English, and today in the islands, as a result of that education, the English-speaking people outnumber those who use Spanish. Mr. Bryan says that this is an outrage—not the education, he approves the education—but that it is an outrage that we should hold these islands at all. Well, of course, that depends upon the question whether or not they are fitted for self-government. While I was in the islands there were some intelligent Filipinos who came to me and wanted to establish a party, by peaceable means, called the party of independence, and they asked me to give them permission to do so. I said, "You can establish it, if you want it. I can not approve it; it is not necessary that I should, and I do not think it is wise now, and I would advise you to delay." They came to me with a written argument on the subject of the fitness of the Filipinos for self-government. They said that they were convinced that the Filipinos were fit for self-government, because they had counted up the number of offices in the provinces, the municipalities and the central government, and they had also counted up the number of educated Filipinos able to fill those offices, and they found that the number of persons to fill offices was at least double that of the offices. Therefore, they said they could have a shift, and when the country got tired of the first shift they could put in a second shift, and so they were fitted for self-government. This same committee came before the Congressional delegation that went out there last year, and they explained why they were fitted for self-government in this wise. They said, "There are seven percent of us who speak Spanish and who are educated, and we are fit for self-government; we are a governing class. In addition to the governing class there are ninety-three percent that are totally ignorant. They are like children. They are a serving class, an obedient class, and in that way with us as a governing class and with them as a serving class, we will be happy;" and one of them suggested that they might bring in some Chinamen as an animal class who might do the work. Now that reveals the conception that the educated Filipino has of popular government. His idea is not to educate the lower class and educate them so that they will have a healthy public opinion, without which you can not have a popular government at all. Their idea is to keep that class as a serving class. If the Democrats came into power and let the islands go, they would have to take them back again in course of time. They would be doing just exactly what we are doing—struggling patiently to educate these people on the way to self-government. They are a fine people in many ways. They are a Christian people. They are the only Christians in the Orient, and that we owe to the Spanish Catholic friars. They are the only Malays that are Christians, and being Christians they look toward Europe and America for their ideals. The greatest encouragement that anybody interested in that race can have is the eagerness with which the ignorant tao—that means a common man—is anxious to have his children go to the schools to learn English. That indicates that they do want something better and something higher. The difficulty we have in dealing with them is from the continual statements by the Democrats on this side—especially by Mr. Bryan—that we are going to leave the islands just as soon as the Democrats get in. What effect does this have upon us? It deprives us of the earnest support of the conservative people of the islands who will be glad to have us stay, because if in two years there is to be a change and the islands are to be left derelict on the ocean, and this serving class is to be in control, then those who favor the Americans during the time of the American government will not be popular with this class which is to govern, and therefore it keeps them all in a state of unrest and uncertainty.

The next subject to which I wish to call your attention is that which has been made an issue in some districts, the attitude of the President and Congress towards the laboring men of this country and the labor unions. In the first place no one recognizes more fully than the President the absolute necessity that there is for the organization of labor. What could a single laboring man do in the necessary controversies that arise between labor and capital with respect to the adjustment of wages and the division of the product of a union of capital and labor against his wealthy employers, especially when that employer is a great corporation? It may be that in the end wages of labor are determined by the relation of supply of labor to the demand for it, but certainly in the long periods of transition, between good times and bad times, and bad times and good times, readjustment of wages on a fair basis, considering the times, is very much affected by the power that the laboring men may gather for themselves by united effort to increase their wages on a rising market and to prevent the too sudden decrease of their wages on a falling market. There is a great deal of human nature in man, and employers when they come to economize their expenditures in more stringent times are apt to look to their pay-roll, which constitutes their chief expenditure, as the place where they can most easily effect a reduction. On the other hand, when business is improving and profits are increasing they are loath to share these profits with the men who do the work and without whose labor no profit could be had.

Hence I say again that the organization of labor into labor unions is absolutely essential to the welfare of the laboring man in the protection of his legitimate interests; and Theodore Roosevelt is the last man who would lay any obstacle in the way of the efficiency of these organizations to accomplish their legitimate purpose. He is himself an honorary member of the Brotherhood of Locomotive Firemen, and he has taken pains at all times and in every public utterance of his where it was at all relevant, and in his recommendations to Congress, to manifest his interest in the welfare of the laboring men of this country and his earnest desire to see that they do not suffer from the aggressions of capital and that the law makes every provision for the defense of their interests and the betterment of their welfare.

Having heard from the complaints of the laboring men that the eight-hour law was not efficiently administered as to contractors in the war department and in the navy department and in other departments of the government, he instituted an investigation and issued most stringent orders which have now put that law into thorough operation. Having found that the rules with reference to the recovery of damages from railroads for injuries to their employees, suffered through the negligence of the railroad companies or their fellow-servants, were not as uniform and not as equitable as they ought to be, he recommended the passage of an employers' liability act for interstate commerce railroads, which passed at the last session of Congress. Having found that in a lower court there was some doubt about the proper construction of the law with reference to the use of appliances on railroad cars which should prevent injuries to brakemen and other employees concerned about cars, and that a case had been lost by an employee thus injured, in one of the Federal courts of California, and that the employee was unable for want of means to take an appeal, he directed his Attorney-General to take up the case—though a private one—as a government case in order to test the validity of the decision of the court below against the workingman. And this appeal at the instance of the government resulted in a complete reversal of the decision of the court below, a construction of the statute favorable to workingmen, and a judgment for the employee.

Complaint was made to him by the great labor organizations, the Brotherhood of Locomotive Engineers, the Brotherhood of Locomotive Firemen, and the Brotherhood of Railway Conductors, that the issuing of injunctions by the lower Federal courts had at times been abused. They pointed out to the President that there were instances in which legal strikes had been carried on without any violation of the rights of the employers, and that injunctions had sometimes issued on the petition of the employers, and at the instance of their attorneys, on misstatements of the facts, against a striking workingman without any notice or opportunity to demonstrate the lawfulness of their proceedings, and that in such cases it had not infrequently happened that although the strikers were pursuing legal methods, and although the strike was in every way within the law, nevertheless they were discouraged and gave up the controversy.

The President conferred with the heads of these organizations, with the Atorney-General, and after a time agreed with them that the best way of avoiding difficulty was to pass a statute requiring that notice should be issued in the granting of such injunctions. This indeed returned to a practice which had been required by statute in the Federal courts some fifteen or twenty years before. A bill called the Gilbert Bill was introduced in Congress by Mr. Gilbert of Indiana, to require that no injunction should issue against a defendant in such cases until he had a chance to be heard in a court and explain just exactly what he intended to do and to show that he did not intend in any way illegally to infringe upon the rights of his employers. The Gilbert Bill was introduced, but then Mr. Gompers, representing the Federation of Labor, came before the committee and said that the bill was not satisfactory to him. He went before the President and the Speaker, Mr. Cannon, and demanded not the Gilbert Bill, but demanded that all injunctions should be abolished and that a bill should be passed which I am about to describe.

The first section of the Gompers Bill provides that no Federal court shall have the power to enjoin men from unlawfully injuring the business of another in a labor dispute. The claim made by Mr. Gompers and those who support the bill, is that under ancient practice in equity injunctions issued only to protect property, and business is not a property right, and that for the lower Federal courts to protect a business from unlawful injury is a judicial usurpation. The Supreme Court of the United States has decided that injunctions may properly issue to protect either a property right or a right of a pecuniary nature. The issue therefore made by Mr. Gompers and his associates is shortly stated thus: Whether the business that a man has built up, the business that he is doing in manufacturing or otherwise, including as it does the good will, may be injured unlawfully by laboring men in a labor dispute, and they be exempted from any interference with such unlawful action by the writ of injunction, so that all he can do to protect his business in a private suit is to bring a suit for damages and to have the matter tried before a jury to determine the amount of the damages. This is of course a remedy which everyone will recognize as wholly inadequate to protect him in his business right. I am willing to submit to any body of laymen the question whether a man's business, involving his good will, that which by advertising and lawful and honest dealing he has made a valuable asset to him, so it passes to his next of kin when he dies, and may be sold by his administrator, is not a right of a pecuniary nature which ought to be protected by injunction just exactly as any property right ought to be. All the courts have decided that this is the case, and the charge that the lower Federal courts or the state courts, and there are a great number who have held that injunctions may issue in such cases, have usurped their authority, falls to the ground. In this view the President declined to recommend the passage of a law abolishing the writ of injunction in labor disputes, and he did so on the ground that to do so would be to place laboring men who were violating the rights of others in a special class enjoying immunity from the remedies of the law.

A farmer might unlawfully injure a man's business, a physician might injure another man's business, a lawyer might injure another man's business, and against them the writ of injunction would issue, but this bill contemplated that it should not issue in such cases against a laboring man. The President is against privileges to any special class and so was against that bill. Therefore he told Mr. Gompers that while he strongly favored the giving of notices in such cases, he would certainly invoke as against lawless workingmen the same writ of injunction that he would invoke against lawless capitalists; that he was in favor of a square deal to all and special privileges to none.

The second section of the Gompers bill in effect legalizes boycotts and blacklisting and forbids their restraint or punishment. These are cruel methods, taken sometimes by employers, sometimes by the employees, to effect purposes which in themselves may be laudable, but the method used is so oppressive and cruel that the commission appointed by the President to investigate the anthracite coal strike in Pennsylvania, upon which was a president of a labor union, reported unanimously that boycotts and blacklisting were cruel and lawless and should not be supported in a civilized society and that they ought to be denounced in the law. I ask you whether under these circumstances a bill which in effect legalizes both ought to receive the votes of members of Congress?

In the hearing before the committee, Mr. Gompers, as representative of the American Federation of Labor, was opposed by the representatives of the great labor unions of the railroads, to which I have referred, and in the statement before the committee it was repeatedly stated that there had never been a President who had shown as much sympathy with the laboring men and with the labor unions as Theodore Roosevelt; so much active sympathy and so great desire not to talk about them, but to do things in their behalf.

Now it is said that this Congress has acted injuriously to labor in regard to the Panama Canal and the employment of labor. The eight-hour law applies to work done directly under the government. The Attorney-General, therefore, held that it applied to the day laborers on the Isthmus. Congress amended the law so that it should apply only to American laborers on the Isthmus and not to aliens. The Isthmus of Panama is in the Tropics. It is impossible for an American laborer to work there except under cover, and all the American labor possible for us to get we use. But it is all skilled labor, engineers, machinists and other skilled mechanics. The common labor the American finds impossible to do because of the terror of the tropical sun and the tropical torrents of rain that fall during the rainy season. We are therefore limited in our employment of common labor to those men who can stand the tropical heat in their day's work and we are now using tropical negroes from the West Indies on the ditch. These men have nothing of the industry of the American workingman. Instead of beginning their work on Monday morning and working industriously and with effect until Saturday night, they do not begin work until Tuesday and they lay off work on Friday, and it is very rare that we can get more than four days a week out of six from them. If you pay them twenty percent more wages they will work just twenty percent less, for they want only to feed themselves and to enjoy their leisure.

Now the eight-hour law in the United States affecting the government is a law passed as a type and standard for other employers for the purpose of encouraging a reduction in the hours of those workingmen who are industrious and put in eight hours of work for six days in the week, so that out of the remainder of the twenty-four hours each day they may rest, may have time for recreation and for intercourse with their families and for such reading as they may be willing to do. The principle of such law and the reasons for recognizing it have not the slightest application to laborers such as I have described, the tropical negroes of the West Indies. We never could get out of them, although we employ them for the week, eight hours a day for six days. We must build the canal, and to allow sentimental considerations, that really have no relevance at all to the work under such conditions, to increase the difficulties that we have found in getting the necessary labor, is to fly in the face of reason. Again, the administration is criticised for investigating the question with a view possibly of employing Chinese labor on the Isthmus.

If Chinese common labor is more efficient than the tropical negro labor, why then should we not employ it, when it does not come into competition in any way whatsoever with American labor, when the work is to be done about two thousand miles away from the territory of the United States, and under circumstances which will not affect in the slightest workingmen in the United States? If yellow labor is able to withstand the effects of the tropical sun, what difference does it make whether we employ black labor or yellow labor if the American laborer cannot do the work? President Roosevelt believes that we ought to use reason and not to be carried away by sentiment that has no basis in common sense.

And now, ladies and gentlemen, I come to another question which seems to be a local question, and yet one in which the President is deeply interested, because it is a question much wider than the State of Idaho, and reaches out into the neighboring states and to the country at large. First I ought to state the position of the President. It is that he favors and has the most active sympathy with all branches of labor and all branches of labor organizations; that he favors and has sympathy with all corporate enterprises that make for the prosperity of the country; but the line he draws, and the line he insists upon, is that if a representative of either steps beyond the law and violates it, he must be punished. Now in the neighboring State of Colorado they had for years a condition in which both miners and state officers and the heads of mining corporations violated the law in a war against each other, and the President is utterly out of sympathy with them all. They brought disgrace upon the State of Colorado, and what he is hoping and praying for is that conditions may not arise in Idaho which shall lead to the same results. He believes that the election of Governor Gooding is one of the most important issues of this campaign. The question, as he views it, is whether an executive officer, charged with the execution of the law, who attempts to bring to trial, and does bring to trial, men charged with a heinous crime, shall be marked for defeat at an election because those men can awaken sympathy the country over because of their associations and affiliations. This is not a prosecution by a corporation. This is a prosecution by the State of Idaho to vindicate it and its community and to punish a heinous crime. It is not an incident in a war between capital and labor. It is merely the punishment of crime. Neither Governor Gooding nor anyone interested in the prosecution says that the men are guilty. What he says, and what the officers of the law charged with the duty of bringing them to trial say, is that there is evidence enough to justify their indictment by a grand jury lawfully impaneled, and therefore that they ought to be brought to trial. It is said that there was injustice in their extradition. All the papers were made regularly; the evidence was set out and was examined by the Governor of this State before he presented his agent with a request for a warrant of extradition. The evidence was examined by the Governor of Colorado before that Governor passed upon it and issued his warrant and the men were brought here. Now it is said that they were not fugitives from justice because when the crime was committed with which they were charged they were in the State of Colorado and the explosion which took the life of Governor Steunenberg occurred in this State. I ask you whether an executive officer did wrong to assume that a man from one State who committed a crime in another, though not personally present in the other, was nevertheless in law to be regarded as a fugitive from the justice of the State in which the crime was committed? Could he not reasonably assume that that was the law until it was decided to be otherwise by the highest court of the land? In other words, might he not assume that there was not a premium to be put upon doing murder across State lines ? If Governor Gooding is defeated in this election for this reason, then the State of Idaho and the people of the State of Idaho will serve notice on the world that criminals, or men charged with crime, who have a wide influence and can awaken a sympathy for themselves, can bring down condemnation upon the officers of the law having the courage to bring them to trial, and that such officer is to be condemned by his own people and turned out of office, or at least not re-elected when he submits himself to their suffrages. The charge is made that Governor Gooding is going to railroad these men to the gallows. I assume—I know—that the State of Idaho has a proper legal procedure for the trial of persons charged with crime; that it includes a petit jury and a court to see that the jury does its duty and is instructed as to the law; that it includes a Supreme Court to which any error committed in that trial can be carried; and that it includes the Supreme Court of the United States to which Federal questions arising as to rights under the Federal constitution can be carried for decision there. The prisoners have enjoyed counsel. They have had funds furnished to them by their friends. There is no right which has been denied them. Why then should the officers of the law who are simply doing their duty be punished by popular disapproval at election? But it is said that this is not an issue in this campaign. Senator Dubois, an old friend of mine, says that I had no business to come to this State to speak on this issue. Though an old friend of Senator Dubois, I differ frequently with him on political subjects, and one of the most frequent differences on political subjects is, "What is the issue of a campaign?" Governor Gooding from one end of this country to the other is receiving threatening letters from those who do not sympathize with the crime charged to Moyer and Haywood but who think that they are not guilty. He is now being opposed in his election by many men who are going all over this State and spending money for the purpose. If then he is defeated, I ask you whether the country is not likely to charge—will not necessarily charge—that the reason for his defeat is because he had the courage to do his duty? One Democratic paper (I do not know but that there are others) in one part of the State invites opposition to Governor Gooding and a vote for his opponent because Governor Gooding brought Moyer and Haywood to this State. In other parts the Democratic papers follow the Democratic platform, which is in favor of law and order and the punishment of those responsible for crime. I assume that the opponent of Governor Gooding is a law-abiding citizen and would obey the law, but he can not be elected without the aid of those who are opposing Governor Gooding on the ground that he did his duty. Therefore I do not care what is said with respect to other issues, the issue of the supremacy of the law is the real issue—the standing up for your officials who have courage in face of explosions, in face of hostile and powerful interests to enforce the law. The supremacy of the law under such circumstances is an issue that overshadows all issues and ought therefore to lead all patriotic citizens, without regard to party, to support your faithful official.

9

The Legislative Policies of the Present Administration

Columbus, Ohio, August 19, 1907

Quickening of Public Conscience in Midst of Prosperity

Members of the Buckeye Republican Club and Fellow-Citizens of Ohio: The present is a period of the greatest prosperity, general comfort and even luxury. Throughout this country, the demand for labor has increased wages to a higher point than ever known before. The compensation of skilled labor now frequently exceeds that of certain professions, like teaching and the ministry. Wealth has accumulated enormously in the hands of individuals and never before have rich men given so freely of their fortunes to educational and charitable objects. Such conditions are apt to dim and dull the eye and the ear of the people to abuses and dishonesty in the body politic and social. In such periods in the history of ancient republics their foundations were sapped and their fall ultimately brought about. Prophets of evil have foretold the same fate for this Republic. They have been refuted. In spite of the general comfort, there have been made manifest by signs not to be misunderstood, a quickening of the public conscience and a demand for the remedy of abuses, the outgrowth of this prosperity, and for a higher standard of business integrity. Every lover of his country should have a feeling of pride and exaltation in this evidence that our society is still sound at the core.

Abuses in Railway Discriminations

I have been invited by your body to discuss the national issues. Some of these involve the abuses over which the public conscience has been aroused, and the proper remedies for their removal. The first, and possibly the greatest, abuse has been in the management of the arterial system of the country which the interstate railroads form. Any unjust discrimination in the terms upon which transportation of freight or passengers is afforded an individual or a locality, paralyzes and withers the business of the individual or the locality exactly as the binding of the arteries and veins leading to a member of the human body destroys its life.

Failure of Old Interstate Commerce Law and Causes

The result of twenty years' operation under the interstate commerce act of 1887, passed to restrain abuses of unjust discrimination and unreasonableness of rates, was that the railroads came to regard the action of the commission it created as of no importance. The delays, due to the necessity of resorting to the courts to try out the merits of every order of the commission, before it became effective, made the remedy of the complaining shipper or locality so slow and burdensome that in contested cases it was no remedy at all. The commission was not, under the old act, authorized to fix reasonable rates. It could only say that a particular rate was unreasonable and order a railroad to change its rate and make it reasonable. The railroad might fix a new rate at anything less than the rate declared to be unreasonable, and if the reduction made was not sufficient, a new action had to be brought to decide that the new rate was also unreasonable.

President Roosevelt's Recommendation— New Rate Bill

Made aware of the moribund condition of railway regulation under the old law and of the widespread abuses which prevailed in railway management,

President Roosevelt, in his message of 1904, recommended that the powers of the commission be largely increased; first, by enabling the commission to fix rates, and second, by making its order effective against the carriers without resort to courts to compel performance. He asked that it be made an administrative tribunal with real power. This was done by the passage of the Rate Bill, in June, 1906. The new act enables the commission to fix rates and gives efficacy to all of its orders by providing that they shall go into effect thirty days after they are made, unless suspended by an order of court, and failure to comply with them is punishable by a fine of $5,000 a day during the delinquency. Express companies, sleeping car companies, and oil pipeline companies are brought under the jurisdiction of the commission as common carriers. The act gives the commission power to fix rates for the various incidental services performed by railways at terminals and on the journey and to require them to be performed for every shipper. By withholding such services from one, and extending them to another, and by imposing varying charges for them, companies have been able in the past to make them a convenient instrument for discrimination. The new law requires the publication of rates charged for such incidental services. Railroads are compelled to furnish cars without discrimination for the movement of traffic. After May, 1908, they are confined in their business strictly to transportation by a provision forbidding them, after that date, to transport for themselves anything but what is intended for their use as common carriers. Experience has shown that the railroads can not be trusted to deal fairly in matters of transportation between themselves and their competitors in an outside business. The new law makes radical changes in the matter of the publication of rates. Under the old law, by means of what was called the "midnight tariff," a railroad company gave favored shippers advance information of a contemplated reduction of rate and immediately restored the old rate when these shippers had profited by it. Thirty days' notice is now required of any change in the rates unless the commission, for good cause, modifies the requirement.

Resembles National Banking Act

Again, the new law enables the commission to prescribe a uniform system of accounting for railroads. Under the old law the commission could call for a report of the railroads and might ask questions of railroads, but it had no way to compel a compliance with its request, and no penalty was provided in the law for failure to make the full report. Under the new law, annual reports must be made under oath, and penalties are prescribed for failure to file them with the commission within a certain time. The commission can call for monthly or special reports. It may prescribe the bookkeeping methods of the carrier and has access at all times through examiners to the carrier's books. The carrier is forbidden to keep any other books than those prescribed. The commission's authority, under the new law, over interstate commerce railroads is thus in many respects like that of the Comptroller of the Currency over National Banks, which has the approval and confidence of the country.

Great Opposition by Railroads— Their Arguments against Bill

Never before was there such a united opposition by the railroad interests to any National measure as they instituted against the Rate Bill. A campaign of education was entered upon, speeches were made in every part of the country and literature was showered upon the members of every community, with the hope of convincing the public that the bill was a dangerous innovation.

The objections urged against it were three: First, it was said to be unwise because it was a departure from the *laissez-faire* doctrine of as little government as possible, and was a long step toward socialism and Government ownership.

Outraged Public Opinion Carried the Bill

The revelations of infidelity to trust obligations in the Insurance investigations in New York, the fraudulent discriminations in the traffic of the coal-carrying roads, disclosed by the inquiry made by the interstate commerce commission, and the disclosure of secret rebates on an enormous scale granted the Standard Oil Company by the railroads in the report of Mr. Garfield, as Commissioner of Corporations, overcame such a specious argument, created a strong public opinion in favor of a radical remedy against all dishonest corporate practices, and held up the hands of those supporting the bill.

Second Objection—Incompetency of Commission to Fix Rates—Proved Too Much

The second ground of opposition was that a tribunal like the commission was utterly unable to fix rates,—that the fixing of rates was such a difficult matter, that only the expert traffic managers of railroads were competent for the work; that each rate was so connected with every other that it was impossible for a body of laymen to reach a safe and just conclusion in respect to any one rate, without creating hopeless confusion. The argument proved too much. If the commission could not fix rates, then neither it nor a court could safely determine whether a rate was unreasonable, for exactly the same expert knowledge was needed to say that a rate was unreasonable as to say what was a maximum reasonable rate. Indeed, in the natural mental process, a maximum reasonable rate must be determined before declaring the rate in question unreasonable. All this inevitably led to the conclusion that there was no remedy either by Commission or Court against unreasonable rates, that the public was helpless, and that the whole matter must still be left to the only experts, the traffic managers of the railroads, although it was the dishonesty, discrimination and injustice of many of them which had been the cause of the trouble. Naturally, the argument had weight neither with Congress nor with the public.

Constitutional Objection by Railroads without Weight

The third and final objection was that the law was invalid in that Congress was thereby delegating its legislative power to another body, and was violating the general constitutional rule that delegated power can not be delegated. The rule has an exception. There may be delegation of legislative power where the purpose in the original conferring of the power can be subserved only by its delegation to an agent. It is admitted that the constitution gives Congress the power to fix rates. Obviously, however, it is impossible for Congress as a body to spend the time and labor to do so. If the power is to be exercised at all, practically it can be done only through a tribunal or an agency like that of the interstate commerce commission. Hence Congress may delegate the power under proper legislative limitations and rules of decision. A similar conclusion has been reached by a number of State courts with reference to the power of legislatures under State constitutions presenting the same question, and while the case has not, with respect to a Federal commission, been brought directly before the Supreme Court of the United States, there is a plain dictum in one decision in favor of the validity of such delegation of legislative power.

Small Vote against Bill

The opponents of the bill were not able with these objections to muster more than seven negative votes in the House of Representatives, or three votes in the Senate.

Opponents of Rate Bill Now Belittle It and Praise Elkins Bill

The opponents of the measure continue to denounce it, but now instead of pointing out its disastrous effect, they say it is a failure and that in the year since its passage, it has not helped a single shipper. They insist that the only effective and all-sufficient law to regulate railways is the Elkins act, passed in 1903, and that this is shown by the fact that all the prosecutions in which convictions have been had against railway companies and favored shippers in the last two years, have been under the Elkins Act, and not under the Rate Bill. Let us look into the facts in regard to this allegation. The chief prosecutions which have been instituted have been criminal indictments against the Sugar Trust and the Standard Oil Company, and certain railways and their agents and officers for taking and giving secret money rebates. They could not have been brought under the Rate Bill, because the acts prosecuted were committed before the passage of the Rate Bill.

Effect of Elkins Bill on Existing Criminal Prosecutions Was to Save Rebate Givers and Takers from Jail

It is true that these prosecutions were instituted under the Elkins Act, but it is also true that had the Elkins bill never been passed, the same acts could and doubtless would have been prosecuted as giving and receiving unjust discriminations against the persons committing them under the amendment to the Interstate Commerce Act of 1889 which the Elkins law supplanted. The Elkins law was really an amendment to the Interstate Commerce Act, enlarging and making more effective the procedure for prosecuting violations of the prohibitions of that law and describing them in more comprehensive form. It gave greater latitude in respect of the district where the offense would be prosecuted and it made the company necessarily responsible in a fine for the act of its agents, without other proof of direct complicity than the agency. Under the 1889 amendment, however, the individuals convicted could have been sent to the penitentiary, whereas under the Elkins Act the punishment by imprisonment was taken away while the fine was increased. The chief effect the Elkins law had on these particular prosecutions which have been given so much prominence, was to make it easier to convict the corporation and to increase its fine, but to save the guilty individual perpetrators from imprisonment.

Railroads Favored Elkins Bill Because of Abolition of Jail Penalty

It is well understood that the Elkins bill was passed without opposition by, and with the full consent of, the railroads and that the chief reason for this was the elimination of the penitentiary penalty for unjust discriminations. The abolition of imprisonment, as a possible penalty, was unfortunate. Experience has shown that a mere fine is generally not enough to deter a corporation from violation of the law, because it then becomes a matter of mere business speculation. The imprisonment of two or three prominent officers of a railway company, or a trust, engaged in giving or receiving secret rebates, would have a greater deterrent effect for the future than millions in a fine.

Rate Bill Restored Jail Penalty

In the Rate Bill, Congress amended the Elkins bill and restored imprisonment as part of the punishment for secret rebates. Had the rebating and
dishonest practices of the railroad companies and the trusts, been as clearly
known to Congress and the public, when the Elkins bill was considered,
as they were when the Rate Bill was passed, the Elkins bill would not have
passed so smoothly.

Narrow Scope of Elkins Bill
as Compared with Rate Bill

I do not wish to decry the merits of the Elkins bill because, aside from its
elimination of imprisonment as punishment, it is a most useful measure,
but its scope is so narrow in respect of the regulation of railways that it can
not be compared in importance of operation and effect to the Rate Bill.
The increase by the Rate Bill in the powers of the commission in supervision, investigation, rate-fixing and effective order-making to prevent discrimination is great. Elaborate machinery for making it difficult to violate
the law without discovery and for discovering violations when they exist,
and for affording affirmative and mandatory relief in requiring railroads to
furnish equal facilities to all, is found in the provisions of the New Rate
Bill. Criminal prosecutions will continue to be under the Elkins law, but as
amended by the new Rate Bill. This is because the Elkins law, as amended,
contains the part of the interstate commerce legislation which prescribes
the punishment for violations of the law and so, in ordinary practice,
comes into operation after the violations have been discovered under the
other provisions of the Rate Bill.

If the Rate Bill Is Ineffective
Why Such Railroad Opposition?

If the Rate Bill was likely to be a failure and to accomplish nothing in the
regulation of their business, the query naturally arises, Why did the railroads
spend so much money and so great effort to defeat it? Why was it, if it had
no effect, that in the interval between the time of its passage and its going

into effect, there were filed with the interstate commerce commission more notices of reduced rates by the railroads than ever had been filed in the previous twenty years of the life of the interstate commerce law? It is true that later on, many rates were properly raised by the railroads because of an increase in wages and other cost of maintenance; but I only cite the prompt action of the railways on the passage of the bill as a recognition by them of the importance of the measure and the increased power of the commission.

Good Effect of Rate Bill Naturally
Not Shown in Statistics

The Rate Law has not been in operation a year, and the beneficial results from its operations though clear, are not ready to be presented in statistical array. Moreover, the chief benefit of the act is likely to be its influence in discouraging attempts to renew the old abuses and such benefits do not appear in statistics. The immediate effect of the act has certainly been to compel railroads to regard the commission now as the important tribunal whose views they must follow. They are manifesting every outward disposition strictly to comply with the law and to avoid prosecution or complaint. The time has gone by in which the action of the commission can be ignored or laughed at. The commission itself has taken up its duties with renewed energy, has proceeded, without awaiting the intervention of the railroads or the filing of complaints, to construe the act by administrative rulings, in order to assist the railroads in complying with the law. With the large powers for correcting evils, which the commission now has, we may reasonably expect a marked improvement in the conduct of the railways of this country.

The Attitude of the Country
toward the Rate Bill

The passage of the Bill was taken, the country over, and properly taken, as a most important step toward the suppression of abuses which had grown up in a period of tolerant prosperity. It was thought to be an effective cure of the arterial system of the country which had become poisoned by dishonesty, injustice and fraud. It was a great solace to the conscience of the country outraged by recent revelations of railway and trust management. Passed at the instance of Mr. Roosevelt, it stands as a monument to the principle which he has incessantly maintained in speech and action, that the laws must be so made that they can be enforced as well against the sins of the wealthy and the powerful as against those of the poor.

Error of Mr. Bryan as to
Court Review in Rate Bill

Mr. Bryan contends that the law was greatly weakened in authorizing, or recognizing judicial intervention to restrain the orders of the commission. This criticism has not the slightest foundation. There can be no judicial appeal in the nature of a complete review on the merits from the commission to the Supreme Court or to the circuit court of the United States, for the commission is not a court of first instance, but only a mere administrative tribunal. The only power a Federal Court could validly exercise would be to decide first, whether the administrative tribunal had followed correctly the limitations upon its course of action imposed by the act of Congress creating it, and second, whether its order taken as an authorized expression of the legislative power deprived the railroad company of its right, under the fourteenth amendment, to derive a fair profit from the use of its property. Whether the Federal courts were expressly given this power in the law or not, they would have had it under their general jurisdiction. If their power had not been recognized and a purpose of Congress had been expressed to prevent an appeal to the courts, the law would have been invalid. The extent of the judicial remedy could not be either diminished or enlarged by Congressional action, with due regard to the validity of the act. Congress was wise, therefore, in not attempting to define what the court should or should not do, and in merely recognizing the right of the companies to appeal to the Federal courts to test the validity of the action of the commission. No victory was gained by either the conservative or the radical party in this regard.

Importance of Courts in Upholding
Constitutional Guaranties

By what I have said, however, I would not for a moment be thought to favor any legislation which would exclude railroad companies or anyone else from a recourse to the courts to protect them in their statutory and constitutional rights. The courts, and especially the Supreme Court of the United States, are the part of our government indispensable in making good those guaranties of life, liberty, property and the pursuit of happiness given in the Constitution and placed there by the people themselves to curb their own hasty action under stress of sudden impulse or with too little deliberation. The administration of exact justice by courts without fear or favor, unmoved by the influence of the wealthy or by the threats of the demagogue, is the highest ideal that a government of the people can strive for, and any means by which a suitor, however unpopular or poor, is deprived of enjoying this is to be condemned. It is important, however, that appeals to judicial remedies should be limited in such a way that parties will not use them merely to delay and so clog efficient and just executive or legislative action.

New Amendments to the Rate Bill
Needed—Classification

The Rate law does not go far enough. The practice under it has already disclosed the necessity for new amendments and will doubtless suggest more. Such is the true method—the empirical and tentative method—of securing proper remedies for a new evil. The classification of merchandise for transportation is a most important matter in rate-fixing, for by a transfer from one class to another, the rate is changed and may work injustice. With the power of rate-fixing, it would seem, should go the power in the commission to classify and to prescribe rules for uniform classification by all railroads.

Amendment Needed to Prevent
Over-Capitalization

Recent revelations have emphasized the pernicious effect of the so-called over-capitalization of railroads which aids unscrupulous stock manipulators in disposing of railway securities at unreasonably high prices to innocent buyers. This evil would not of itself justify Federal restraint or control because such stock and bonds are usually issued under State charters. The practice, however, has a tendency to divert the money paid by the public for the stock and bonds which ought to be expended in improving the road bed, track and equipment of railways into the pockets of the dishonest manipulators and thus to pile such an unprofitable debt upon a railway as to make bankruptcy and a receivership probable in the first business stringency. This result, in an interstate railway, necessarily interferes with, and burdens, interstate commerce, and justifies the exercise of the regulative power of Congress to stop the practice. A railroad company engaged in interstate commerce should not be permitted, therefore, to issue stock or bonds and put them on sale in the market except after a certificate by the interstate commerce commission that the securities are issued with the approval of the commission for a legitimate railroad purpose. The railroads that are honestly conducted would accept the certificate of the commission as a valuable one in the markets of the world, and only railway stock manipulators, who look to the floating of watered securities as their best source of profit, would have reason to complain.

Amendments against Purchase of Stock in Competing Lines and against Common Directors

A much-used means of eliminating competition among interstate lines serving the same territory is the acquisition by one company of the stock in another and the election of directors to represent that stock. This process is facilitated by the uncontrolled power to issue securities beyond the needs of the company for its legitimate business and would be curbed by the restriction proposed. The evil ought further to be directly restrained by making it unlawful for an interstate railway to acquire stock in a competing line. This is a simpler remedy of meeting the evil than by recourse to the anti-trust law under the Northern Securities case. In addition to this, competing lines should be prohibited from having directors or officers in common.

Proposed Amendments Plainly Constitutional

These suggestions of additional legislation in respect to the supervision and control of interstate railways have been made by the interstate commerce commission and I heartily concur in them. They are plainly within the Federal jurisdiction under the interstate commerce clause. I do not think that in order to accomplish a good which the Federal Government with its greater resources and wider geographical reach can bring about more quickly and efficiently, the constitutional limits upon Federal action should be blurred out or an undoubted Federal power should be expanded by doubtful construction into a field which really belongs to the State. But the right of Congress to take any action, not confiscatory, in the most rigid control of interstate commerce can not be denied.

Suggested by Harriman Consolidations

The measures taken and proposed are radical perhaps, viewed from the standpoint of the *laissez-faire* doctrinaire whose ideas have been allowed to prevail in respect of railroad management down to the present; but no one can read the report of the commission on the history of the union of the Southern Pacific and Union Pacific systems with the Illinois Central system without trembling at the enormous power that one man, by the uncontrolled use of the stock and bond issuing power of interstate railways under State charters, has acquired in respect of a vital part of the country's business and without looking for some means of remedying such a dangerous tendency which, if not stopped, will lead to the absorption of all the railroads of the country into one hand.

Rate Bill and Proposed Amendments
Not Socialistic, but the Opposite

The contention on behalf of the railroads, already noticed, that such supervision as the Rate Bill and these suggested amendments afford, is socialistic and tends to Government ownership, is utterly without basis. Efficient regulation is the very antidote and preventative of socialism and Government ownership. The railroads, until now, have been permitted to wield without any real control the enormously important franchise of furnishing transportation to the entire country. They have constructed 230,000 miles of road. In certain respects they have done a marvelous work and have afforded transportation at a cheaper rate, per ton, per mile and per passenger, than in any country in the world. They have, however, many of them, shamelessly violated the trust obligation they have been under to the public of furnishing equal facilities at the same price to all shippers. The watering of stock and bonds and the over-capitalization of some of them for the profit of their managers have prevented the needed improvement of their railroads in construction and equipment. The tremendous demand for increased facilities due to the enormous growth of business shows the inadequacy of their equipment and construction. While they might not have been expected to meet in full such an extraordinary demand, the obligations some of them have assumed in the form of stocks and bonds leave no doubt that, had the money they represented been put into the roads in good faith, the shortage of cars and equipment and inadequacy of road bed and track would not be so great. They discharge a public function. They have been weighed in the balance and found wanting. The remedy for the evils must be radical to be effective. If it is not so, then we may certainly expect that the movement toward Government ownership will become a formidable one that can not be stayed.

Objections to Government Ownership

I am opposed to Government ownership—

First, because existing Government railways are not managed with either the efficiency or economy of privately managed roads and the rates charged are not as low and therefore not as beneficial to the public;

Second, because it would involve an expenditure of certainly twelve billions of dollars to acquire the interstate railways and the creation of an enormous national debt.

Third, because it would place in the hands of a reckless executive a power of control over business and politics that the imagination can hardly conceive, and would expose our popular institutions to danger.

Proposed Railway Regulation
Not Inconsistent with Individualism

The supervision proposed need not materially reduce the legitimate operation of individualism in railway enterprise. It will indeed limit the opportunity to accumulate enormous fortunes through over-capitalization or secret rebates, but the legitimate profit which comes from close attention to operation, to efficiency of service, and economy in details and from broad conceptions of new methods of reducing cost without impairing the service will not be disturbed in the slightest. There is no attempt to take away the property of the railway companies; there is no furnishing of public money to the enterprise and no public officers are required to administer the property. There is no more attempt in this law to make transportation a Government business than there is in the National Banking act to making banking a government business.

Favors Railway Rate Agreements If Submitted to and Approved by Interstate Commerce Commission

The movement of competing railway companies to consolidate arose originally from fear that the antitrust act forbade them to make agreements as to uniform tariffs. If they were now permitted to make such agreements subject to the approval of the interstate commerce commission, such a tendency would lose much of its force. It is impossible to prevent competing railways from seeking to make their tariffs uniform in order to prevent an unending and disastrous tariff war, and though such agreements are against the law, it is perfectly apparent that tacit arrangements for uniformity exist. These arrangements do not prevent the operation of competition, from time to time as one company finds that it may acquire new business without loss by a reduction of rate and insists on it, but they do prevent a tariff war which helps neither the public nor the railway by violent fluctuations in rates. As the public now asserts the right to fix maximum rates and thus to eliminate one phase of competition, it is logical to permit an agreement on rates, if approved by the interstate commerce commission, the tribunal appointed to fix rates. The President and the commission both recommend a provision permitting such agreements. In this way, there would be restored that respect for law which many railroad men in the last decade seem to have lost. Moreover, every company under such a system would be a policeman to see to it that every other company obeyed the agreement and the law, and strictest obedience would be secured.

Physical Valuation

Mr. Bryan is most insistent, in discussing rate regulation, that the present physical value of all roads in the country should be ascertained for the purpose of fixing rates by allowing to the railroad companies only a fair profit on such valuation. Whenever the interstate commerce commission deems it important as an aid in fixing rates to determine what it would cost now to rebuild any railroad, it has complete power to do so; but it would doubtless be found in respect to most of them that in spite of over-capitalization and lack of economy in construction, land for terminals and right of way and the cost of construction, have increased so enormously that the total of their securities upon which they pay dividends and interest is not much if any in excess of present physical value. More than this, physical valuation, as the President pointed out in his Indianapolis speech, and as the Supreme Court had in effect said before him, is only one of a number of data to be considered in reaching what is a fair profit upon the investment; and in determining a particular rate, the proper relation between that rate and the total net profit of operation is so complicated with an infinite variety of other circumstances that it is most difficult in rate-fixing to use the latter to affect the former. The importance of fixing rates, complained of as too great in and of themselves, is much exaggerated; for the overwhelming evidence is that, on the whole, rates in this country, especially as compared with those of all European railroads, many of which are owned and operated by the government, are low. The chief evil consists in unjust discrimination in rates between individuals and localities. I do not object to valuation, if thought relevant to any issue, but I merely deprecate the assumption that it is to be the chief means of a great reform in rates.

Frightful Loss of Life and Limb among
Railway Employees Requires Stringent Regulations

The frightful loss of life and limb among the railway employees of this country, reaching more than 4,000 killed and 65,000 injured in one year, has properly attracted the attention of Congress and the Legislatures. It makes apparent that service in connection with trains of a railway is an extra-hazardous business and may well call for Government supervision and exceptional rules to secure the safety of the passengers and reduce the danger to employees. Congress, years ago, passed stringent laws for the adoption of safety devices to protect both employee and passenger on interstate railways. With the same purpose, it has recently limited the hours of continuous service for which employees on such railways may be engaged.

Statutory Rule for Liability of Interstate Railways to Employees

Finally, it has regulated the rules for the liability of an interstate railroad company to an employee injured in its service. This is a most important measure, for an unfortunate lack of uniformity has existed heretofore in respect to the rules of liability in such cases, dependent on the court in which the case has been tried. The new statute makes everything uniform as to interstate railroads. It has introduced into Federal law what is called the comparative negligence theory by which if an employee is injured, proof of negligence on his part does not forfeit his claim for damages entirely unless the accident was due solely to his negligence. If there was negligence by the company, the jury is authorized to apportion the negligence and award compensation for the proper part of the damage to the employee and the question of negligence is always for the jury.

Abolition of Fellow-Servant Rule

The most important provision of this law, however, is that abolishing what is known as the fellow-servant rule, by which an employee injured can not recover from his employer for injury sustained through the negligence of a co-employee. This rule was incorporated into the law by Chief Justice Shaw, of Massachusetts, on the ground of public policy. It was acquiesced in by the Courts of England and of this country. Whatever may have been the wisdom of the rule originally, a change of conditions justifies its abrogation. Public policy can be changed by statute, so that this exemption from liability is not secured by the constitution to the railroad companies. The abolition of the exemption certainly furnishes a strong motive to the railroad companies for the exercise of greater care in the selection, supervision and control of all of their employees, which tends not only to the safety of their employees, but also to the safety of their passengers.

New Law Will Lead to Settlement
of Most Claims without Suit

With these changes, all claims by employees against railroad companies, except in a few extreme cases, will doubtless be settled by the railway companies without litigation, just as they now settle without suit substantially all claims for injuries to passengers. The validity of this law is under consideration by the Supreme Court. The only serious doubt in regard to its constitutionality grows out of some carelessness of language in limiting its application to interstate railways and, therefore, even if the present law should fall, there will be no difficulty in reënacting it in proper form.

Trusts

I pass now from railway regulation and the abuses arising in the discharge of a public function to the evils which have grown out of the combinations existing in private business, and so come to the subject of Trusts. The combination of capital in large plants to manufacture goods with the greatest economy is just as necessary as the assembling of the parts of a machine to the economical and more rapid manufacture of what in old times was made by hand. The Government should not interfere with the one any more than the other. In the proper operation of competition the public will soon share with the manufacturer the advantage in lowered prices. When, however, such combinations not only lower the cost to themselves, but are able to control the market and maintain or raise the old prices, the public derives no benefit and is helpless in the hands of a monopoly.

Anti-Trust Law

Fear of the existence of such an abuse led to the passage of the anti-trust law, in 1890. It recognizes two forms in which this evil may be maintained. One is by an agreement among a number of different manufacturers of an article for the maintenance of the price of the article and the suppression of competition. This is denounced when the contract is in restraint of interstate trade as a criminal offense against the United States, punishable by fine and imprisonment, and a conspiracy which may be restrained by injunction in a civil suit. The other form is denounced, with similar remedies against it, as a monopoly of interstate trade, and covers the union of the conspiring companies into one company which, by owning all the plant or nearly all the plant, engaged in the manufacture of the product and by use of other devices, controls the prices. The Supreme Court of the United States has not defined what a monopoly under this section of the anti-trust law is.

Definition of Unlawful Monopoly

I conceive that it is not sufficiently defined by saying that it is the combination of a large part of the plants in the country engaged in the manufacture of a particular product in one corporation. There must be something more than the mere union of capital and plant before the law is violated. There must be some use by the company of the comparatively great size of its capital and plant and extent of its output, either to coerce persons to buy of it rather than of some competitor, or to coerce those who would compete with it, to give up their business. There must, in other words, be an element of duress in the conduct of its business toward the customers in the trade and its competitors before mere aggregation of plant becomes an unlawful monopoly. It is perfectly conceivable that in the interest of economy of production, a great number of plants may be legitimately assembled under the ownership of one corporation. In such a case it is either not a trust, if the term involves unlawfulness, or it is a lawful trust, if a trust merely means a company which has assembled a large part of the manufacturing plant of any product. It may be, as Mr. Bryan, in his controversy with Senator Beveridge, says, that there is a limit in the union of capital and plant that will effect economy, and that after that limit is reached, the increase of the plant or the capital rather enlarges the risk in the management of the business, and is likely to increase the cost of production rather than to diminish it. If so, then, when a corporation goes beyond that limit, there is a reasonable presumption that it is doing so for the purpose of monopolizing trade.

Mere Aggregation of All Plants in One Ownership Does Not Suppress Competition

It must be borne in mind that in a country like this, where there is an enormous floating capital awaiting investment, the time within which competition by construction of new plants can be introduced into any business is comparatively short, rarely exceeding a year, and is usually even less than that. Many enterprises have been organized on the theory that mere aggregation of all or nearly all existing plants in a line of manufacture, without regard to economy of production, destroys competition. They have most of them gone into bankruptcy. Competition in a profitable business will not be excluded by the mere aggregation of many existing plants under one company, unless the company thereby effects great economy or takes some illegal method to avoid competition and to perpetuate a hold on the business.

Illegal Devices Badges of Unlawful Trusts

Frequently contracts have been made with customers by which they are required to deal exclusively with the Trust, on the threat that if there is not this exclusive dealing, then at a time when they most need the product, it will not be sold to them at all, or only at a very high price, and one prohibitive of profit on their part. Again, the tremendous wealth and resources of the Trust are exerted to destroy a rival in a particular locality by selling at a very low price in that neighborhood and driving him out of business, and then raising the prices. This can be easily detected by the inequality of the prices which the Trust asks for the same commodity in different localities under the same conditions. Such or like methods bring the company within the description of a monopoly, at which the anti-trust law is directed. I am inclined to the opinion that the time is near at hand for an amendment of the anti-trust law defining in more detail the evils against which it is aimed, making clearer the distinction between lawful agreements reasonably restraining trade and those which are pernicious in their effect, and particularly denouncing the various devices for monopolizing trade which prosecutions and investigations have shown to be used in actual practice. The decisions of the courts and the experience of executive and prosecuting officers make the framing of such a statute possible. It will have the good effect of making much clearer to those business men who would obey the laws the methods to be avoided.

Secret Rebates Most Effective
to Maintain a Monopoly

Another and perhaps the most effective method in the past for an unlawful trust to maintain itself has been to secure secret rebates or other unlawful advantage in transportation, by threat of withholding business from the carrier. This is undoubtedly what has enabled the Standard Oil Company and the Sugar Trust, and other great combinations, to reap an illegal harvest and to drive all competitors from the field. If by asserting complete Federal control over the interstate railways of the country, we can suppress secret rebates and discriminations of other kinds, we shall have gone a long way in the suppression of the unlawful trusts.

Answer to Mr. Bryan's Question:
What Should Be Done to Trusts?
Government Action

Mr. Bryan asks me what I would do with the trusts. I answer that I would restrain unlawful trusts with all the efficiency of injunctive process and would punish with all the severity of criminal prosecution every attempt on the part of aggregated capital through the illegal means I have described to suppress competition.

There has been great activity in the Department of Commerce and Labor and in the Department of Justice in an effort to investigate and restrain the continuance of such unlawful methods, and the success which has attended this effort in the dissolution of a number of such trusts where they consisted of several companies or partnerships united by a contract in restraint of trade has been gratifying. In the case of those who have made themselves into one corporation, their restraint is more difficult. It involves enormous labor on the part of the Government to prosecute such a combination because the proof of the gist of the offense lies underneath an almost limitless variety of transactions. In the outset, it can be very much more easily reached by bill in equity than in a criminal prosecution and the questions of law arising may be more quickly settled. When the law is declared so that the corporation understands exactly the limits upon its action, and it then pursues its previous illegal methods, nothing but criminal prosecution ought to be resorted to.

Why Trust Promoters Have Not Been Imprisoned

Mr. Bryan is continually asking why have some of the managers of unlawful trusts not been convicted and sent to the penitentiary? I sympathize with him in his wish that this may be done, because I think that the imprisonment of one or two would have a most healthy effect throughout the country; but even without such imprisonment I believe that the prosecutions which are now on foot and the injunctions which have already been issued, have had a marked effect on business methods. One reason for the small number of sentences of imprisonment in trust prosecutions is that the revelations of unlawful trust methods and dishonesty have been chiefly made known in secret rebates, and as I have already said, the Elkins act, until amended by the Rate Bill, only prescribed fines as a mode of punishment in such cases.

Juries Hesitate to Imprison by Their Verdicts

Again, it is difficult to induce juries to convict individuals of a violation of the anti-trust law, if imprisonment is to follow. In the case of the Tobacco Trust, the Government declined to accept a plea of guilty by the individual defendants, offered on condition that only the penalty of a fine be imposed, and the result was that the jury did not hesitate to stultify itself by finding the corporation guilty and acquitting the individual defendants, who had personally committed the acts upon which the conviction of the corporation was based. In the early enforcement of a statute which makes unlawful, because of its evil tendencies, that which has been in the past regarded as legitimate, juries are not inclined by their verdicts to imprison individuals. The course which the Government has pursued of resorting to civil processes first, and clarifying the meaning of a general statute which needs definition, is probably the best course to pursue. As the criminal prosecutions go on (and many such prosecutions have now been begun), if the violations of the trust law are continued, undoubtedly some shining marks will be hit, but the vigor with which these prosecutions have been continued has created an anxiety among those engaged in doubtful enterprises that has either driven them out of the business or made them careful not to give occasion for further complaint.

Bryan's "Extirpation Root and Branch"

Mr. Bryan says: "He would extirpate trusts, root and branch." If Mr. Bryan's language is more than mere rhetoric and he means to seize the property, to divide it up and sell it in pieces, and disassemble the parts, then I am not in favor of his method of dealing with trusts, because I believe that such large combinations legitimately conducted greatly add to the prosperity of the country. The attitude of the Government toward combinations of capital for the reduction in the cost of production should be exactly the same as toward the combinations of labor for the purpose of bettering the conditions of the wage-worker and of increasing his share of the joint profit of capital and labor. They are both to be encouraged in every way as long as they conduct themselves within the law. They both wield enormous power, and if wielded for good, can be of inestimable benefit. Their power for evil when in the control of unscrupulous men is such that, if it is to be restrained, it needs the use of all the means which the executive and the courts can lawfully command. I think it entirely possible by the rigorous prosecutions of the law against illegal combinations and by the equal and just operation of railways, to prevent a recurrence of what we have had in the past and to restrain within the bounds of legitimate and useful business, all these great corporations.

Federal License of All Interstate Business Corporations

Mr. Bryan's method of suppressing unlawful trusts would be to require every person, partnership or corporation, engaged in interstate traffic, to take out a Federal license, and by withholding such licenses from illegal trusts, he would make them impossible. It is probable that a statute embodying this plan, could be drawn which would stand the test of the Constitution. It would, however, have to contain some provision for ultimate judicial determination of those applicants for license who were violating the anti-trust law and thus involve the same litigation we now have. There is danger that its effect would be so to clog the channels of legitimate inter-state trade that after it had been tried for a short time, the people of the country would regard it as burdensome and demand its repeal. It is important that, in new legislation to stamp out evils, we should not so annoy the law-abiding in the community as to lose their sympathy in the reform. This plan has had the approval of Mr. Garfield and others. I was at first inclined to think that this was a practical method, but fuller consideration, for the reasons given, makes me doubt. The decision of the Supreme Court that a corporation can not refuse to disclose facts which will criminate itself, makes less important the advantage which the license system was supposed to furnish in keeping the business of a corporation under observation. Until it is clearer than at present that the evils of unlawful combinations can not be suppressed without it, it seems to me such a plan ought not to be tried.

Evil of Swollen Fortunes

One of the results of the conditions and evils which I have been describing has been the concentration of enormous wealth in the hands of a few men. I do not mean to say that all the large fortunes are to be traced to unlawful means but it is quite clear that many of those described as swollen are due to rebates, or to some form of unlawful monopoly, or to over-capitalization. Of course, great enterprises organized and managed by men of transcendent ability should result in great profit to them. It is proper compensation when they share with the people the profit from the economies that they introduce in the business by reducing the price. The captains of legitimate industry, therefore, are entitled to large reward, and it is impossible to impose a fixed limitation upon the amount which they may accumulate.

Legislation, Not Confiscatory, Having Tendency to Divide Such Fortunes and to Discourage Their Accumulation Not Socialistic

On the other hand, it is not safe for the body politic that the power arising from the management of enormous or swollen fortunes should be continued from generation to generation in the hands of a few, and efforts by

213

laws, which are not confiscatory, to divide these fortunes and to reduce the motive for accumulating them are proper and statesmanlike and without the slightest savor of socialism or anarchy. The law of primogeniture was abolished in states where it had been adopted, merely for the purpose of securing a division of the land among the children of the man who owned the land. Many of the provisions of our public land laws are drawn to discourage the union of large tracts in one ownership, and to encourage small holdings.

Best Remedy to Be Found in State Legislation

The State legislatures have complete control of what shall be done with a man's property on his death. He has no right to leave it by will and his children or heirs have no right to receive it which the legislatures may not modify or take away. The States, therefore, can best remedy the dangers of too great accumulation of wealth in one hand by controlling the descent and devolution of property and they ought to do so. They can adopt the French method, which requires the division of a large part of a man's fortune between all his children and gives him absolute power with respect to only a fraction. This would secure a division in the second generation and a probable change for the better in respect to such fortunes. Many of the States have already and properly adopted a graduated inheritance tax which not only reduces the great fortune but lessens the motive for its accumulation.

Federal Government May Properly Lend Its Aid— Favors Graduated Inheritance Tax

Federal action for a Federal end may legitimately have an indirect effect to aid the States in reforms peculiarly within their cognizance. When, therefore, the Government revenues need addition, or readjustment, I believe a Federal graduated inheritance tax to be a useful means of raising government funds. It is easily and certainly collected. The incidence of taxation is heaviest on those best able to stand it, and indirectly, while not placing undue restriction on individual effort, it would moderate the enthusiasm for the amassing of immense fortunes.

Income Tax

A graduated income tax would also have a tendency to reduce the motive for the accumulations of enormous wealth, but the Supreme Court has held an income tax not to be a valid exercise of power by the Federal Government. The objection to it from a practical standpoint is its inquisitorial character and the premium it puts on perjury. In times of great national need, however, an income tax would be of great assistance in furnishing means to carry on the government, and it is not free from doubt how the Supreme Court, with changed membership, would view a new income tax law under such conditions. The Court was nearly evenly divided in the last case, and during the Civil War great sums were collected by an income tax without judicial interference and, as it was then supposed, within the Federal power.

Does Not Favor Immediately Such Federal Legislation but on Next Readjustment of Revenues

I do not favor Federal legislation now to reduce such fortunes either by a constitutional amendment to permit an income tax or by a graduated inheritance tax, but whenever the Government revenues need an increase or readjustment, I should strongly favor the imposition of a graduated inheritance tax and, if necessary for the revenues, a change in the constitution authorizing a Federal income tax, with all the incidental influence of both measures to lessen the motive for accumulation.

The suppression of monopolies and the abolition of secret rebates and discriminating privileges by the railroads, will lessen the possibility of such enormous accumulations as those which have already taken place. The evils of too great concentration of money or of any kind of property in a few hands are to be best remedied by the gradual effect of a long course of legislation and not by measures, having an immediate and radical effect, that are apt to involve injurious consequences to the general business community.

After a Review of President Roosevelt's Policies, Concurs in Them

I have thus reviewed at great length what have properly come to be known as President Roosevelt's policies and have discussed them with what I hope you will think is entire candor. I have attempted to point out one or two instances in which I would qualify details of future policies which he has sketched, but with these minor exceptions as to method, I am glad to express my complete, thorough, and sincere sympathy with, and admiration for, the great conserving and conservative movement which he has with wonderful success initiated and carried so far against bitter opposition, to remedy the evils of our prosperity and preserve to us the institutions we have inherited from our fathers.

Criticism That Mr. Roosevelt's Policies Are Socialistic Absurd

Critics of President Roosevelt denounce his policies as socialistic and likely to impair the institution of private property. The institution of private property next to that of civil liberty is the most important factor in all that is good in modern society. It is indispensable to individualism and is one of the two chief means by which man raised himself from a low estate near to that of the beasts of the field to his present condition. But if the people are not convinced that it is possible to eradicate the evils and abuses arising from the unscrupulous use of wealth and corporate combination under the system of private property, the movement toward its abolition and the adoption of socialism in some form will gain great strength. President Roosevelt would stop this movement by a demonstration that it is possible under the system of private property, by efficient Government regulation, supervision and prosecution, to stamp out the evils which have created our social unrest. He knows what a futile remedy socialism will prove to be. Socialism looks to a dead level of life, to an absence of all motive for material progress, to a stagnation in everything. It involves a lack of individual freedom and requires an official tyranny to carry out its system that finds no counterpart in modern Government. It offers no real remedy for the evils that appear from time to time as the accompaniment of our progress. And yet, President Roosevelt knows and everyone must realize, the plausible force with which socialistic doctrines can be pressed upon a discontented people who see real wrongs in the body politic and social.

Policies Framed to Defeat Socialism

For this reason, he takes the most conservative course in insisting on adopting measures entirely consistent with the principle of private property in order to stamp out the evils which have attended its abuse. There is nothing either radical or severe in the reforms he proposes. What is there in the tenet of private property that prevents close government regulation of the exercise of a public franchise like that of interstate railways, or the enactment of criminal laws or civil procedure to restrain the evils which result from the improper use of the right of property in combinations of capital to suppress competition and to monopolize trade, or the adjustment of tax laws or laws of descent in such a way as to reduce the motive for accumulating fortunes so great that the power they give their individual owners is politically dangerous?

The Railroads—Not Mr. Roosevelt— Responsible for Restrictive State Legislation

The critics I have referred to are in the habit of charging to Mr. Roosevelt responsibility for all the recent State legislation looking to the restraint of corporations and especially for that which cuts down the passenger rates on State railways. This is most unjust, for whether such legislation is proper or oppressive, the impetus that carried it into law was given not by Mr. Roosevelt but by the evils that he has been attempting to remedy within the Federal jurisdiction. If the State measures are unjust to the property rights of the railways, they may be corrected in the courts. If they are unwise, they will react against the communities in which they operate by making the service poorer and in other ways, and the reaction will lead to their repeal. The railways can blame no one but themselves if the revelation of their flagrant violations of law and of their unjust administration of a public trust have led to an outburst of popular indignation and have brought on temporary excess.

Slump in Wall Street Prices
Not Due to President's Policy

Again, every time that there is a fall in the prices of stocks in Wall Street, those who are injuriously affected condemn the President with great bitterness as responsible for their losses. Just at present there has been a very serious depression in the values of marketable securities, and it is said that the President's attitude toward corporations has been the cause of this. Such critics fail to observe that there has been a similar decrease in the marketable value—not only of railway stocks but of Government consols abroad, and that there is a stringency in the markets of the world. But more than this, if the prosecution of dishonesty and illegal practices, like the giving and taking of rebates and the destruction of competition by monopoly, is to injure the market for stocks on the stock exchange, then this is a burden that must be borne and must be charged—not to the head of the nation, whose duty it is to enforce the law, but to the violators of the law whose pursuit of criminal methods has been so successful and far-reaching as to make their prosecution a serious threat against the stability of the market. It is not true that the President is engaged in a raid against all corporations. It is not true that he proposes to rip up past transactions, when by reason of the injury to innocent purchasers such a course would do more injustice than good. His only policy and sworn duty is to prosecute, with the fullest vigor, the corporations and individuals whose flagrant violations of the laws make it necessary to do so, in order that complete reform may be effected in our business methods with respect to the evils which I have described.

Radical Differences between Mr. Roosevelt's
and Mr. Bryan's Theories of Government

These same critics like to say that Mr. Roosevelt has "out-Bryaned" Mr. Bryan in his policies and Mr. Bryan has lent color to this saying by the claim that he was their original inventor. No one who has given the slightest attention to the attitude of Mr. Roosevelt and Mr. Bryan upon the social and political questions of the day can for a moment miss the radical difference between the two.

Mr. Roosevelt's Trust in Both People and Individuals

Mr. Roosevelt believes not only in the people but also in the individual as the unit who, multiplied, makes up and gives quality to the people. He thinks that there is no royal road to the elevation of a people but by the improvement in the intelligence and moral character of the individual. He believes in the possibility of the individual's being honest, courageous and just and able to resist the influence of "the money power" to wean him from the path of duty. He believes that the people can select individuals who may be trusted, as public officers—executive, legislative and judicial—to wield, without abuse and in the interest of the people, the powers needed to conduct an efficient government. He has faith in the maintenance of an honest, courageous and efficient representative popular legislature that will give the rich and poor equal protection and opportunity before the law.

Mr. Roosevelt's Belief in Strong and Efficient Government

Mr. Roosevelt believes in the necessity for a strong government that can and will make both rich and poor obey the law, and he would have the officers charged with its maintenance render due account of their stewardship to their masters, the people. Mr. Roosevelt knows no favorite in matters of lawlessness, be he rich or poor, corporation president or member of a labor union. The courts must be strong enough to restrain them all. Mr. Roosevelt believes our present government the best one possible for us and in every way adapted to the genius of our people. He has the utmost confidence in the capacity of the people through their representatives, and by the means provided in the Constitution by our fathers, to remedy the evils that arise in our material progress.

Mr. Bryan's Theories Based on Distrust of Individual and Failure of Representative Government

Mr. Bryan's whole system of remedies, on the other hand, for the evils that both Mr. Roosevelt and he and many others recognize, is based on his distrust of the honesty, courage and impartiality of the individual as an agent on behalf of the people to carry on any part of government, and rests on the proposition that our present system of representative government is a failure. He would have government ownership of railways because he does not believe it is possible to secure an interstate commerce commission that the "money power" can not and will not ultimately own. He would have the initiative and referendum because he distrusts representative government and has no confidence in the ability of the people to find men who will conscientiously, and free from the influence of "the money power," represent them in preparing and voting legislation. Because he distrusts the ability of judges to resist the malign influence of the "money power," he would take away from courts the power to enforce their own orders until a jury is called to tell the court whether the order has been disobeyed, and thus, in practice, though not in theory, the jury would come to pass on the correctness and justice of the court's order.

Mr. Bryan Seeks Judicial Procedure That Will Restrain Wealthy Wrongdoer but Will Give Freedom of Action to Lawless Poor— Instance Oklahoma Constitution

Mr. Bryan seems to be seeking some system of administering law under which the rich wrongdoer shall be certainly restrained, while the lawless poor shall escape. He would have his judicial machinery adjusted to restrict the violations of law by a corporation but would give freedom of action to the lawless members of a labor union. Indeed in the constitution of Oklahoma, which he says is the greatest constitution ever written, this anomaly prevails. No one can be punished for violating an order of injunction or restraint except after a verdict of a jury deciding that the violation was committed, and yet in the same constitution, a corporation commission of an executive and administrative character, a body of laymen, authorized to make orders against railroads and other corporations is empowered, if its orders are not obeyed, to change itself into a court and after giving due process of law by a hearing to enforce its own orders by a fine of $500 a day until the order is performed.

Such Discrimination Impossible— Offers Immunity to Rich

Such a discrimination in practical legislation can not be maintained for a moment. Courts and judicial procedure are made for all and must operate equally for and against all. The only method by which wealthy and powerful malefactors can be restrained is by maintaining the power of the courts, and the minute the power of the court is weakened in the supposed interest of the lowly and unfortunate accused of wrongdoing, the lawless rich are furnished the immunity they seek. The wealthy wrongdoers could easily escape the restraint of the law through the rents in its meshes Mr. Bryan would make for the benefit of those with less influence and means.

Mr. Bryan's a Weak and Nerveless Government

In all his proposed reforms, Mr. Bryan seems to give little attention to securing efficiency and force in government so that the evils he recognizes may be suppressed. The government which his system of remedies would tend to produce would be nerveless. Estopped by his own expressed fear of power put in the hands of any individual, he would find difficulty in wielding it when most needed.

Absurdity of National Referendum

The representative government that has served us well for 130 years has not been for Mr. Bryan sufficiently expressive of the will of the people. Election of Senators by the people is not enough for him. We must call upon fourteen million electors to legislate directly. Could any more burdensome or inefficient method be devised than this? I believe that a referendum under certain conditions and limitations in the subdivisions of a State on certain issues may be healthful and useful, but as applied to our national government it is entirely impracticable. If it is difficult for the people to use proper judgment in the concrete question of the personality of the representatives they are to select to carry on their national government, as Mr. Bryan's theory assumes, how much more difficult for them to give sufficient attention to the settlement of the many questions of policy and procedure in complicated statutes which the people have always been willing to leave to the decision of their representatives, skilled in the science of legislation, whose general views on the main political issues of the day are well understood. Think of the possibility of securing a vote of fourteen millions of electors on the 4,000 items of a tariff bill. The opportunity to retire a representative who fails to be truly representative is all that the people wish and need to enforce their will.

Certainly it is difficult for an impartial observer to find anything in the actual government of Mr. Roosevelt that harmonizes with that which would be the government under Mr. Bryan if he could carry out his theories. Mr. Roosevelt is doing everything in his power to avoid the condition which Mr. Bryan's theories when put in practice would bring about.

The Protective Tariff—Its Revision—
Its Relation to Trusts

I come now to the question of the tariff, its revision, and its relation to the unlawful trusts. The Dingley tariff was adopted immediately after the election of Mr. McKinley. Since that time we have passed through the Spanish war and have had a decade of prosperity and an increase and expansion of trade unexampled in the history of this or any other country. The Republican principle of the protective tariff is, as I understand it, that through the customs revenue law a tariff should be collected on all imported products that compete with American products, which will at least equal a difference in the cost of production in this country and abroad, and that proper allowance should be made in this difference for the reasonable profits to the American manufacturer. The claim of Protectionists, and it has been abundantly justified in the past, is that protection secures a high rate of wages and that the encouragement it gives to the home industry operating under the influence of an energetic competition between

American manufacturers, induces such improvement in the methods of manufacture and such economies as to reduce greatly the price for the benefit of the American public and makes it possible to reduce the tariff without depriving the manufacturer of needed protection and a good profit.

Business System Rests on Protective Tariff— Free Trade Revision Disastrous

The present business system of the country rests on the protective tariff and any attempt to change it to a free trade basis will certainly lead only to disaster.

Duty of Republican Party to Prevent Excessive Tariff Rates

It is the duty of the Republican party, however, to see to it that the tariff on imported articles does not exceed substantially the reasonably permanent differential between the cost of production in the foreign countries and that in the United States, and therefore when changes take place in the conditions of production likely to produce a very large reduction in the cost of production in the United States, it is time that schedules be re-examined and if excessive that they be reduced so as to bring them within the justification for the rule, by which the amount of tariff to be imposed under the protective system is properly determined.

Temptations to Monopoly in Rates Exceeding Protective Principle

Whenever the tariff imposed is largely in excess of the differential between the cost of production in the two countries, then there is formed at once a great temptation to monopolize the business of producing the particular product, and to take advantage of profit in the excessive tariff. This denies to the people altogether the economies of production that competition under a protective tariff should develop.

Reason for Thinking Some Schedules Excessive

In the enormous progress in the manufacturing plants and the improvement in methods which have been brought about in the last ten years in this country, there is the strongest reason for thinking that in many industries the difference between the cost of production in this country and abroad has been reduced. This is an opinion of mine formed *a priori* because I am a sincere believer in the efficacy of the protective system ultimately to cheapen the cost of production. The opinion has been confirmed by conversation with manufacturers and others who knew something of what they speak.

Confirmation by Action of National Association of Manufacturers

I am not myself a tariff expert and am not sufficiently familiar with the cost of production of the various articles covered in the many schedules to point out the particular ones in which such a change has taken place; but my general conclusion formed as above finds striking support in the action of the National Association of Manufacturers of the United States upon this very question. A committee appointed by that body for the purpose, investigated the question whether the tariff had not in respect to many articles by a change in conditions become excessive.

Association All Protectionists

This National Association of Manufacturers is composed almost wholly of protectionists, and I think we may safely say, therefore, of Republicans. I am advised that the Association represents all classes of manufacturers in this country and that a majority of the manufacturers of consequence are members. The committee reports: "We are all Protectionists—there are a very few brilliant exceptions, but so few that we may repeat the statement, 'We are Protectionists.' " The committee lays down in its report the following doctrine, which seems to me of the orthodox Republican type: "Protection, as the word implies, requires that the Tariff Schedules be such as *protect* our manufacturers against undue pressure from foreign competition, and maintain our high wage scale and standard of living. The *minimum* measure of protection is, therefore, as President Roosevelt said, 'The difference in the cost of production in this country and abroad.' These Protective Schedules, thus figured, must carry with them a very ample margin for safety. It must make full allowance for the possibility of hard times abroad and good times here; for dumping, and all other contingencies. This done, it is truly protective; and it is only so, as it covers these features and nothing more."

Many Schedules Excessive

After referring to the fact that there were some articles in which the tariff was hardly high enough, the conclusion of the committee was stated as follows:

"Confining ourselves to the protective principle, we find many schedules—some of them upon the prime necessities of life—returning the Government no revenue of consequence, and yet under the claims of the protective theory, bearing a tariff schedule—not merely equal to the difference in the cost of production here and abroad, with all reasonable contingencies allowed for—but decidedly in excess of the total wage cost of production in this country.

"We find some of these schedules many times in excess of the difference between the cost of production here and abroad. We find that individuals who are at the top, both in stock holdings and in management in some of these same industries, declare privately that these schedules are wrong, and that the best interest of those industries themselves, as well as the interests of the country at large, require adjustment at the earliest possible moment. They say that now is the time for revision, while the country is so prosperous that adjustment may easily be made to new conditions."

Vote of Association

In that body of members of 1,800—350, or 20 percent, were radically opposed to revision; 8 percent were opposed to revision at this time lest it unsettle business; 55 percent wished revision; and 17 percent were indifferent or uninformed. Taken by industries, out of 77 different industries tabulated, 56 voted for revision, casting a total of 1,510 votes; 16 industries voted against revision, casting a total of 102 votes; 5 industries were each tied in their votes, casting a total of 28 votes.

The Association then by resolutions passed by a large majority declared itself in favor of a revision of the tariff at the earliest practicable date.

Significance of This Report and Action Should Bring Matter before Congress for Investigation

I have not cited the report or action of the National Association of Manufacturers as conclusive upon the character of the present schedules, nor do I assume that the manufacturers of the country embrace all the classes who are interested in maintaining the protective system, for I fully recognize that other classes, especially the farmers, are vitally concerned in some of the schedules. All that I maintain is that when after a tariff law has been in force ten years and a representative body of protectionists in principle and in interest, whose business makes them familiar with the facts and who have no motive for misrepresentation, adopt such a report as the one I have quoted from, it makes a case for investigation into the existing tariff by Congress for the purpose of determining how much revision is needed.

Schedules for Committees and Congress

The investigation in the end will be conducted by the Committee of Ways and Means of the House of Representatives and by the Finance Committee of the Senate. The schedules are for them to recommend and for Congress to fix after they hear evidence of the cost of production in this country and the cost of production abroad, and the conditions existing in each trade, and if it shall turn out that popular opinion founded on such substantial evidence as that which I have cited here should prove to be unfounded, then the revision of the tariff will be confined to minor inequalities. But if the result of the investigation justifies the report of the National Association of Manufacturers, then the revision of the excessive schedules should be substantial, and the motive for the organization and maintenance of unlawful trusts to monopolize the manufacture and sale of articles in such schedules will be taken away.

Prosperity Argument against Revision

Objection is made to revision on the ground that we are enjoying business prosperity, that this will be disturbed by a proposal to change the tariff, and that we should wait until hard times before we revise. I can not follow the argument. The revision proposed is to be by the Republican party and is not to be a departure from the protective principle but in conformity with it. It will affect only those persons injuriously who are making an unreasonable profit out of an excessive rate. The present prosperity is not dependent on such a profit. If it were, then it would not be the prosperity of the whole business community, but only of a few unduly favored at the expense of the community. In the present temper of the people, general prosperity has not prevented the remedying of other abuses and injustice. I don't know why it should prevent this.

Controlling Reasons for Delay in Revision till after Presidential Election

I had occasion in a speech which I delivered at Bath, Me., now about a year ago, to express my individual opinion as in favor of an immediate revision of the tariff, but I there pointed out, and I only refer to it to repeat it and emphasize it, that the revision of a tariff involves so many different interests the country over that it could not be undertaken successfully by the Republican party, and therefore ought not to be undertaken at all, until the party as a whole is in favor of it. I ventured to express the opinion that the sentiment in favor of a revision in the Republican party was crystalliz-ing to such a point that in a short time we might expect to have action upon the subject. What has happened in the last year has only served to confirm the view I then expressed, and it now seems to me that even most of the extremists in the matter of the tariff are of opinion that it would be not only unwise, but unsafe, for the party to fail in its next national plat-form to pledge itself to a revision of the tariff as soon after the next Presi-dential election as possible. Those of us who favor immediate revision can well afford to wait until after the next Presidential election in order to se-cure substantial acquiescence by all Republicans. Certainly a delay of ac-tion for eighteen months ought to furnish a reason for no protectionist to invite the certain business disaster that Democratic revision on free trade lines would involve. More than this, full time should be given for the operation of a new tariff upon the business of the country before the people express their opinion of it. The passage of a bill by the next Congress would mean the consideration by Congress of the tariff in the midst of a Presidential campaign with all the opportunity for misrepresentation of its effect which its practical operation for a year or more would refute. Furthermore, with a Presidential election four years removed, we can count on a revision less affected by political considerations than if made in the heat of a national campaign.

Other Subjects Omitted

There are other subjects I should like to discuss—Porto Rico, Cuba, the Philippines, Santo Domingo, the Navy, the Army and our foreign policy, the race question and the war amendments, and the order of the President dismissing one hundred and seventy men of the 25th Infantry.

Brownsville Order

The attitude of the President and the War Department and the reasons for the action taken in respect to the 25th Infantry were sufficiently set forth in the communications by the President and by me, sent to Congress with the evidence then taken. Since that time, the Senate Committee on Military Affairs has taken 3,200 printed pages of evidence in the same matter, and the hearing is not concluded. Until the hearing is closed and the Committee makes its report, it would be premature for me, in view of my official relation to the matter, to express an opinion as to the effect of the Senate evidence on the issue which the President decided. The other topics I must pass over for lack of time.

Advantages of Republican Party in Leadership of President Roosevelt

I can not close without comment on the position of advantage for the coming National campaign which President Roosevelt, by the intense earnestness, vigor, courage and success with which he has pressed the reforms that rightly bear his name, has secured to the Republican party. A trimming, do-nothing, colorless policy in face of the proof of business, railway and corporate abuses would certainly have driven the party from power, however little responsibility for them could be justly charged to it. It was not political advantage which the President sought in these reforms but the real betterment of conditions which he has effected. Still the belief of the people in his sincerity, his courage and his amazing quality for doing things on their behalf has won for him a hold on the American public, at which even his bitterest opponents marvel and which finds few if any parallels in the political history of this country. Fortunate a party with such a leader.

10

The Panic of 1907

*Delivered before the Merchants Association
of Boston, Massachusetts, December 30, 1907*

Gentlemen of the Merchants Association of Boston: I am glad to be here. For more than two years I have been trying to accept your kind invitation. I do not feel strange in this New England company. My father was born in Vermont. My mother was born in Boston; my two grandfathers were born in Mendon, Worcester County; much of my boyhood was spent in Millbury, and I was educated at Yale. While I can not claim to be one of you, I like to boast that I have enjoyed the good influence of the same traditions.

I had expected to talk to you about the Philippines tonight. That was one of the reasons why I accepted the invitation so lightly. It is a subject easy for me to talk about. It may be it is getting a little stale. For instance, I have found that one of the best methods of discouraging my friends, the correspondents of the press in Washington, from pursuing embarrassing inquiries into other matters, is to insist on discussing with them for publication interesting phases of the Philippine situation. They leave forthwith. But I had supposed that, however dead the Islands might be as a topic inviting discussion and attracting attention elsewhere, one could rouse some excitement over it still in Boston. I have been warned, however, that here, too, there were subjects more absorbing, at least for business men. So, when I was honored by an invitation for this morning, to address the Ministers of Boston, whose profession carries them naturally into a consideration of other worlds, I said my say in respect to the Philippines, and the, to me, very absorbing national problem, which I hope and believe we are working out successfully. It follows that for this company, I must find another subject.

During the last three months, the country has suffered from a severe monetary panic. Even yet the clearing-house certificates linger in your bank exchanges as emphatic evidence of its severity and the extreme measures which had to be taken to avoid greater disaster. Doubtless many of my hearers have not yet recovered from the intense nervous strain and mental suffering to which they have been subjected since the middle of October. The panic has been given a certain political bearing and importance. For this reason, I have selected as my topic of tonight: The Panic of 1907, its Causes, its Probable Effects, and the Relation to it of the Policies of the National Administration.

What did cause the panic? Writers upon financial subjects who have given their lives and constant attention to matters of this kind, who are able to institute a comparison of the present panic with previous panics, and who are entirely familiar with the conditions preceding all of them, substantially agree upon the causes. Panics and industrial depressions are the result of the characteristics of human nature, which manifest themselves in business as elsewhere. The world generally has a certain amount of loanable capital available for new enterprises or the enlargement of old ones.

In periods of prosperity this capital with the instrumentalities for enlarging its potentiality by credits is put into new enterprises which are profitable, and the increase in free capital goes on almost in arithmetical progression. After a time, however, expenses of operation and wages increase and the profit from the new enterprises grows smaller. The loanable capital gradually changes its form into investments less and less convertible. Much of that which might be capital is wasted in unwise enterprises, in extravagance in living, in wars and absolute destruction of property, until the available free capital becomes well-nigh exhausted the world over, and the progress of new enterprises must await the saving of more. Men continue to embark in new enterprises, however; the capital fails them, and disaster comes.

For eight or nine months last past, there were many indications that the loanable capital of the world was near exhaustion. This result was brought about not only by the enormous expansion of business plants and business investments, which could not be readily converted, but also by the waste of capital in extravagance of living and by the Spanish war, the Boer war, and the Russian-Japanese war, and in such catastrophes as Baltimore and San Francisco. It became impossible for the soundest railroads and other enterprises to borrow money for new construction or reconstruction. The condition was not confined to this country, but extended the world over and was made manifest in the countries of Europe even before it was felt here.

Secondly, the conclusion cannot be avoided that the revelations of irregularity, breaches of trust, stock-jobbing, over-issues of stock, violations of law, and lack of rigid State or National supervision in the management of some of our largest insurance companies, railroad companies, traction companies and financial corporations shocked investors and made them withhold what little loanable capital remained available. Such disclosures had much more effect, probably, abroad than they had here, because here we were able to make distinctions, while there, at a remote distance, the revelations created distrust in our whole business fabric.

When, therefore, two or three institutions, banks and trust companies, supposed to be solid, were found to have their capital impaired by stock-jobbing of their officers, the public were easily frightened and the run upon the banks began. The question then became not one of loanable capital but of actual money to be used in the transactions of the day,—a very different question, though, of course, closely related.

It would seem that our system of currency is not arranged so as to permit its volume to be increased temporarily to counteract the sudden drain of money by the hoarding in a panic. It is probable that the stringency which reached its height on that dark day of October twenty-fourth, might, in part, have been alleviated, had we had a currency which could automatically enlarge itself to meet the tremendous demand of a day or a week or a month, while public confidence was being restored. The National Administration, together with many of the large capitalists of New York and elsewhere, put their shoulders under the load and by various devices of an unusual character have brought about the present condition of gradually increasing confidence.

The injurious consequences to follow from this panic are not likely to be so long drawn out, or to result in such disastrous industrial depression, as the panic of 1893, or the panic of 1873, and this, for the reason that the condition of the country makes it so much easier to resume business gradually, to accumulate capital, and then to renew the enterprises which had to be abandoned for lack of it. In the first place we have a gold currency with no suggestion now of a departure from the gold standard. In 1893, the pressure for free silver was on, and the threat of National repudiation had much to do with the delay in the return to prosperous times. Our Government finances now are in excellent condition and we have a large surplus. Our farming communities in the West today are not under the weight of mortgages and of debt which distressed them in 1893 and in 1873. They are prosperous and wealthy.

Again, the railroads, which make up a large part of the wealth of this country, are on a much solider foundation than they were in 1893. Then many of them had to be taken into the hands of receivers and immense amounts expended by means of receivers' certificates, displacing and destroying the value of vested securities in order to put roads in a safe and income-earning condition. The railroads today are in a better physical condition than they have ever been in their history. But few of them have recently been built into new territory in which business has to be created by introducing a new population.

Again, the balance of trade is with us. We were able to settle for the hundred millions of gold that we withdrew from Europe in order to meet the demand for money in the markets in New York by the excess of our exports over our imports in the single month of October.

All these things point to the probability of a restoration of confidence and, after a proper liquidation and an industrial depression of some months, to a resumption of business on a normal basis.

Modern business is conducted on a system of credit which, in normal times, increases the facility with which the work of manufacture, production and sale can be carried on, a thousand-fold beyond the limit of earlier days, and enables a total of many billions to rest on a very small percentage of actual money passed. Every manufacturer, every merchant, is, under modern conditions, dependent in the successful conduct of his business upon bank credits extended at regular seasons. The banks themselves in turn acquire the means of granting these credits largely from the money of their depositors. And in loaning from their deposits, the banks rely on the improbability that more than a certain part of the deposits will be called for at any one time. A lack of public confidence in the banks creates a common desire among bank depositors to withdraw their money. The fright which seizes the creditor—the depositor—and leads him to hoard his money, spreads like wildfire and is as unreasoning and unreasonable as the spirit of a mob. A run on the banks ensues. The banks then call on their debtors, and the tremendous structure depending upon credit tumbles. Meantime, men who properly count themselves as millionaires, who are honest, conservative, solid business men always responding to their obligations, find themselves as helpless under such a financial cataclysm as they would be in an earthquake.

Gradually, reason resumes its sway, but the injury to credit and the blow which has been struck at the normal business progress has more or less permanence. Values have shrunk, plans for new and increased business enterprises must be abandoned, and liquidation and house-cleaning take place. The business men who have had to stand the strain—who have seen their fondest hopes crushed, and have only been able to come through the crisis with the greatest effort and most substantial financial loss—are naturally sore and depressed. They believe, and generally they are right, that this disaster has come upon them without fault of theirs. It is unjust to them. No matter how many symptoms of the coming trouble there may have been, panics always come with a shock and a tremendous surprise and disappointment. And hardly is the panic over but a fierce discussion arises as to the cause of its coming. With various motives, editors and public speakers rush to the front to fasten upon some thing or some one the responsibility for what has happened. It is entirely natural that, in the condition of mind in which the suffering business men are left by the great strain and trial, such suggestions should receive marked attention and that the

more definitely the personality of the scapegoat can be fixed, the more pleasure it gives the victims of the catastrophe.

This mental attitude of the business community which I have described as likely to be found after every financial panic is clearly present
today. The economic and political history of the last four years gives it
especial importance, because it offers to certain elements in the business
and political community an exceptional opportunity. Let me invite your
attention to that history. It is one of a giant struggle between the National
Administration and certain powerful combinations in the financial world.
These combinations, for lack of a better name, are called "trusts." They
engaged in different lines of manufacture and production, and by assembling large amounts of capital into one mass in a particular line of business,
managed, by artful and skillfully devised but illegal methods of duress, to
exclude competition and monopolize the trade. They became the dictators
to great railroads, however powerful, and by threatening a withdrawal of
patronage secured unlawful and discriminating rebates, greatly increasing
their profits, and still more completely suppressing competition. Managed
with conspicuous business ability, these trusts went into legitimate foreign
trade and largely increased our country's exports. The profits which they
had realized enabled them to engage in other enterprises carried on by legitimate methods until the hold which they acquired in the business community gave them a position of vantage which it seemed hopeless to
combat. The basis of their original success and the maintenance of their
power was the violation of the Sherman Anti-trust law and the Interstate
Commerce law, and for a time both laws were but dead-letters upon the
statute books of the United States. The purpose of the administration of
Mr. Roosevelt was to make these men, however powerful and wealthy, to
know that the laws upon the statute books were living things and must be
obeyed. It was not proposed that the legitimate enterprises that were carried on with the capital of these men should be destroyed. It was not proposed that the foreign trade which inured to the benefit of the whole
country should be struck down; but it was determined that those who were
making the statutes a dead letter should be subject to restraint by injunction processes and punishment by indictment—not as a matter of
revenge—not to gratify the exercise of power, but to eradicate systematic
lawlessness from our business system. In this struggle the Administration

has been greatly aided by the popular sympathy awakened by revelations as to breaches of trust by the managers of some of the great insurance companies; by revelations as to mismanagement in the internal affairs of great railroad companies, by the disclosures as to the enormous amount of rebates extorted from the railroad companies by these trusts; and by the conscienceless stock-jobbing and over-issue of bonds and stocks shown to have occurred in the management of some of our great corporations.

There was a moral awakening among the people, and the hands of the Administration were held up in the work which it was doing. On the other hand, the men and the interests which were the subject of attack were not idle. They had their partisans—guilty and innocent. The guilty, of course, wished to defeat the Administration by any means. The innocent were those who had become involved with trust magnates in legitimate business transactions and to whom the attitude of the Administration seemed one of general opposition to the whole business community.

One of the great manifestations, one of the monuments in this moral progress, was the passage of the railroad rate bill. It met the opposition of many of the railroads, not because they were in sympathy with the trusts, for I think they in many respects had been more sinned against than sinning, but because they resented that close control, that rigid supervision which the public demanded, in view of the possibilities which the disclosure as to their past transactions revealed. The fight made by the Administration has been a noteworthy one. And now, after the victory has been won, after there has been introduced into the hearts of all men, and especially of those leaders, these trust managers and financial opponents of the administration, the fear of the law—the panic comes on. The trust magnates solidly intrenched with great financial resources are not the ones who suffer the most from it. It is the men who have had no such unlawful or fruitful method of making money—the great body of business men and the wage-earners. This is the feature of the panic that arouses one's deepest sympathy and regret.

The agents and sympathizers and defenders of the trusts and others innocent, but mistaken, now rush forward to place the blame of the present conditions upon the Administration. They seek to use the panic as an argument for giving up the moral victory which has been won. Apparently they would take a retrograde step back to the conditions that existed five and six and ten years ago, when, unhampered by statute law, these trusts were building the financial bulwarks behind which they are now fighting. They rely upon the soreness and the mental strain and suffering, through which all the honest business men of the community have had to pass, as a golden opportunity for driving home their attacks upon the Administration and for paralyzing the onward movement toward supremacy of the law.

I have set forth what I believe to be the real explanation of the panic. Let us examine the specifications of our opponents now made to show that the Administration is responsible. In the first place, it is said that the policy of the Administration has been directed for the last four years against organized capital, and that it has thereby frightened investors. I deny it. The course of the Administration has been directed against such organized capital as was violating the statutes of the United States—and no other. It had every consideration and desire to aid and assist organized capital which was engaged in legitimate business.

It is true that the execution of the policy of the Administration has involved the bringing to the light of public criticism the violations of law by influential and powerful corporations, and their prosecution. Through the investigations of National and State tribunals there have been revealed, as I have already said, breaches of trust, stock-jobbing, over-issue of stocks and mismanagement in some of our largest corporations. They have properly been severely condemned by all, including the President. Knowledge of these things doubtless affected our credit in Europe and hastened the panic; but those who are morally responsible for such a result are the guilty managers, not those who, in the course of their official duty, have made known to the business world the facts, and commented on them.

It is said that the Administration has arraigned the whole business community as dishonest. I deny it. The President has condemned the law-breakers. He has convinced those who have unlawfully accumulated enormous powers and capital that they are not immune. He has put the fear of the law in their hearts. They have been acute enough to attempt to protect themselves by giving the impression that his action has been directed against the whole business community. It is true that the business men of our community, as a whole, are honest, and their methods are sound. The President has never said otherwise. Indeed, it is chiefly in the interest of the great body of honest business men that he has made his fight for lawful business methods.

Again, it is said that the Rate Bill, for which the Administration is responsible, caused the present panic. Could anything be more absurd? The object of the Rate Bill was merely to bring the railroads under closer supervision of a tribunal which could act upon complaints of individuals suffering from their injustice. The immediate effect of its passage was the voluntary reduction of rates. Subsequently, under normal circumstances justifying it, the rates of the railways generally were increased. The continuance of the abuses of the railway management was made by the Rate Bill much more difficult, but the Rate Bill has not had the slightest effect upon the legitimate business earnings of the railways. The utter hollowness in the cry that the Rate Bill caused the panic, is seen in the fact that those who now venture to advance this proposition have been for more than a year contending that the Rate Bill was a humbug and a fraud because it had no effect whatever—because it had given promise of a reduction of rates and no reduction of rates followed.

Then State legislation against railroads is pointed to as a cause for shrinkage in the value of the stocks and for the panic. Mr. Roosevelt and the National Administration are not responsible for this. It was occasioned by the same revelations of lawlessness and discrimination in railway management that made the Federal Rate Bill a necessity. If the State measures have been too drastic, the cause of the injustice is not with the National Government.

Instead of making a panic, the national policy, of ending the lawlessness of corporations in interstate commerce, and of taking away their power of issuing, without supervision, stocks and bonds, will produce a change in their management and remove one fruitful cause for loss of public confidence.

The business men in the past have sympathized with the effort to eradicate from the business system of this country the influence and control of those who have achieved success by illegal methods. Is all this to be changed by the panic? Is it proposed, because of it, to repeal the Rate Bill? Shall we dismiss the prosecutions for violations of the anti-trust law? Shall we permit and encourage rebates and discriminations by railways? Is this the condition of sanity to which we are invited to return? Shall we join in the sneer at the fight of the Administration for honesty and legality in business as a youthful attempt at an alleged moral regeneration of our business system? No panic, however severe, can make wrong right. No man who sincerely believed the Administration right in its measures to punish violations of law, can now turn from the earnest support of that policy today.

I believe myself to be as conservative as anyone within this company. I believe that in connection with personal liberty, the right of personal property is the basis of all our material progress in the development of mankind, and that any change in our social and political system which impairs the right of private property and materially diminishes the motive for the accumulation of capital by the individual, is a blow at our whole civilization. But no one can have been an observer of the operation of the exercise of the right of property and the accumulation of capital and its use in business by the individual and the combination of capital by the combination of individuals, without seeing that there are certain limitations upon the methods in the use of capital and the exercise of the right of property, that are indispensable to prevent the absolute control of the whole financial system of the country passing to a small oligarchy of individuals.

The combination of capital is just as essential to progress as the assembling of the parts of a machine; and hence, corporations, however large, are instruments of progress. But when they seek to use the mere size or amount of the capital which they control to monopolize the business in which they are engaged, and to suppress competition by methods akin to duress, they should be restrained by law.

Again, I am earnestly opposed to the government ownership of the interstate railways, which are the arterial system of this country. Those railways should continue to be managed by private corporations. Government ownership of railways means State socialism, an increase in the power of the central government that would be dangerous. It would be a long step away from the individualism which it is necessary to retain in order to make real progress. But no one could defend a railway system in which the unlawful discriminations by secret rebates and otherwise were practically without limit in the interest of the trusts and against the ordinary shipper. These abuses can only be reached and ended by closely regulating the railways and putting them under the tribunal which can insist upon publicity of business and in cases of complaint can direct the exact remedy for the wrong.

If the abuses of monopoly and discrimination can not be restrained; if the concentration of power made possible by such abuses continues and increases, and it is made manifest that under the system of individualism and private property the tyranny and oppression of an oligarchy of wealth can not be avoided, then socialism will triumph and the institution of private property will perish.

The Administration has been thus far successful in showing that dangers from individualism can be effectively regulated, and that abuses in the exercise of private property can be restrained. Thus a great conservative victory has been won and the coming of socialism has been stayed.

The question which you have ultimately to meet is not whether we shall return to a condition of unregulated railways and unregulated trusts; but it is whether we shall maintain a strict system of regulation of railways and trusts or whether we shall turn the country over to the advocates of Government ownership and State socialism. Anyone who seeks a retrograde step from the policy of the Administration, on the theory that it would be a real step toward conservatism, is blind to every political sign of the times.

If one attempts to fix the center of the conservatism of the country, he is likely to fix it in New England. If he is seeking a community where appeals to righteousness and justice awaken a response, he will find it in New England. Hence it is that I have ventured at this time and under the circumstances I have described, to discuss the political aspects of this panic, and to appeal to you, whether Democrats or Republicans, not to allow an acute condition involving pecuniary loss and mental strain, serious as it is, to lead you from the broad, impartial, just and patriotic view of the situation. In this widespread catastrophe, I have the deepest sympathy with the great body of business men and wage-earners, who I know are honest, and who have to bear the brunt of it. And I feel the greatest solicitude and anxiety for their recovery; but I urge them not to allow their resentment at conditions to be made a weapon against the public weal.

11

Southern Democracy and
Republican Principles

Lexington, Kentucky, August 22, 1907

It is a great pleasure for me to be given the opportunity to address an audience like this of a state lying next to my own, and one with which I have been more or less familiar since boyhood. I can well remember how often, in early years, I looked over from the suburbs of Cincinnati, where I was born and brought up, to Kentucky, and I discovered the signs of coming summer in the apple, peach and cherry trees that flung out their beautiful banners of blossoms on the green hills immediately opposite.

As one looks over this blue grass region far-famed as it is for its beautiful women, magnificent horses and other things, a country that God has blessed in so many different ways—and observes the wealth and prosperity of its inhabitants, and the comfort which they enjoy on every hand, he is moved to inquire why it is that in the governmental control of this great United States, so fair, so educated, so intelligent a community as that of Kentucky wields comparatively so small an influence on the general government. Why is it that Kentuckians are not in the councils of the Nation? It is true they have their Congressional and Senatorial representatives, but why is it that in framing the policies—foreign and domestic—with which we have to do as a nation, Kentuckians, like their brethren of all the South-ern states, have so little to say? This patent fact in respect to the Govern-ment at Washington has not failed to escape the attention of the leading men who represent the South in Congress, and it has called for regretful comment with explanations that, with deference to those who make them, I submit are not the true ones. The reason why the South exerts so little political influence in the guidance of the nation is because one single issue has made it the perpetual tail of the Democratic party, so that however small the Northern head, it wags that tail. The South has permitted the shadow of an issue that circumstances in this state ought long ago to have removed from political controversy to bind it solidly to the Democratic party, no matter what principles or candidates that party has adopted.

The specter of so-called negro domination, the threat of a recurrence to the days of reconstruction, however weighty they might have been at one time in the history of the far Southern states, have never had any sub-stantial weight or reason for being in this great State of Kentucky, for the colored people of the state were never so numerous as the white voters. The force of inertia keeping voters in the Democratic party on the race issue was in this state always a mere sentiment without reason. Neverthe-less, Kentucky has trailed along with her sisters further south. It has always been regarded as a solid Democratic state, no matter what the Democratic party did in its convention, no matter whom it nominated. Under those circumstances, with human nature as it is, why should the Northern Demo-crats pay the slightest attention to what the Kentucky Democrats desired? Why should the Northern Republicans, who could not expect a majority in Kentucky, pay the slightest attention to what the people of Kentucky wished? Why should the President take into his Cabinet a representative from Kentucky? Kentucky, while an agricultural state, is developing great manufactories. It is developing great mining industries—and all of them are more or less dependent for their success upon the protective tariff. There are a number, I doubt not, of sincere protective tariff men among the Democrats of Kentucky, and yet throughout these forty years since the war, they have come forward solidly and stolidly to vote the Democratic ticket merely because of the feeling on the race issue which they derived from their far Southern brethren. Now is not it time for a manly and highly intelligent electorate to commune with itself and to say to itself at the polls, it shall establish its right to be considered by both parties as a factor in making up national policies and in selecting national candidates?

We have arrived in the history of the politics of this country at what seems to be a repetition of that condition which existed at the end of Monroe's second administration, called the era of good feeling. After violent outbursts against President Roosevelt for his expressed sympathy with the colored man, the men of the South generally have come to recognize the sterling virtues and courage and independence of our President, and I venture to say that there is no section of the country in which he is more popular than he is in the South today. It was not an exaggeration when a gentleman of Texas, who greeted the President on behalf of one of the cities of that state, said to him: "Mr. President, we welcome you to a state where you have more friends and fewer voters than any state in the Union." That was true. That was an anomaly, and what I ask you today is, is there any reason for the existence of such an anomaly—whether the time has not come, especially for men of Kentucky, in which there was never the slightest occasion for the race feeling, to support President Roosevelt, not only in expressions of good will, not only in praise and approval, but also in that which counts, in casting their ballots in behalf of the party and its candidates, of which he is the head.

I propose with your permission for a little while to take up the race question. It is a question that it is difficult to deal with impartially and in a spirit of friendliness and charity toward all sides, so as to avoid irritating phrases and bitter responses. And yet when one comes into a Southern community, with that regarded as perhaps the chief question of the day, one can not be frank and courageous, and avoid it. I know that the discussion by a Northern man of the question is apt to rouse on the part of the Southern Democrat the objection that he does not understand the question, that he does not know the difficulties of it, and that if he can't take it up with sympathy with the attitude of the white man in the South, he had better not take it up at all. On the other hand, he is liable to encounter the criticism of the colored men, who, with a natural sensitiveness and interest in their race, and remembering the wrongs and oppression to which their race has been subjected in times past, resent on the part of the Northern man any attitude which does not involve condemnation of the attitude of the Southern white man, or which manifests the slightest consideration for his view. I am not a pessimist with respect to the race question. I am convinced that it is working itself out, and I am convinced that nothing has so much contributed to its gradual solution as the 13th, 14th and 15th amendments.

The 13th amendment abolished slavery. There have been some intermittent attempts on the part of extreme men in the South at times to revive a system of involuntary servitude, called peonage, which, however, is subject to prosecution under the Federal law, and which we may expect to be eliminated in due course. The 13th amendment on the whole has been entirely effective to release the slaves.

In the 14th amendment the colored man has been guaranteed against state or other action or any effort to deprive him of life, liberty or property without due process of law. Under this amendment and in conformity to it, those who were slaves, and the colored people who have been born since, have been able throughout the Southern states to earn and save their money and to make themselves useful members of the community. By the 13th amendment four millions of them were taken from their masters and turned out upon the world to enjoy freedom. In the outset this certainly seemed to be a heavy burden—that they who had been wont to depend on others not only for their food and clothing but for the guidance of their lives, should now be made to depend upon themselves to find the work and earn the wages with which they might stand up and support themselves as free citizens of this country. It was a long, hard, severe lesson through which these four millions, now increased to eight, had to go. There were but five percent of them who were literate; ninety-five percent were in the darkness of utter ignorance. For a time general education was thought to be the best means of uplifting the race, and undoubtedly the removal of illiteracy was a great boon to it; but in the past two decades under the influence of General Armstrong, Dr. Frisell and Booker Washington, the wisdom of making the education manual and industrial for the benefit of the great bulk of the race has been made manifest. The colored people have been taught by their greatest leader, Mr. Washington, that the way for the negro to build himself up is to make himself useful as a laborer—unskilled and skilled—as a farmer and as a business man in the community of which he forms part. As he lives in an agricultural country he should learn that the best home for the negroes is the farm and that the best property which he can accumulate is farm land and farm equipment. I shall not stop to give you the statistics showing the great progress that has been made by the negro race in the South in literacy, in the enormous increase in the farm holdings by colored men and the great proportion of the agriculture of the South that they carry on. We are apt to forget this real improvement in the diatribes that we occasionally hear from men who seem to have a lack of sympathy with the progress of the colored race and who lose themselves in denunciation of the entire race on account of a comparatively small criminal class that formed the dregs of the Southern population.

I shall not rehearse the history of reconstruction or of the bloody days of the South that followed it, or of the fraud and oppression and violence with which the 15th amendment was nullified in the far Southern states. Suffice it to say that the negro vote in those days was made to count for nothing. But, as always happens where law is flouted and fraud and violence are allowed to have full sway, the good people in the community found that the triumph of such methods had a tendency to create a demoralization in all walks of life. Therefore, we find in every Southern state a movement on the part of the good element in the Democratic party to introduce new laws and new constitutions, which shall make the exclusion of the negro from the ballot square with the law. So we have these constitutional amendments which introduce educational and property qualifications for electors, with clauses called "grandfather clauses," which permit voting on a basis of ancestry. The grandfather clauses are supposed to permit the poor ignorant white to vote and to exclude the colored man. I do not hesitate to say that if that is the result, it is a violation of the 15th amendment. But these grandfather clauses have generally expired by limitation according to their terms, and now the method of excluding the negro from the ballot is to have a law of ineligibility apply in its terms equally to black and white, and to secure a discrimination in favor of the white by executing the law rigidly against the black and allowing the white to vote. I deplore such methods. An exclusion of both black and white on the ground of ignorance and irresponsibility, measured by proper standards, is not subject to criticism if impartially enforced. But an unlawful discrimination in the execution of the law is different perhaps in method, but still is fraud, like the original violence and ballot-stuffing of previous years. Nevertheless the fact of the step is a good sign. It is an indication that the conscience of those who have violated the law is in some measure being stirred, and with the law on the statute book we may reasonably hope that ultimately the law will come to be fairly enforced, for we may reasonably hope that the colored men of the South, under the influence of Booker Washington and his supporters, will continue to go into business, to go on farms, to possess themselves of property and to become respected members of the communities in which they live, and when they exercise independence of judgment in respect to political issues, we may be sure that gradually the right to vote will be accorded them and they will exercise a far more useful influence as intelligent and solid members of the community for the benefit of their race than the ignorant members of their race would have exercised, had they been allowed to vote. In this way through devious ways, which can not be justified or approved, we may still reach a result that will square with the requirements of the Federal constitution and will give to the negro every political and economic right, and will confer great benefit upon the colored race.

The negro is necessary to the South as a laborer—skilled and unskilled. The South could not get along without him. The world over today there is a demand for labor, and were the negro to be withdrawn from the South the difficulties agriculture would labor under can hardly be overstated. The negro is an American. He has no other country than this, and can have no other country than this, and called upon to defend it he lays down his life as freely as the white man sacrifices his. Ours is the flag he loves—the only one he knows. It is our duty to see to it that his path is made as easy as we can, that his progress is as incessant as proper encouragement can make it. His best friend, the one that can do most for him and the one in many respects who sympathizes with him most, is the Southern white man. He understands his defects. He knows his virtues. And if the negro responds to the opportunities for improvement as Booker Washington points them out, we can be sure that he will grow in the estimation of his white fellow-citizens of the South, and that the great problem which has burdened the South, with its race issues, will be largely solved. It is plain that the party of intelligent Southerners who are sympathetic with Booker Washington and the evangel he is preaching to his people is growing in force and influence.

Propositions are made to repeal the 15th amendment. Such propositions are foolish. The people of this country would never consent to such a retrograde step. It may be that the 15th amendment is today nullified in many states. Nevertheless it stands there as a monument and a mandatory restriction upon state laws and as an ideal toward which politically the South must work. The 15th amendment does not require that every negro shall vote. All that is required is that he should not be excluded from voting because he is a negro. If he lacks educational qualification, property qualification, or any other qualification that the state may lawfully impose as a rule of eligibility for its voters, then he may be excluded provided that everyone else who lacks similar qualifications is equally excluded. The 15th amendment is merely intended to secure him in his political rights from race discrimination by the states. It is not intended to give him affirmative privileges as a member of his race. Its strict enforcement does not involve the amalgamation of the races—does not involve social association or equality. It does not involve negro domination, and to permit the question now at this late day—forty years after the war—to control the votes of intelligent men in respect of issues that are living and that affect their welfare, is to indicate on their part a lack of sense of proportion which I can not think will continue to manifest itself among the voters of the South. If only under the influence of President Roosevelt's administration some of the Southern states, including Kentucky, could be led into the Republican column in accordance with the real sympathies of the voters of those states, it would be a crowning glory of his administration. It will not necessarily work for the benefit of the Republican party in the end, because the closeness with which the Southern states have united in support of Democratic candidates and the Democratic party has introduced a similar cohesion among the Northern states and we might expect much more independence of voting at the North if the voters there were not confronted with the solidarity of the South. As an American citizen and lover of my country, however, I long for the time when the South shall be received again into the councils of the nation, and when the people of that section shall resume the influence to which they are entitled and which they themselves deny themselves by being frightened at a mere ghost of the past.

It may be said that when I say the South denies itself the opportunity to take part to influence the course of the Government and to determine its policies, I ignore the fact that by the oppression of the negro vote, the white Democrats of the South in point of representation in the Senate, and in the House per capita, wield a far greater influence on the legislation of the country than do the Northern voters per capita, because in the representation they get the benefit in the proportion of all their colored adults over twenty-one, while they exclude them from exercising the ballot. This is true and it is an injustice; but the very injustice leads many a Northern voter to support the Republican party and to keep it in control, and thus prevent the Southern states, following as they do the Democratic party, from taking any part in the executive control of the Government or to exercise any substantial influence.

Why should not the Democratic voters of Kentucky who really sympathize with Theodore Roosevelt and his policies, come into the Republican party and uphold the standard which he carries? What is there about his policies that they do not approve? Let us examine as between him and Mr. Bryan, who represents the Democracy today. First, do they believe that the tariff is a robbery of the many for the enrichment of the few? Do they think it is wiser to destroy our present business prosperity, which has as its basis the protective tariff system? If so, then they are right to continue to vote with Mr. Bryan; although it will probably be found, should Mr. Bryan come into office with a Democratic House and Senate behind him, that a tariff bill produced by a Democratic House and Democratic Senate, to be signed by a Democratic President, would be just such another botch as was the Gorman-Wilson tariff bill, a hybrid which was neither real protection nor real free trade, and was only productive of disaster to the business interests of the country.

Then let us take the question of our policy with our dependent possessions, including Puerto Rico, Cuba and the Philippines. As to Puerto Rico there is not much question except as to whether we shall bring a million people of that island into our political system so as to make them citizens and ultimately make them a state and give them two senators and an appropriate number of representatives. Upon that question neither party has spoken and I do not know that any issue is raised. With respect to Cuba there seems to be no dispute, and that it is our duty to go ahead and prepare the island for peaceful government and turn it back to the republic, the functions of which are temporarily suspended.

Coming then to the Philippines, there we do have a sharply drawn issue between Mr. Bryan and Mr. Roosevelt, and upon that issue I venture to say that men of the South are largely with Mr. Roosevelt. In the Spanish-American War, which was brought about quite as much by the earnest sympathy of the South as by the feelings of the Republicans of the North, we were carried by the exigencies of battle to the Philippine Islands and almost before we knew it. By Dewey's victory and what followed we were put in a position that required us to decide, whether having fought with the Filipinos as allies against Spain in a war to free them from what they regarded as oppression by Spain, we should thereafter agree with Spain to turn them back to that same sovereignty. That seemed treachery to an ally. Consequently could we turn the islands over to the insurgents with whom we had been fighting as allies? They had nothing but a military government, and that in the four or five months when they exercised any power had proven to be a colossal failure, in which the tyrannies were quite as great as they were in the Spanish times. Aguinaldo and his government were utterly unable to give security of peace, law and order to the three hundred islands with their population of 8,000,000. In the interests of the people themselves it was absolutely necessary that we should take the other alternative, establish a government in the Islands ourselves and attempt to teach the people something of the principles of self-government in order that ultimately we may be able, if they desire, to turn over the government to them. Mr. Bryan asserts that the Filipinos are entirely capable of self-government and ought to be permitted to control the Islands, however ignorant, however lacking in political experience they may seem to be. Now I submit to you, and I submit to the whole Southern people, whether we can safely trust a people, the great majority of whom are without political experience, to govern themselves and produce a modern civilization. Can we avoid the trust which has been thrust upon us? Can we avoid the responsibility which is ours by reason of fate and say to these people, "Take over your government; you have had no experience; you can begin your factional guerrilla warfares and we will move out of the Islands." Is there not an obligation on the part of a great, rich, intelligent and capable nation like ours, when fortune has thrust us into control of 8,000,000 of people like these, to establish a government in which law and order shall be preserved and in which the rights of the humblest may be maintained and to remain there until we can be certain of its continuance? Were we to leave, there is every prospect that tyranny would be reintroduced and there would only be class government, and that the uplifting of the people would cease. The principles of the Declaration of Independence do not require the immediate surrender of a country to a people like this. If they did, then it would be utterly impossible to defend rules which exclude women from the ballot, rules which exclude minors from the ballot, rules which exclude ignorant and irresponsible male adults from the ballot. Do the people of the South contend that the difficult science of self-government is so implanted in the breast of every human being, be he Hottentot, Esquimaux or any of the uncivilized races, or even one of those partly civilized or those having no experience in government, that he ought not to be assisted in the maintenance of a government which shall secure law and right? We are engaged in a great altruistic work in the Philippines. We promised that we would gradually increase their measure of self-government as they might show themselves fit, that we would lead them on and on in this direction, and the necessary inference is that ultimately when they became fit for self-government, if they desire, then they shall have it. But to throw them out now upon the world entirely incapable of maintaining permanently a government in which law and order shall be supported, would be to run away from the plain duty of a nation conducted on the principles of Christian civilization.

We have been in the Philippines now nearly ten years. For four years we were engaged in suppressing the disorder due to two insurrections and the Spanish-American War. Since that time we have been slowly laboring against the burdens which have come upon the people both from war and also from famine and pestilence and the destruction of their one instrument of agriculture—the water buffalo. Gradually we can see improvement in the business of the islands. Gradually we can see the restoration of all the conditions favorable to a prosperous future. If we can only open to the markets of the United States the products of those Islands, it will greatly aid them without in the slightest degree injuring the similar agricultural interests of the United States, and ultimately doubtless we shall come to this. The more generously we treat the Islands, the more carefully we look after their interests, the more will be our reward in the matter of growth of commerce between the two countries, and the more satisfactory will be our contemplation of the policy of altruism which we shall have pursued in reference to a generous, graceful, light-hearted Oriental Christian people.

Thirdly, how with reference to railway regulations? Do you favor Mr. Bryan's policy or do you favor Mr. Roosevelt's? Mr. Bryan wishes to purchase all the interstate railways of the nation, some 230,000 miles in extent, costing upward to the nation of $14,000,000,000, and to operate them as a government institution. Shades of Thomas Jefferson! Think of what he would have said of such an accumulation of power in the executive of his republic. Even a man of the dullest imagination trembles at the thought of the power which the executive might exercise with that instrument under his control. And why does Mr. Bryan favor Government ownership? It is because he thinks that the tribunal appointed to regulate the railroads— the interstate commerce commission—must necessarily come under the influence and domination of the railways of the country. In other words, he does not believe in the possibility of securing individuals who are able, courageously, and with an eye single to the interests of the republic, to administer and enforce the laws and regulations with reference to the wholesome, just and efficient conduct of the railways of this country. It is a great arterial system. When it is poisoned, when it is conducted dishonestly, when there is discrimination against it, then the person or the locality against whom that discrimination is exercised, is palsied and withered. It is a great trust that railways by the enjoyment of the franchise of public transportation take over and exercise, and it is essential that they should discharge that trust honestly and impartially to all individuals and localities. Mr. Roosevelt believes in the individual. He believes that it is possible under our system to select men who, courageous, brave, free from the influence of the power of money, will discharge the functions placed upon them and see to it that the public interests are conserved. Now are you with Mr. Bryan or against him, or are you with Mr. Roosevelt or against him? I need not ask the question, for I know that in this State of Kentucky a majority of the Democrats on this point are with Mr. Roosevelt. Why then should not they vote their sentiments?

Upon the question of trusts how is it? Mr. Bryan uses a great deal of rhetoric in connection with the trusts. He would extirpate and root them

out. Now what is a trust? A trust is a great combination of capital in manufacturing plants which produce a large part of the product of any particular
line of merchandise. If by trusts you mean an illegal trust or if the term is
to be taken as an illegal combination, then the definition should be extended. It means a large combination of capital for the production of any
commodity in which the combiner aims by reason of the extent of the plant
and by methods of duress to drive out competition and to monopolize
the trade. Now combination is the law of being of our present business
community. A machine for manufacturing that which was made by hand
before is formed by the assembling of many parts, and by the joint action
of all of them the more rapid, and generally the more efficient, manufacture of the article in question is secured. Always it is more economical than
hand production. So the combination of capital is a means of reducing
the cost of production, so that the lowered expense results in much of the
enormous strides that we have made in our commercial and manufacturing
life. The public can no more dispense with it, and the government has no
more right to suppress it, than any other good movement in other useful
means of profit. Combination is what enables the laborer today to secure
the proper measure of the joint profit between him and the capitalist. He
unites with his fellows in the trades unions, lays up money to be used in
times of stress when in the constant and necessary recurring strife between
labor and capital for a division of the joint profit, he may support himself
or his fellows in temporary idleness. The spirit of combination has created
these enormous trades unions, which wield a power for good that can
hardly be over-estimated. And yet the Government has no more business
to suppress combination of capital than it has combination of labor, and
the Government will never suppress either as long as the enormous power
which each uses is confined within the limits of lawfulness and is not per-
verted to deprive men, communities, or the public, of that which should
be theirs. But when combinations of capital are used not alone to produce
economy in production but methods are adopted and devised by which
the combination drives out of business smaller concerns engaged in competition, or uses devices by which customers are compelled to deal with
the combination and abandon their smaller competitors—that is, when
they introduce an element of coercion into the business, it becomes a trust,
and an unlawful trust. Now, the question is whether that trust shall be

destroyed, whether the parts of it shall be disassembled and we shall go back to the single factories, or whether the leaders of that trust shall be punished for violating the law and required by such punishment and by injunction to return to the lawful administration of their business and to confine themselves to a legitimate form of competition and to the maintenance of their prestige in business by reducing the cost of production and sharing that cost with the public in reduced prices. If Mr. Bryan can be believed, he is in favor of driving them all out of business. Mr. Roosevelt is in favor of punishing them, of eliminating lawlessness and maintaining the useful combination. On which side of that question are the Democrats of the South going to range themselves?

Mr. Roosevelt is in favor of a large navy. He is in favor of a navy commensurate to the size of the country, so that no country may insult us or offend our dignity or subject us with impunity to a course which we otherwise would not take. In other words, he is in favor of a navy to keep the peace. He would be mild in manner and sweet in disposition, but he would have it understood that his anger could be aroused, and when aroused that he knew how to strike and had the means withal to strike effectively. Mr. Bryan, if I understand him, would have no navy, but he would have a navy that was prepared over night. We should be in a pusillanimous position— one in which we could effect no good.

We have not yet reached the millennium when everything is to be settled by arbitration and by peaceful influence. We are not looking out into the world for conquests or exploitations. We are not seeking to take anything which is not ours. We are not seeking to deprive any nation of what is its own; but in international life there is a great opportunity for the exerting of a peaceful, moral influence among nations. A nation of 80,000,000 people should not hesitate to prepare itself, to make its healthful influence as effective as possible. And I don't care whether you are a member of the strictest peace society, or whatever your principles, if you answer yourself, deep down in your heart truthfully, you know that a nation that is able to defend itself, a nation whose coast is properly protected for the resistance of modern war attacks, and whose navy is a formidable fleet of modern ironclads, exerts much more influence to secure justice than the nation whose defenses are to be improvised in a week, whose navy is to be constructed of shallops and swivel guns or converted merchant-men. Are you with Mr. Bryan or are you with Mr. Roosevelt on that issue?

Finally, Mr. Bryan wishes to have the judges of all the Federal Courts elected. He wishes to take away the power to issue injunctions, conferred upon the courts as perhaps their most effective arm to bring about justice, and all because he does not think men can be found capable of wielding the power necessary to make an efficient government and necessary to make an efficient court, without running the risk of having them corrupted by the influence of wealth and the influence of corporations. Mr. Roosevelt be-lieves that it is possible and necessary if we have government at all to have a government strong enough, efficient enough, and with power enough, to make both wealthy and poor obey the law. And under the combinations that we have today of labor unions on the one hand, and wealth and capital on the other, if we would keep them both within the law, in exercising their enormous power, we must have courts that are to be strengthened and not weakened. And if we can not find the public agents in our individ-uals who can exercise that government power without danger, then we might as well go out of the governing business. Mr. Bryan would create a favorite class of lawless workingmen. Mr. Roosevelt would have no favor-ites, but would treat the wealthy and the poor alike, and would bring them within the control of the law. Are you with Mr. Roosevelt or are you with Mr. Bryan on that issue?

Now I am aware that it is said that Mr. Bryan is not the Democratic party, and that the Democratic party is not Mr. Bryan. Your own distin-guished fellow-citizen, Mr. Henry Watterson, is engaged in giving out at various times most interesting views on public questions which assume that there is a difference between what Mr. Bryan thinks and what the Demo-cratic party thinks. But everybody knows that Mr. Bryan is to be the next candidate for the Presidency, and that Mr. Bryan's influence is controlling in the Democratic party, and that what he thinks makes up the real plat-form of the party. Now I know the Democrats of the South many of them have no sympathy whatever with the principles that actuate Mr. Bryan. And I say to them as courageous men who can look situations square in the face, are they longer to permit themselves to be led at the tail of the wagon, pursuing a course with which they have no sympathy merely be-cause of the traditions of the past and a ghost of a former issue?

They have an opportunity in the present election to make an effective Declaration of Independence. The Democratic party is hopelessly divided by the arbitrary conduct of an iron machine and the time is ripe for a change. The Republican party has nominated a strong ticket. Mr. Willson, the candidate for Governor, a member of the Bar of high standing, of great ability and representing the best elements of Republicanism in the state, may well command your suffrages because you may be confident that he will make a dignified, honest, courageous and efficient governor of the commonwealth. His colleagues on the ticket should appeal to you in the same way. Now is the accepted hour to break away from the dead bonds of the past and range yourself under the banner of the party of progress, efficiency and reform under the leadership of Theodore Roosevelt.

12

Labor and Capital

Delivered before the Cooper Institute,
New York City, Friday, January 10, 1908

Ladies and Gentlemen: I am going to ask your attention tonight to the subject of labor and capital, their common interest, their necessary controversies, their lawful acts and the legal remedies for their abuses.

Origin of Institution of Property

Looking back to a time when society was much ruder and simpler, we can trace the development of certain institutions that have come to be the basis of modern civilization. We can hardly conceive the right of personal liberty without private property, because involved in personal liberty is the principle that one shall enjoy what his labor produces. Property and capital were first accumulated in implements, in arms and personal belongings, the value of which depended almost wholly on the labor in their making. As man's industry and self-restraint grew, he produced by his labor not only enough for his immediate necessities, but also a surplus, which he saved to be used in aid of future labor. By this means the amount which each man's labor would produce was thereafter increased. There followed at length the corollary that he whose savings from his own labor had increased the product of another's labor was entitled to enjoy a share in the joint result, and in the fixing of these shares was the first agreement between labor and capital. The certainty that a man could enjoy as his own that which he produced or that which he saved, and so could dispose of it to another, was the institution of private property and the strongest motive for industry beyond that needed merely to live.

This is what has led to the accumulation of capital in the world. It is the mainspring of human action which has raised man from the barbarism of the early ages to modern civilization. Without it he would still be in the alternating periods of starvation and plenty, and no happiness but that of gorging unrestrained appetite. Capital increased the amount of labor's production and reduced the cost in labor units of each unit produced. The cheaper the cost of production, the less each one had to work to earn the absolute necessities of life, and the more time he had to earn its comforts. And as the material comforts increased, the more possible became happiness and the greater the opportunity for the cultivation of the higher instincts of the human mind and soul.

All Benefited by Increase of Capital

It would seem, therefore, to be plainly for the benefit of everyone to increase the amount of capital in use in the world, and this can only be done by maintaining the motive for its increase.

Security of Capital Great Benefit to Labor

Labor needs capital to secure the best production, while capital needs labor in producing anything. The share of each laborer in the joint product is affected not exactly, but in a general way, by the amount of capital in use as compared with the number of those who labor. The more capital in use the more work there is to do, and the more work there is to do the more laborers are needed. The greater the need for laborers the better their pay per man. Manifestly, it is in the direct interest of the laborer that capital shall increase faster than the number of those who work. Everything, there-fore, which legitimately tends to increase the accumulation of wealth and its use for production will give each laborer a larger share of the joint result of capital and labor. It will be observed that the laborer derives little or no benefit at all from wealth which is not used for production. Nothing is so likely to make wealth idle as insecurity of invested capital and property. It follows, as a necessary conclusion, that to destroy the guaranties of prop-erty is a direct blow at the interest of the workingman.

The last two generations have witnessed a marvelous material develop-ment. It has been effected by the assembling and enforced coöperation of simple elements that previously had been separately used. The organization of powerful machines or of delicate devices by which the producing power of one man was increased fifty or one hundred fold was, however, not the only step in this great progress. Within the limits of efficient administra-tion, the larger the amount to be produced at one time and under one management the less the expense per unit. Therefore the aggregation of capital, the other essential element with labor in producing anything, be-came an obvious means of securing economy in the manufacture of every-thing. Corporations had long been known as convenient commercial instruments for wielding combinations of capital. Charters were at first conferred by special act upon particular individuals and with varying pow-ers, but so great became the advantage of incorporation, with the facility afforded for managing great corporations, and the limitation of the liability of investors, that it was deemed wise in this country, in order to prevent favoritism, to create corporations by general laws, and thus to afford to all who wished it the opportunity of assuming a corporate character in accordance therewith.

The result was a great increase in the number of the corporations and the assumption of the corporate form by seven-eighths of the active capital of the country. For a long time it was contended that the introduction of machines to save labor would work an injury to those who made things by hand, because it enabled the capitalist to reduce the number of hands that he employed. The argument was a strong one, but the result has shown that it was erroneous in that it did not take into account two things—first, that the saving made by machinery so increased the profit on the capital and thus made so much new capital that while the demand for labor in one factory or business was reduced, the number of businesses and factories grew so that on the whole the demand for labor increased greatly; and, second, the use of machinery so reduced the cost of production and price of both the necessities and comforts of life that the laborer's wages in money were given a substantial increase in purchasing power.

Panic Shows Labor's Interest in Welfare of Capital

What has been said, it seems to me, shows clearly enough that the laborer is almost as keenly interested in having capital increase as the capitalist himself. As already said, anything that makes capital idle, or which reduces or destroys it, must reduce both wages and the opportunity to earn wages. It only requires the effects of a panic through which we are passing, or through which we passed in 1893 or 1873, to show how closely united in a common interest we all are in modern society. We are in the same boat, and financial and business storms which affect one are certain to affect all others. It was not so much so in olden times, when the population was scattered, and when each family supplied almost all of its own wants, when it raised its food on the farm and made its clothes in the winter, and depended but little on what it sold, and bought practically nothing. Now we live in a society that is strictly cooperative. Destroy the buildings of a city like San Francisco by an earthquake, and then learn the complete dependence that all the urban population has upon the rest of the country for more than a week's life. As the population increases, as the cost of production for our necessities and comforts is reduced by having them made in great quantities, and at a low price, we become dependent on the working of this coöperative mechanism to such a point that a clog in any of the wheels which stops them causes stagnation and disaster.

Therefore, to come back to my original proposition, the laboring man should be the last to object to the rapid accumulation of capital in the hands of those who use it for the reproduction of capital. The thoughtful and intelligent laborer has therefore no feeling of hostility toward combinations of capital engaged in lawful business methods.

The capitalist, however wealthy, who is willing to devote his nights and days to the investment of his capital in profitable lawful business or manufacture, and who studies methods of reducing the cost of production and economizing expenses therein, should be regarded with favor by the workingman, because, while his motive is merely one of accumulation, he is working not only for himself but for labor and for society at large. The inventors on the one hand, and the men of judgment, courage and executive ability, who have conceived and executed the great lawful enterprises, on the other, have reaped princely profits, which the world may well accord them for the general good they have done. The wealth they accumulated is not wrested from labor, but it is only a part of that which has been added to the general stock by the ingenuity, industry, judgment and ability of those who enjoy it. If, with the growth in the population, the condition of man is to improve, new plans for the use of capital to better advantage must be devised, which shall, at the same time, increase capital more rapidly than the population and reduce the cost of living.

What has been said should not be misunderstood. The men who have by economic organization of capital at the same time increased the amount of the country's capital, increased the demand and price for labor and reduced the cost of necessities, are not philanthropists. Their sole motive has been one of gain, and with the destruction of private property that motive would disappear, and so would the progress of society. The very advantage to be derived from the security of private property in our civilization is that it turns the natural selfishness and desire for gain into the strongest motive for doing that without which the upward development of mankind would cease and retrogression would begin.

Fair Laws for Capital Should Be Favored by Labor

It is greatly in the interest of the workingman, therefore, that corporate capital should be fairly treated. Any injustice done to it acts directly upon the wage-earners who must look to corporate wealth for their employment. Take the large body of railroad employees. Any drastic legislation which tends unjustly to reduce the legitimate earnings of the railroad must in the end fall with heavy weight upon the employees of that railroad, because the manager will ultimately turn toward wages as the place where economy can be effected. So in respect to taxation, if the corporation is made to bear more than its share of the public burdens, it reacts directly, first, upon its stockholders, and then upon its employees. In the election of 1896, when the cry was for free silver, a great many wage-earners in that campaign of education were enabled to see that while the serious impairment of the standard value by going on to a free-silver basis might work advantageously for the debtor class, the laboring man belonged to the creditor class. The wage-earners had no debts of any amount to pay; they were benefited by having their wages paid in the best currency possible; and they were directly interested that their employers with capital should collect the debts due them in the same medium in which those debts had been contracted. The truth was that the wage-earners were in effect part of the moneyed classes of this country in the sense that their interest and that of the capitalist were identically the same in requiring the honest payment of debts.

We are suffering now from a panic. It was brought on, in my judgment, by the exhaustion of free capital the world over, by the lack of an elastic system of currency and also by a lack of confidence in our business fabric produced in Europe through the revelations in certain great corporations of business dishonesty, corruption and unlawfulness. It had been necessary for us to purify some of our business methods; but the purification can not stop the panic. It will doubtless make another in the far future less likely. Meantime all must suffer, both the innocent and guilty, and the innocent more than the guilty. Certainly the laborer who is thrown out of his employment by the hard times is innocent and suffers more than the capitalist, whether innocent or guilty, who has money to live on meantime until prosperity shall be restored.

The conclusion I seek to reach is that the workingman who entertains a prejudice against the lawful capitalist because he is wealthy, who votes with unction for the men who are urging unjust and unfair legislation against him, and who make demagogic appeals to acquire popular support in what they are doing, is standing in his own light, is blind to his own interests and is cutting off the limb on which he sits. It is to the direct interest of the workingman to use careful discrimination in approving or disapproving proposed legislation of this kind and to base his conclusion and vote on the issue whether the provision is fair or just, and not on the assumption that any legislation that subjects a corporation to a burden must necessarily be in the interest of the workingman. What I am anxious to emphasize is that there is a wide economic and business field in which the interests of the wealthiest capitalist and of the humblest laborer are exactly the same.

Where Labor and Capital Are Necessarily Opposed—Labor Unions Necessary

But while it is in the common interest of labor and capital to increase the fruits of production, yet in determining the share of each in the product, their interests are plainly opposed. Though the law of supply and demand will doubtless in the end be the most potent influence in fixing this division, yet during the gradual adjustment to the changing markets and the varying financial conditions, capital will surely have the advantage unless labor takes united action. During the betterment of business conditions, organized labor, if acting with reasonable discretion, can secure much greater promptness in the advance of wages than if it were left to the slower operation of natural laws, and in the same way, as hard times come on, the too eager employer may be restrained from undue haste in reducing wages. The organization of capital into corporations with the position of advantage which this gives it in a dispute with single laborers over wages, makes it absolutely necessary for labor to unite to maintain itself.

For instance, how could workingmen, dependent on each day's wages for living, dare to take a stand which might leave them without employment if they had not by small assessments accumulated a common fund for their support during such emergency? In union they must sacrifice some independence of action, and there have sometimes been bad results from the tyranny of the majority in such cases; but the hardships which have followed impulsive resort to extreme measures have had a good effect to lessen them. Experience, too, is leading to classification among the members, so that the cause of the skilled and worthy shall not be leveled down to that of the lazy and neglectful. This is being done, I am told, by what is called the maximum and minimum wage.

Controversy Concerns More Than Wages

The diverse interests of capital and labor are wider considerably than the mere pecuniary question of the amount of wages. They cover all the terms of the employment and include not only the compensation but also the circumstances that affect the comfort and condition of the workingmen, including the daily hours of work, the place in which they work, the provisions for their safety from accident, and everything else that is germane to the employment.

Good Effect of Labor Unions—Legislation

The effect of the organization of labor, on the whole, has been highly beneficial in securing better terms for employment for the whole laboring community. I have not the slightest doubt, and no one who knows anything about the subject can doubt, that the existence of labor unions steadies wages. More than this, it has brought about an amelioration of the condition of the laborers in another way. The really practical justification for popular representative government rests on the truth that any set of men or class in a political community are better able to look after their own interests, and more certain to keep those interests constantly in mind, than the members of any other class or set of men, however altruistic. This truth is fully exemplified in the course which legislation has taken since labor has organized and has made a systematic effort to secure laws to protect the workingman by mandatory provision against the heartlessness or negligence of the employer. Labor unions have given great attention to factory acts which secure a certain amount of air and provision for the safety of employees, to the safety-appliance acts in respect to railroads, to fixing the law governing the liability of railroads to their employees for injuries sustained by accident, to the restriction of child labor in factories, and to similar remedial legislation. The interest of the workingman has been more direct in these matters than even that of the philanthropists, and he has pressed the matter until in the legislation of nearly every state the effect of his influence is seen.

Wise Attitude of Capitalist toward Organized Labor

What the capitalist, who is the employer of labor, must face is, that the organization of labor—the labor union—is a permanent condition in the industrial world. It has come to stay. If the employer would consult his own interest, he must admit this and act on it. Under existing conditions the blindest course that an employer of labor can pursue is to decline to recognize labor unions as the controlling influence in the labor market and to insist upon dealing only with his particular employees. Time and time again one has heard the indignant expression of a manager of some great industrial enterprise that he did not propose to have the labor union run his business; that he would deal with his own men, and not with outsiders.

The time has passed in which that attitude can be assumed with any hope of successfully maintaining it. What the wise managers of corporate enterprises employing large numbers of laborers will do, is to receive the leaders of labor unions with courtesy and respect and listen to their claims and arguments as they would to the managers of any other corporate interest with whom they were to make an important contract affecting the business between them. At times some labor leaders are intoxicated with the immense power that they exercise in representing thousands of their fellow-workers and are weak enough to exhibit a spirit of arrogance. Dealing with them is trying to the patience of the employer. So, too, propositions from labor unions sometimes are so exorbitant in respect to the terms of employment as literally to deprive the manager of the control which he ought to retain over the laborers employed in his business. This is to be expected in a comparatively new movement and is not to be made a ground for condemning it.

On the other hand, the arrogance is not confined to one side. We all of us know that there are a number of employers who have the spirit of intolerance and sense of power because of their immense resources, and that their attitude is neither conciliatory nor likely to lead to an adjustment of differences. The wise men among the employers of labor and the labor leaders are those who discard all appearance of temper or sense of power and attempt by courteous consideration and calm discussion to reach a common ground. One of the great difficulties in peaceful adjustments of controversies between labor and capital is the refusal of each side to take time to understand the attitude of the other. The question which troubles the capitalist, of course, is how an increase in wages or a maintenance of wages will affect the profits of his business. The question which troubles the workingman is how much he can live on and what he can save from his wages. And these things are affected by many different circumstances, including, on the one hand, the condition of the market for the merchandise which is being manufactured and the other elements in the cost of operating the enterprise, and, on the other, the rate of rent and the price of necessaries of life. If the leaders of the workingmen believe that the employer is considering their argument and weighing it, and the labor leaders manifest an interest in the conditions with reference to expense and profit of the employer, the possibility of an adjustment is much greater than when each occupies a stiff and resentful attitude against the other.

The great advantage of such organizations as the Civic Federation is that they bring capitalists and labor leaders together into a common forum of discussion and cast a flood of light in which each party to the controversy derives much valuable information as to the mental attitude and just claims of the other. I do not think it a mere dream either to hope that by reason of this friendly contact between employers and labor leaders, labor unions may be induced to assist the cause of honest industry by bringing to bear the moral force of the public opinion of the union to improve the sobriety, industry, skill and fidelity to the employer's interests of the employee. Indeed, the rules of some labor unions already contain evidence of a desire to effect such a result.

Arbitration

This brings me to the question of arbitration. It goes without saying that where an adjustment can not be reached by negotiation, it is far better for the community at large that the differences be settled by submission to an impartial tribunal and agreement to abide its judgment, than by resort to a trial of resistance and endurance, by lockouts and strikes and the other means used by the parties to industrial controversies in fighting out the issues between them. Not infrequently one side or the other—but generally the capitalist side—will say in response to a suggestion of arbitration that there is nothing to arbitrate; that their position is so impregnable from the standpoint of reason that they could not abide judgment against them by any tribunal in a matter subject to their voluntary action.

In such a case, arbitration as a method of settlement is impossible, unless the system of compulsory arbitration is adopted. It is a very serious question whether under our Constitution a decree of a tribunal under a compulsory arbitration law could be enforced against the side of the laborers. It would come very close to the violation of the thirteenth amendment, which forbids involuntary servitude. It has been frequently decided that no injunction can issue which will compel a man to perform his contract of employment, and that on the ground that while the breach of his contract may give rise to a claim for damages, he can not be compelled, except in the peculiar employments of enlistment in the Army and service on a ship, specifically to perform a labor contract. Hence, compulsory arbitration does not seem to be the solution.

Massachusetts Plan

A method has been adopted in Massachusetts and some other states, and, indeed, has practically been adopted by President Roosevelt, in respect to the settlement of these labor controversies which has substantial and practical results. That is a provision of law by which an impartial tribunal shall investigate all the conditions surrounding the dispute, take sworn evidence, draft a conclusion in respect to the merits of the issue and publish it to the world. There often are disputes between great corporate employers and their employees which eventuate in a strike, and the public finds it impossible to obtain any reliable information in respect to the matter because the statements from both sides are so conflicting.

We can not have a great labor controversy or a great strike without its affecting injuriously a great many other people than those actually engaged in it. The truth is, that the class of capital and the class of labor, represented on the one side by the managers of the great corporations and on the other side by the leaders of the great labor unions, do not include all the members of the community by a great deal. In addition to them are the farming community, the small merchants and storekeepers, the professional men, the class of clerks, and many other people who have nothing to do with manual labor—skilled or unskilled—and who do not own shares in the stock of industrial or other enterprises requiring capital to carry them on. These are the middlemen, so to speak, in the controversy. The views of the members of this body make up the public opinion that, it is so often said, finally decides labor controversies. It is for the information of this body in the community that such a provision as that of the Massachusetts law is admirably adapted. That statute does not provide for compulsory arbitration, but it comes as near it in practical affairs as our system of constitutional law will permit.

Anthracite Coal Arbitration

One of the instances, most striking in the history of this country, of the possibility of bringing capital and labor together to consider the question from a standpoint of reasonableness and patriotism is the settlement of the Pennsylvania anthracite coal strike. That, of course, was by arbitration. And it was brought about through the influence of the President, who had no official relation to either side, but who as the first citizen of the country was deeply interested in preventing the cataclysm to which things seemed to be tending in the anthracite coal region. The permanence of the settlement which was there effected is a triumphant vindication of what was done. And it illustrates the possibilities when opponents in such controversies can be brought face to face and in the presence of impartial persons be made to discuss all the circumstances surrounding the issue.

Strikes Costly

I shall not stop to cite statistics to show the enormous loss in the savings of labor as well as the savings of capitalists which strikes and lockouts have involved. Time was when the first resort of the labor leader was to order a strike. But experience has taught both sides the loss entailed, and strikes are now much less lightly entered upon, especially by the more conservative labor unions. Everybody admits their destructive character and that all means should be resorted to to avoid them. Still, there are times when nothing but a strike will accomplish the legitimate purpose of the laborer.

Legal Right to Strike

And, now, what is the right of the labor union with respect to the strike? I know that there has been at times a suggestion in the law that no strike can be legal. I deny this. Men have the right to leave the employ of their employer in a body in order to impose on him as great an inconvenience as possible to induce him to come to their terms. They have the right in their labor unions to delegate to their leaders the power to say when to strike. They have the right in advance to accumulate by contribution from all members of the labor union a fund which shall enable them to live during the pendency of the strike. They have the right to use persuasion with all other laborers who are invited to take their places, in order to convince them of the advantage to labor of united action. It is the business of courts and of the police to respect these rights with the same degree of care that they respect the right of owners of capital to the protection of their property and business.

Change of Public Sentiment toward Unions

I have thus considered the necessity and justification of labor unions and their legal power. Those leaders of labor unions who have learned to pursue conservative methods have added greatly to the strength of their cause, and have given the unions a much better standing with the great body of the people who are neither capitalists nor laborers, and only favor the greatest good for the greatest number. I am inclined to think that the popular resentment against the revelations of corporate lawlessness may have had something to do with this change of sentiment.

A resort to violence, or other form of lawlessness, on behalf of a labor union, properly merits and receives the sharpest condemnation from the public, and is quite likely to lose the cause of labor its support in the particular controversy.

Necessity for Considering Abuses

I have been discussing the relations of capital and labor and the lawful scope of their action, on the assumption that they do not violate the law or the rights of any member of the community, and I am glad to say that I believe that this assumption is correct with respect to the great majority of those engaged as capitalists and of those engaged as wage-earners; but it would be a very insufficient consideration of the relations of labor and capital if I did not take up the abuses, lawlessness and infractions of others' rights, of which some of the combiners of capital and some of the wage-earners—members of labor unions—have been from time to time guilty and did not consider further the remedy for the restraint of these evils.

Abuses of Capital Combinations

For the sake of clearness in examining into the character of corporate evils and abuses which need restraint and punishment, we may divide corporations guilty of them into industrial corporations organized for the purpose of manufacture and sale of merchandise, and into railroad and other corporations organized for the transportion of passengers and goods.

Industrial Corporations

Let us deal first with industrial corporations. The valuable consideration moving to the public for conferring the franchise necessary in the incorporation of such companies is the public benefit to be derived in the lowering of prices. The temptation to the managers, however, when the enterprises become very large, is to suppress competition and maintain prices, and thus to deny to the public its proper share in the benefit sought to be attained and to appropriate to the corporate owners all the profit derived from improved facilities of production.

One method of suppressing competition is by agreements between all the large concerns engaged in the same business to limit the output and maintain prices. Such agreements are usually secret and are difficult for public officials to obtain proof of; but when these agreements do become public and are successfully prosecuted, this method is enjoined and abandoned, and the independent corporations that acted together under secret agreements to maintain prices are absorbed into one great corporation, so that the large proportion of the producing capital in a single industry is placed under one control. Then competition with the trust, thus formed, is excluded by ingenious contracts of sale with middlemen, distributers, and retail dealers, who are coerced by the agents of the trust into a maintenance of retail prices and a withdrawal of all patronage from smaller independent and competing producers through the knowledge and fear that the trust in times of active demand for its products will either refuse to sell or will sell only at discriminating prices to those who do not comply with its demand.

Abuses of Railway Corporations

The second class of corporations—that is, the railway and transportation companies—have misused their great powers to promote the unlawful purposes of these industrial combinations. One of the largest elements going to make up the selling price of a commodity in any part of the country is the cost of transportation from the place of manufacture. If one business concern can secure lower rates of freight in the transportation of its merchandise to its customers than another, the former will necessarily drive the latter out of business. This is exactly what has happened. The largest concerns controlling enormous shipments and able as between competing roads to determine which shall enjoy the profits of the transportation, have induced and sometimes coerced the railway companies into giving them either secret rates or open public rates so deftly arranged with a view to the conditions of the larger concern, as to make it impossible for its would-be business competitors to live. The rebate of a very small amount per hundredweight of goods shipped by any one of the great industrial corporations will pay enormous dividends on the capital invested. The evils of railroad management can be summed up in the words "unjust discrimination."

Interest of Wage-Earners in Suppression of These Abuses

Wage-earners are not injuriously affected in their terms of employment directly by such violations of law by combinations of capital as I have described. But they are very seriously affected in another way. The maintenance of such unlawful monopolies is for the purpose of keeping up the prices of the necessities of life, and this necessarily reduces the purchasing power of the wages which the wage-earners receive. This is a serious detriment to them and a real reason why they should condemn such corporate abuses and sympathize with the effort to stamp them out. It is not that they should sympathize with an effort to destroy such great corporate enterprises because they employ enormous numbers of wage-earners and lawfully and normally increase the capital from which the wage fund is drawn, but they should and do vigorously sustain the policy of the Government in bringing these great corporate enterprises within the law and requiring them to conduct their business in accordance with the statutes of their country. I have already said that they should discriminate in respect to legislation affecting their corporation, and should not assume that simply because it burdened the enterprise from which they derived their wages it was in their interest; but I would invoke with the utmost emphasis their approval of the present interstate-commerce law as needed to keep the railroads within the law.

Violence in Interest of Capital

In rare instances corporate managers have entered into a course of violence to maintain their side of a labor controversy. They have justified it on the ground that they were simply fighting fire with fire, and that if the labor union proceeded to use dynamite they would use dynamite in return. I can not too strongly condemn this course or this argument. No amount of lawlessness on the part of the labor striker will justify lawlessness on the part of the employer. Such a course means a recurrence of civil war and anarchy.

A second abuse which employers are sometimes guilty of is what is technically known as blacklisting, by which laboring men, solely because they may have been advocates of a strike, or have been against a compromise in a labor dispute, are tagged by one employer of labor, and all other employers of labor are forbidden on penalty of business ostracism to give them a means of livelihood. This is unlawful and should be condemned. It is the counterpart of the boycott, or indeed it is itself a boycott in one form, to which I shall make reference hereafter.

Abuses of Labor

What are the abuses which not infrequently proceed from some of the members of united labor? They are, first, open violence and threats of violence to prevent the employment of other workingmen in the places which such members have left on a strike, with the hope that they will thus prevent their former employer from being able to carry on his business. Of course this is the most effective method, if successful, of bringing the employer to terms. If the demand for labor is such that many persons of the same craft as those who strike, not members of the labor union, are idle, it will be easy for the employer to replace the strikers. They will be out of a job and he will continue his business.

It follows, therefore, that the wisest time for skilled or other labor to strike is when there is a great demand for labor, and it is difficult for the employer to replace those who leave him. But if there are other laborers available, then there are only two ways by which the strikers can accomplish their purpose, either by actual or threatened violence to those who would take their places, or by persuading them in the interest of all labor that they should join their union, receive the benefits of the common fund for support during enforced idleness, and join in the refusal to aid the employer in his extremity. Violence and threatened violence are of course unlawful and are strongly to be condemned. Persuasion not amounting in effect to duress is lawful.

Boycotts

Another method by which wage-earners sometimes attempt to coerce their employer into acquiescence in their demands is what is called a boycott. It is a method by which the striking employees and their fellows of their union attempt to coerce the whole community into a withdrawal of all association from their former employer by threatening the rest of the community that if they do not withdraw their association from such employer they will visit each one of them with similar treatment. This is a cruel instrument and has been declared to be unlawful in every court with whose decisions I am familiar. The Anthracite Strike Commission, which was selected at the instance of President Roosevelt and which had upon it such a distinguished jurist as Judge George Gray, of Delaware, and Mr. Clark, the president of one of the great labor organizations of the country, and other men entirely indifferent as between labor and capital—men selected by agreement between the employers and the employees in that great controversy—used the following language in respect to the boycott:

"It also becomes our duty to condemn another less violent, but not less reprehensible, form of attack upon those rights and liberties of the citizens which the public opinion of civilized countries recognizes and protects. The right and liberty to pursue a lawful calling and to lead a peaceable life, free from molestation or attack, concerns the comfort and happiness of all men, and the denial of them means the destruction of one of the greatest, if not the greatest, of the benefits which the social organization confers. What is popularly known as the boycott (a word of evil omen and unhappy origin) is a form of coercion by which a combination of many persons seek to work their will upon a single person or upon a few persons by compelling others to abstain from social or beneficial business intercourse with such person or persons. Carried to the extent sometimes practiced in aid of a strike, and as was in some instances practiced in connection with the late anthracite strike, it is a cruel weapon of aggression, and its use immoral and antisocial."

To say this is not to deny the legal right of any man or set of men voluntarily to refrain from social intercourse or business relations with any persons whom he or they, with or without good reason, dislike. This may sometimes be un-Christian, but it is not illegal. But when it is a concerted purpose of a number of persons not only to abstain themselves from such intercourse, but to render the life of their victim miserable by persuading and intimidating others to refrain, such purpose is a malicious one, and the concerted attempt to accomplish it is a conspiracy at common law, and merits and should receive the punishment due to such a crime.

I may add that the same Commission visited black-listing with similar condemnation.

Legal Remedies for Abuses

What are the remedies by which a person injured may be protected against the illegal acts of combinations of capital and of combinations of labor? First, if the injury sought to be inflicted is one which will be inadequately compensated for in money damages, one can apply to a court of equity to prevent the injury from being done, and that court can, in advance of the proposed violation of the plaintiff's rights, determine exactly what those rights are and advise the defendant accordingly; or he can wait until the acts are performed and then, by suit for damages, he can make himself whole if he can.

Remedy by Injunction Preferred

In cases of unlawful combinations of capital, as well as of such combinations of labor, the method in equity by securing an injunction seems to be preferred by those who are about to be injured. In every statute which has been enacted to denounce the improper use of capital to secure illegal restraints of trade and illegal monopolies, a specific provision has been inserted enabling those who are injured or affected to bring an equity proceeding to enjoin the carrying on of the improper methods about to be attempted. In the same way, when labor unions or members of labor unions or workingmen on a strike resort to methods destructive of the business of their employer and his property, the employer deems it the most convenient method of defending himself to apply to a court of equity for an injunction against those who give indication of their intention to carry on such methods.

Criticism of Injunction Remedy

This remedy by injunction has been very severely denounced and criticized, on the ground that it places in the hands of a judge legislative, judicial and executive powers; that it enables him to make the law for one case against a particular individual and if he does not abide by it to try him and punish him. When this objection is analyzed it is found to be unjust.

Criticism Unjust

An injunction suit does not differ in the slightest degree from a suit brought after the event, so far as the function of the court is concerned in declaring the law, except that the court declares the law in respect of anticipated facts rather than in respect of those which have happened. He has no authority to make law. In an injunction suit, as in any other suit, he merely interprets the law and applies it to the circumstances. His judgment in the one case involves exactly the same precedents and the same rules of law as in the other. In order to save the party plaintiff from having to bring suit to recover for an injury that he is going to suffer, he says, "This is an unlawful injury; and as you threaten to do it I enjoin you from doing it."

Prevention Better Than Cure

Certainly, prevention is better than cure, and it is no wonder that a man who is about to have his business injured or his property destroyed prefers to prevent the injury rather than to allow it to occur. Neither a suit in damages nor a criminal prosecution is likely to bring him back his property or to restore his loss. Moreover, in cases of boycott, in many states, there is no provision for criminal prosecution.

History of Writ of Injunction

I wish to invite attention to this writ of injunction, which is one of the most beneficial remedies known to the law, and to trace its history and show how useful it has been in the past for the purpose of preventing injustice.

Originally, in England, from which we get our procedure and most of our law, the King was supposed to decide cases through his judges of the King's bench or of the common pleas. The common law was rather rigid and severe, especially in holding persons to the letter of their contracts, and judgments went for the plaintiff on this strict interpretation that really shocked the conscience. And so, after a while, the people began to appeal to the King to save them from the severity of his own courts. He turned the matter over to the lord keeper of the great seal, and said, "Work out equity in this case." The way the lord keeper worked it out was not to issue any direction to the court of King's bench or the common pleas; but he took hold of the plaintiff in the suit and threatened him with excommunication if he did not stop the suit and do that justice which equity required.

In other words, he enjoined the plaintiff from proceeding with the suit in the court of the King's bench or of the common pleas, as the case might be, and brought him into what grew to be a court of equity known as the court of chancery. As the lord keeper in those days was an ecclesiastic, he exercised power over the consciences of the litigants, and the threat of excommunication was generally sufficient to enforce what he wished. Subsequently, the lord keeper ceased to be a bishop and became known as the lord chancellor, and after the court of equity had been established, violation of the injunction was punished by imprisonment instead of excommunication.

Usefulness of Writ

Let me take a case that illustrates the usefulness of the writ of injunction. At common law, when a man wished to borrow $500 on his farm which was worth $10,000 he gave a mortgage to secure it. The mortgage was a conveyance of the title to the land with the condition that the title should become absolute if the money was not paid on the date mentioned in the mortgage. If the money was not paid, the creditor could put the debtor out of possession by suit and for $500 become the owner of a farm which was worth $10,000. In such a case the lord keeper said to the plaintiff: "Here, you are trying to get this farm for $500 when it is worth $10,000. That is not equitable, and I will not let you do it. I will enjoin you from continuing that suit, because you are after something that is unjust, and I will make you come in before me and settle this, and if the defendant is not able to pay the $500 and interest we will sell the farm and pay you the $500 and interest and turn over the balance to the defendant." That was an equitable decision, and it was made effective by the power of injunction.

A man leases a farm, with a row of beautiful trees, to a tenant. The tenant advises him that he is going to cut the trees down during his tenancy. What is the landlord to do? Is he to let the tenant cut his trees down and then sue him for the value of the trees? No. Equity suggests the remedy that he go into court and enjoin the man and prevent injury which could not be compensated for in damages.

A man owns a lucrative business and a numerous set of people conceive a prejudice against him or a desire to injure him, and institute a boycott against him and threaten everybody that they will withdraw their patronage, which is valuable, from anybody that has anything to do with him. In that way he loses a lot of customers. Now, is not it better that he should apply to the court to enjoin them from taking that course, and inflicting injury on him that he can not measure in damages, than that they should be permitted to destroy his business and he should have the burden of a lawsuit afterwards, with all the uncertainty as to damages and the doubt about getting his money even if he secured a judgment?

So, too, where a body of strikers by continued acts of violence, trespass, constituting a nuisance, attempts to stop his business, it is peculiarly difficult for him to estimate the injury he suffers, and a judgment for money would be a very inadequate remedy.

Abuse of Writ of Injunction

But it is said that the writ of injunction has been abused in this country in labor disputes, and that a number of injunctions have been issued that ought never to have been issued. I agree that there has been abuse in this regard. President Roosevelt referred to it in his last message. I think it has grown chiefly from the practice of issuing injunctions *ex parte;* that is, without giving notice or hearing to the defendant. The injustice that is worked is in this wise: Men leave employment on a strike, intending to conduct themselves peaceably and within the law. The counsel for the employer visits a judge, presents an affidavit in which an averment is made that violence is threatened, injury to property and injury to business. And accordingly on this affidavit the judge issues a temporary restraining order *ex parte* against the defendants who are named in the petition or bill. The broadest expressions are used in the writ—frequently too broad. The defendants are workingmen, not lawyers. They are not used to processes of the court. The expressions of the writ are formidable. A doubt arises in their minds as to the legality of what they are about to do. The stiffening is taken out of the strike, the men drop back and the strike is over, and all before they have had a chance in court to demonstrate, as they might, that they had no intention of doing anything unlawful or doing any violence.

Favors Requiring Notice

Under the original Federal judiciary act, it was not permissible for the Federal courts to issue an injunction without notice. There had to be notice and, of course, a hearing. I think it would be entirely right in this class of cases to amend the law and provide that no temporary restraining order should issue at all until after notice and a hearing. Then the court could be advised by both sides with reference to the exact situation, and the danger of issuing a writ too broad or of issuing a writ without good ground would generally be avoided.

Favors Requiring a Different Judge in Contempt Proceedings from the Judge Issuing Injunction

There is another objection made, and that is that the judge who issues the writ has a personal sensitiveness in respect to its violation that gives him a bias when he comes to hear contempt proceedings on charge of disobedience to the order, and makes it unfair for him to impose a punishment if conviction follows: I think few judges on the bench would allow such a consideration to affect them, but I agree that there is a popular doubt of the judge's impartial attitude in such a case. For that reason, I would favor a provision allowing the defendant in contempt proceedings to challenge the judge issuing the injunction, and to call for the designation of another judge to hear the issue. I do not think it would seriously delay the hearing of the cause, and it would give more confidence in the impartiality of the decision. It is almost as important that there should be the appearance of justice as that there should be an actual administration of it.

Objection to Trial of Contempt by Jury

But now it is said, Why not have a trial by jury? The reason why this is objectionable is because of the delay and of the character of jury trial. It would greatly weaken the authority and force of an order of court if it were known that it was not to be enforced except after a verdict of jury. Never in the history of judicial procedure has such a provision intervened between the issue of an order of court and its enforcement. I am quite willing to hedge around the exercise of the power to issue the writ of injunction with as many safeguards as are necessary to invite the attention of the court to the care with which he shall issue the writ; but to introduce another contest before the writ shall be enforced, with all the uncertainties and digressions and prejudices that are injected into a jury trial, would be to make the order of the court go for nothing.

Plaintiff Entitled to Ancient Remedy of Injunction

What the plaintiff in such cases is asking to secure is protection of his property and his business from a constant series of attacks. An injunction offers a remedy which is not given either by criminal prosecutions or the suit for damages. The plaintiff is not trying to punish somebody; he is trying to protect himself after the court shall have defined what his rights are. That right has been his in cases of this general character for years, and why should he be asked to give it up now?

Labor Unions Should Carry Decisions They Condemn to Courts of Last Resort

If, whenever a court issues an injunction that is improperly worded, that goes too far, or that ought never to have been granted, the labor union interested will take the matter up to the court of last resort, it will secure a series of decisions that will prevent the issue of injunctions such as some of those of which they now complain. The labor union has a fund, and it could not be devoted to a better purpose than fixing the law exactly as it should be under the decision of the court of last resort. I should not object at all to the definition of the rights of employer and of the withdrawing employee in labor controversies by statute. I should think that an excellent way of making clear what is lawful and what is unlawful. But until that course is pursued, the rights of the parties to such controversies should be carefully defined by courts of last resort, and when this is done courts of first instance will keep within lawful bounds.

Conclusion

I fear I have wearied you with this long discussion. I have attempted to treat the matter from an impartial standpoint and without prejudice for or against capital, or for or against labor. There is a class of capitalists who look upon labor unions as vicious *per se*, and a class of radical labor union- ists who look upon capital as labor's natural enemy. I believe, however, that the great majority of each class are gradually becoming more conciliatory in their attitude, the one toward the other. Between them is a larger class, neither capitalist nor labor unionist, who are without prejudices, and I hope I am one of those. The effects of the panic are not over. We must expect industrial depression. This may be fruitful of labor controversies. I earnestly hope that a more conservative and conciliatory attitude on both sides may avoid the destructive struggles of the past.

13

The Achievements of
the Republican Party

*Delivered before the Young Men's Republican Club
of Missouri, Kansas City, February 10, 1908*

Fellow-Republicans: We meet today to celebrate the memory of Abraham Lincoln. One of the bases for the everlasting gratitude which the country owes him is the part he took in the successful establishment in national political control of the Republican Party. Lincoln was a party man, as all men must be who expect to leave their individual impress upon the political character of the Nation.

A modern government of a people of 80,000,000 is complicated under any system. The difficulties of its management are not lessened when we commit its control to all males over the age of twenty-one, and call it a Republic. How is it possible to reduce the varying views of the entire population to one resultant executive force which shall carry on this machine of government in the public interest and for the public weal? The problem has been solved by the institution of parties. A party can not be useful unless those who are members of it yield their views on some issues and unite with respect to the main policies to be pursued. The resultant solidarity is necessary to secure efficacy. The sense of responsibility for the continued successful operation of the government must furnish cohesive power.

The party is the more efficient, in which the members are more nearly united on the great principles of governmental action. Though a party has its platform, and on the faith of it has been elected to power, many issues may unexpectedly arise in the course of an administration not controlled by the party's declared principles. The disposition of such issues must depend on the ability and courage of the party leaders. A party may divide on a new issue until by a process of education the sounder view prevails, and the party becomes united again in the enforcement of the new principle. As a party shows itself homogeneous, able to grasp the truth with respect to new issues, able to discard unimportant differences of opinion, sensitive with respect to the successful maintenance of government, and highly charged with the responsibility of its obligation to the people at large, it establishes its claim to the confidence of the public and to its continuance in political power. We are apt to deny to parties characteristics and traits like those of a person, but I venture to think that a history of political parties in which the description is clothed with life and truth must always treat them as having some personal attributes.

The course of the Republican Party since its organization in 1856, and its real assumption of control in 1861, down to the present day, is remarkable for the foresight and ability of its leaders, for the discipline and solidarity of its members, for its efficiency and deep sense of responsibility, for the preservation and successful maintenance of the government, and for the greatest resourcefulness in meeting the various trying and difficult issues which a history of now a full half century has presented for solution. It was born of a desire to maintain inviolate the union of the States. Its essence was that of nationalism, and its spirit was that of sacrifice, no matter how great, to maintain the integrity of our whole country. The federalism of Washington, Marshall and Hamilton was the guide of its constitutional construction, and it did not hesitate, when the issue was presented, to submit its view of the great fundamental instrument of our government to the arbitrament of a long and bloody war. The leader of the Republican party during the Civil War was Abraham Lincoln. In all the varieties of controversy with which it has since had to deal, it has never lost the inspiration of his leadership.

When the Republican Party entered upon the war in 1861, the only issue it was willing to fight out was that of the preservation of the Union.

It did not then assume the burden of the complete abolition of slavery. There were many in its ranks who pressed for such a declaration, but the time had not come. The course of war made abolition inevitable, and Mr. Lincoln, who was the greatest politician of his age, led his party a long way by the Emancipation Proclamation. Even as he did this, he created a division in his party. It was one of the first instances in which the party showed its own power of self-preservation by gradually convincing the minority of the righteousness of the new issue.

After the martyrdom of Lincoln came the period of reconstruction and the adoption of the so-called War Amendments. The Thirteenth Amendment gave to the negro the boon of freedom, but it left as children in the world four or five millions of people, not five percent of whom could read or write, and all of whom had been dependent upon others for what they ate and wore and did. Their emancipation was, of course, the first great step in their elevation as a race, but it involved at first great hardship and suffering and discouragement, as all great changes in existing conditions must. Still the Thirteenth Amendment has accomplished its purpose.

The Fourteenth Amendment secured to the negro the equal protection of the laws of the State in which he lived. This is the amendment which, second to his emancipation, has become the most important in his development. Living in the same community in which he had been a chattel, the great danger was that legislation would be enacted which might prevent him from enjoying the same benefit from the guaranties of life, liberty and property that were extended to his white fellow-citizens. It was of the highest importance to him to be assured of those economic rights in the enjoyment and pursuit of which lay the hope of his future progress.

The opportunity of the Southern negro lay, first, in education; second, in the skill of his hands as a laborer and in his industry as a tiller of the soil; and, third, in his capacity to save from his earnings sufficient to enable him to accumulate capital to buy land and establish his economic independence. Thus could he make himself useful to the community in which he lived and secure the respect which would certainly come to one showing himself indispensable to the growth and prosperity of the South. Thus would flow all the incidents of power and influence to which he aspired. When we regard the history of the forty years through which the colored man of this country has been obliged to struggle, the progress which he has made, material and educational, is wonderful.

The third great War Amendment—the Fifteenth—forbade any State to deprive the negro of his vote on account of his color or previous condition of servitude. The operation of this amendment has not been as successful as that of the Thirteenth and Fourteenth. Nor is this surprising. Consider the condition of things immediately after the war. Here was a masterful people, who had been used to a social condition in which the negro occupied a servile status, brought by law to face the prospect of sharing political control with the poor, ignorant and bewildered masses, who but the day before had been their property. Declarations of equality and popular rights and universal suffrage offer but a feather's weight against the inevitable impulses of human nature. It was impossible that with the elements I have stated, there should not have been developed fraud and violence and illegality. It was impossible that that which was written on the tables of the fundamental law or in the statute book should be immediately carried into effective execution. After a long struggle, the history of which I shall not recall, the negro's vote in the Southern States was made to count for nothing. Then the leaders of the South in many States came to realize the dreadful demoralization of all society if law was to be flouted and fraud was to constitute the basis of government. So they cast about to make the law square with the existing condition by property and educational qualifications which should exclude most of the negro vote.

This very desire to avoid the violent methods which were wont to overcome the colored vote in the South itself indicates a turn for the better. It is said, however, and with truth, that these election laws are intended to be enforced by means of the discretion vested in election officers, so as to exclude the ineligible colored men with rigor and to allow the ineligible whites, who ought also to be excluded, to enjoy the franchise. Deplorable as this is, still the situation is by no means a hopeless one for the Southern negro and the political power that he may in the future exercise. In the first place, if he continues to increase in intelligence by the acceptance of his educational opportunities, and if industrially he becomes a power, and thus gradually increases the number of his race who are eligible to vote in accordance with law, he will introduce into the electorate a body of individuals well qualified to act with common sense and judgment, and who, by their very position in the community, will give weight to the vote they cast. Their position and influence as a growing representation of their race, qualified to exercise the right of suffrage, will become stronger and stronger. Such a gradual acquisition of political power will secure them real influence and an opportunity to help their race to further progress. The greatest friend the Southern negro is likely to have is the broad-minded Southern white man who sympathizes with the colored man and knows his value to the South. Nor is it unreasonable to hope that the men who have already sought to come within the law, and avoid violence, will ultimately see the wisdom and righteousness of the equal enforcement of the law of eligibility against white and black. While I fully recognize the fact that the Fifteenth Amendment has not accomplished all that it was intended to accomplish, and that for a time it seemed to be a dead letter, I am confident that in the end it will prove to be a bulwark equally beneficial with that of the Thirteenth and Fourteenth Amendments to an unfortunate, down-trodden, struggling race, to whom, in view of the circumstances under which they were brought to this country and the conditions of bondage in which they were continued for more than two centuries, we owe every obligation of care and protection. That which has been done for the benefit of the negro race is the work of the Republican Party. It is one of those great issues presented by the exigencies of the war which the party has had the firmness and courage to meet. The party has not yet been entirely successful in fully working out the problem, but nearly all that has been done has been done at its instance or with its aid.

Another issue which the Republican Party found itself pursued by as an outgrowth of the war was the question of money, and on that the party showed a marked capacity for reaching a unanimous and sound conclusion after much controversy within its ranks. In order to maintain the government during the dark days of the war, we departed from the gold and silver monetary medium and issued as currency paper promises of the Government to pay. The students of finance today are disposed generally to think that the issue of greenbacks was not necessary to sustain the government, and that it might have been possible to conduct the enormous operations of the war and still retain gold and silver coin. However this may be, we found ourselves at the end of the war with a great volume of greenback currency and no means of redeeming it. For a time many members of the

Republican Party seemed to think that the wise course to pursue was to reduce the evil by increasing our irredeemable obligations. They imbibed the theory of fiat currency, that the government might create money and pay all its debts by merely printing promises to pay. Gradually the greenback heresy was eliminated. The Republican Party sloughed off its diseased members and took the firm, solid and righteous position that it would redeem every dollar of its bonds and of its other indebtedness in coin of the United States. On the 1st of January, 1878, specie payments were resumed and the paper of the government became as good as gold.

In the decade between 1880 and 1890, the greater production of silver had cheapened the metal in comparison with gold, and quack remedies for financial troubles, in the form of the greater use of silver money, seized a large part of the electorate, both Republicans and Democrats. The silver question was fought out for twelve or fifteen years, and in that time many of the Republican leaders supported doctrines which now would seem heretical. Gradually, however, the lines were formed. The Democracy under Mr. Bryan advanced the theory that the free coinage of silver, which was in effect repudiation of half of every debt, was the solution of all our difficulties, while the Republican Party, gradually and reluctantly, took its position in favor of the single gold standard and against any depreciation of it to make easier payment of debts. In the great battle of 1896 the Republican Party again stood for the maintenance of the integrity of the nation. The fight was against odds produced by a great industrial depression, and against the most sophistical arguments. The Republican Party maintained a campaign of education among the wage-earners and the farmers, which ultimately led to the complete defeat of this second financial heresy which had threatened the integrity of our business structure.

One of the great policies to which the Republican Party has been pledged from the beginning has been the protective system, by which industries have been diversified and domestic manufactures and farm productions have been enormously developed. The method consists in the imposition of customs duties upon imported products equal to the difference in the cost of producing the article in foreign countries and in this country, allowing for a reasonable profit to the home producer. Our whole business structure rests on the system, and the wage-earners dependent on it are myriad. The system has continued without a break from the time of the Morrill Tariff in 1861 until the present day, except that during the second administration of Mr. Cleveland an attempt was made to pass a revenue tariff, which failed, but resulted in the passage of a tariff which illustrated no theory of taxation at all and only brought disaster. There was put in force by the Republicans a new tariff in 1890, called the McKinley Tariff, which was repealed by the Gorman-Wilson Tariff of 1893, which in turn was repealed by the Dingley Tariff of 1897. In the ten years which have elapsed since the enactment of the Dingley Tariff, the conditions have so changed as to make a number of the schedules under that tariff too high and some too low. This renders it necessary to re-examine the schedules in order that the tariff shall be placed on a purely protective basis. By that I mean it should properly protect, against foreign competition, and afford a reasonable profit to all manufacturers, farmers and business men, but should not be so high as to furnish a temptation to the formation of monopolies to appropriate the undue profit of excessive rates.

In 1898 came the war with Spain. While both parties lent their aid in Congress and there was an outburst of patriotism in all sections, the war, for which we were so little prepared, had to be conducted by the Republican Party. Whatever efficiency was displayed in its maintenance was due to that Party, and the ability with which it could meet a new issue. After the Spanish War, comparatively so short and bloodless in its extent, there have developed national questions for settlement of greater importance than any save those of the great Civil War. The Republican Party has marched up to their solution with the same courage, the same skill and the same persistence that it has shown in respect to all the questions arising in its history. After peace with Spain was signed, Congress left to McKinley to pioneer in respect to the government of Puerto Rico, Cuba and the Philippines, imposing only as to the Cuban policy the condition that there should be an early date for turning over that island to the people of Cuba in accordance with the self-denying ordinance known as the Teller resolution. Congress did not interfere in the Philippines for a full four years, and in that time McKinley had worked out a policy which substantially received the full confirmation of Congress and to which the Republican Party is today pledged. The policy of expansion is what distinguishes the administration of McKinley and adds another to the list of patriotic victories of the Republican Party. By this policy the United States has become a world power. In the course of it we have built up a navy, not large enough as yet, but large enough to be respectable and to make our influence felt for peace and good international morals the world over.

In every one of these policies which I have thus enumerated—in the war of the Union—the building up and protection of the negro race with the war amendments—in the maintenance of the sacredness of our promises to pay contained in the greenbacks and in the national bonds—in our maintenance of the national integrity by an adherence to the gold standard and a refusal to enter upon the free coinage of silver—in the support of a policy of protection under which our manufactures and our farm productions have found a prosperity never before known in the world—in the policy of expansion and the development of the unfortunate peoples intrusted to our care by Providence—and in our progress toward world-wide influence—we have encountered the official and persistent opposition of the Democratic Party. At times we have been beaten. Only twice, however, in all that remarkable history of 48 years have we lost the confidence of the people of the United States to the point of their turning over the government to a Democratic executive. I venture to say that neither in this nor any other country can be disclosed such a remarkable record of arduous deeds done as in that history of a half a century of the Republican Party.

By reason of circumstances I need not detail, the influence of the Republican Party has been little felt south of Mason and Dixon's line. It is true that in Maryland, West Virginia, Kentucky and Missouri the Republican Party has been often in the majority, but in the other Southern States a contest has seemed hopeless. The time has come, in my judgment, when it is the duty of our party to make an earnest effort to win to our support the many Southerners who think with us on every living national issue and have only been kept from our ranks by the ghost of the past.

During the present administration the Republican Party has been called again to meet a great national need and to save the country from a growing danger. In the enormous industrial development and the accumulation of capital due to the combination in corporate form of the wealth of the country, there have arisen abuses which have threatened to undermine our whole business fabric. The intense desire for gain, stimulated by the prospect of enormous profits, produced a reckless spirit with reference to the methods of acquisition. Official investigations have disclosed a lack of business integrity on the part of some charged in a fiduciary capacity with the custody and management of great accumulations of capital. Other official investigations showed the eagerness with which certain industrial combinations were willing to use their patronage to induce or compel railroad companies to grant to them unjust and secret discriminations and rebates. The fact that the Interstate Commerce law was violated with perfect impunity became known to the public at large, and a conviction seized the people that there were many engaged in the management of corporate wealth who regarded the statutes of their country as dead letters and themselves as a privileged class. Their corrupting influence in politics and in respect of State and national legislation was naturally becoming greater and greater as their wealth grew and their associations spread. We were passing into a régime of an irresponsible plutocracy. During the last four years there has been a great moral awakening to this danger among the people and a popular demand that the lawbreakers—no matter how wealthy or how high or powerful their position—shall be made to suffer. Under the leadership of Theodore Roosevelt the Republican Party has not faltered in its determination to meet the requirements of this situation and to enact such legislation as may be necessary to bring to a close this period of illegitimate corporate immunity.

At the instance of the President Congress was called upon to pass an amendment to the Interstate Commerce law known as the Rate Bill. What has been the effect of the Rate Bill? Everyone who knows anything about the management of railroads knows that there has been a revolution in respect to their obedience to the law. No longer are special privileges granted to the few—no longer are secret rebates extended to build up the monopoly of the trusts. The railroads are operating within the law, and the railroad directors and officers and stockholders ought to rise up and call blessed the men who are responsible for the passage of the Rate Bill. It may be that it has not reduced rates where it was expected. It may be that it has not furnished local relief at various points, as was hoped, but it has put the railroad business in this country on an honest basis, has eliminated from the operation of the railroads privilege and discrimination, and has enabled railroad men to look their fellows in the face without a consciousness that they are conducting a business in violation of law. It has put every railroad man in the country on his good behavior, and has created a complete change of attitude on the part of him and of his subordinates in respect to the statutes of his country.

I am not now speaking of what may be accomplished, but what has been accomplished—not what the result of litigation under a new law has been or will be, but I am speaking of the result of the movement which found expression in the passage of the Rate law.

Another policy proposed as a means of regulating railway rates is that of the improvement of our national waterways. Much money has been spent on sea harbors and the mouths of our rivers at the sea, but comparatively little upon the internal waterways which nature has furnished to the country, and which form highways of travel from one border of it to the other. The call from the country for the development of a well-thought-out plan for the improvement of all these waterways is so emphatic that it can not longer be resisted. That which has been done is largely piece work. What is needed now is the consistent development of this method of inter-communication, so that a certain amount a year can be assigned to the execution of the plan. The direct effect in the transportation of merchandise will doubtless be most beneficial, while the indirect effect of regulating and reducing excessive railroad rates will be even of greater benefit.

Other corporate abuses have been made manifest besides discrimination in rates. They consist in using the corporate form of investment to float bonds and stocks whose par value is far in excess of the real money value invested in the enterprise—a practice which, in addition to deceiving and defrauding the public, involves consequences with reference to reckless corporate management that are most demoralizing. Legislation looking to the restraint in this regard of interstate commerce railways has been recommended to, and doubtless will receive, the careful consideration and approval of the National Legislature.

Under the stimulus of the revelations in respect to the illegal combinations of wealth for purposes of monopoly, prosecutions under the Interstate Commerce law and the anti-trust law by the Executive have been important and effective, and the whole weight of the Republican Administration has been thrown in favor of holding up to a strict compliance with the anti-trust law those who in times past had regarded it as of no effect.

In the midst of this reform movement for the elimination from our business methods of illegal monopoly and discrimination, our country has been visited by a severe financial panic. The panic was doubtless chiefly due to the exhausting of the free capital of the world by reason of the over-investment in enterprises that have not been as productive as expected. The enormous industrial expansion had at last tied up nearly all the world's capital which was available and the new investments had to halt. This result was world-wide. In addition to this general condition, the revelations concerning the management of a number of our large corporations affected the confidence of European investors in our whole business fabric. Then our monetary system is not of such an elastic nature as to meet the emergency produced by sudden fright on the part of the holders of money, who withdraw it from business uses and hoard it against disaster. The result has been an industrial depression which we all hope and believe from the conditions prevailing will be of short duration. But those who have been made to feel the lash of public criticism by this moral awakening have been quick to seize upon and hold up the panic as a result of the measures taken or agitated to stamp out corporate abuses and illegality, and they have not been slow most unjustly to attack the Republican Administration, and Mr. Roosevelt at its head, as the responsible authors of this industrial depression. There are those who have been members of the Republican party who differ with Mr. Roosevelt in respect to the proper course to be taken in stamping out these abuses of corporate wealth. The great bulk of the Republican Party, however, stands solidly at his back in the work which he and the representatives of the party in Congress are doing.

His recent message, urging the reënactment of the employers' liability act, which, because of bungling language, was declared unconstitutional, and asking additional power for the interstate commerce commission, has given rise in certain quarters to much criticism. I have read the message with care, and I am bound to say that the measures which he recommends to Congress, and the position he takes with respect to them, are all of a most conservative character. His position in favor of a general employers' liability act, which shall put the burden of the trade risk upon the employer, except where the injury is due solely to the negligence of the employee, is in the line of the best considered modern legislation of Europe and England. It will secure uniformity and reasonableness of compensation for the family of the deceased or injured employee, instead of the inequalities and uncertainties of court trials, which under our present system give excessive damages to some and deny any recovery to others equally meritorious. The President stands forth stoutly for the power of the Courts and the efficacy of their orders, but properly calls attention to the abuses to which the reckless issuing of *ex parte* injunctions in labor cases has given rise.

The message contains an answer to the charges made that the Administration is responsible for the industrial depression which has followed; and the sharpness and emphasis with which this unfounded attack is met, have heartened the great body of the people as by a bugle call to renewed support of the policies of this Administration.

From beginning to the end the message shows his earnest desire to protect the honest business man and the honest laborer, and to secure to them the possibility of living under an equal administration of the law. He would not destroy or injure the stock of innocent holders for value though it had its inception in the machinations of unprincipled promoters; but he would make the law to prevent a recurrence of such methods, He takes the utmost pains to point out that railroads should be relieved from the restrictions of the anti-trust law, and that that law should be amended so as to give greater freedom for corporate action in combinations that are not hurtful to the public. No man can find within the four corners of the message anything to shake in the slightest the guaranties of life, liberty and property secured by the Constitution. The measures he recommends, and the positions that he takes, are in accord with the conservative position of the Republican party which has ever looked upon the right of property as only less sacred than the right of liberty, and which has ever made the goal of all its efforts the equal protection of the laws.

Vigorous action and measures to stamp out existing abuses and effect reforms are necessary to vindicate society as at present constituted. Otherwise, we must yield to those who seek to introduce a new order of things on a socialistic basis.

The Republican Party follows the Administration upon this social and moral reform—approves its attitude in favor of vested rights, of maintaining the power of the courts, of rendering more equal by legislation the basis of dealing between employer and employee, of strengthening the regulative power over railroads and other interstate corporations, and of prosecuting those lawbreakers who continue to defy public opinion. Roosevelt leads his party as Lincoln led his—as McKinley led his—to meet the new issues presented, to arm our present civilization, and fit it with a bold front to resist the attacks of socialism, and to transmit to the coming generations unharmed the great institutions of civil liberty inherited from our fathers.

14

Recent Criticism of the Federal Judiciary

Delivered before the American Bar Association,
Detroit, Michigan, August 28, 1895

Within the last four years, the governors of five or more States have thought it proper in official messages to declare that the Federal courts have seized jurisdiction not rightly theirs, and have exercised it to the detriment of the Republic, and to urge their respective legislatures to petition Congress for remedial action to prevent future usurpation. One legislature did present a memorial to Congress reciting the grievances of the people of its State against the Federal judiciary and asking a curtailment of the powers unlawfully assumed by them.

The principal charge against the Federal courts, which an examination of these documents discloses, is that they have flagrantly usurped jurisdiction, first, to protect corporations and perpetuate their many abuses, and second, to oppress and destroy the power of organized labor.

These charges against the Federal judiciary have not been confined to messages from State governors. They also come from persons who, although not holding high office, have a standing before the bar which entitles them to respectful attention. Much of what is found in the official communications I have referred to concerning the treatment of corpora-tions by the Federal courts has taken form from the articles and addresses of the editor of the *American Law Review*. This gentleman, well-known as an able and prominent law-text writer, has given much attention to the Federal decisions on corporate matters and has expressed his condemna-tion of many of them in language that has lacked nothing in freedom, emphasis or rhetorical figure.

The one judicial system to which all the members of this Association bear the same relation is that of the United States, and when I was honored with an invitation to address them it at once occurred to me that I might properly ask their attention to a temperate discussion of the justice of these criticisms.

I have since been oppressed with the thought that the theme might with more propriety be left to one having no official relation to the Federal courts, but circumstances have prevented any change from my original im-pulse. I can only hope that my recent admission to the inferior ranks of the Federal judiciary and my humble position therein will prevent the sug-gestion that what is here to be said has anything in it either of a personal defense or of a *quasi* official character.

The opportunity freely and publicly to criticise judicial action is of vastly more importance to the body politic than the immunity of courts and judges from unjust aspersions and attack. Nothing tends more to ren-der judges careful in their decisions and anxiously solicitous to do exact justice than the consciousness that every act of theirs is to be subjected to the intelligent scrutiny and candid criticism of their fellowmen. Such criticism is beneficial in proportion as it is fair, dispassionate, discriminat-ing and based on a knowledge of sound legal principles. The comments made by learned text writers and by the acute editors of the various law reviews upon judicial decisions are therefore highly useful. Such critics constitute more or less impartial tribunals of professional opinion before which each judgment is made to stand or fall on its merits and thus exert a strong influence to secure uniformity of decision. But non-professional criticism is by no means without its uses, even if accompanied, as it often is, by a direct attack upon the judicial fairness and motives of the occupants of the bench; for if the law is but the essence of common sense, the protest of many average men may evidence a defect in a judicial conclusion though based on the nicest legal reasoning and profoundest learning. The two important elements of moral character in a judge are an earnest desire to reach a just conclusion and courage to enforce it. In so far as fear of public comment does not affect the courage of a judge but only spurs him on to search his conscience and to reach the result which approves itself to his inmost heart, such comment serves a useful purpose. There are few men, whether they are judges for life or for a shorter term, who do not prefer to earn and hold the respect of all, and who can not be reached and made to pause and deliberate by hostile public criticism. In the case of judges having a life tenure, indeed, their very independence makes the right freely to comment on their decisions of greater importance because it is the only practical and available instrument in the hands of a free people to keep such judges alive to the reasonable demands of those they serve.

On the other hand, the danger of destroying the proper influence of judicial decisions by creating unfounded prejudices against the courts, justifies and requires that unjust attacks shall be met and answered. Courts must ultimately rest their defense upon the inherent strength of the opinions they deliver as the ground for their conclusions and must trust to the calm and deliberate judgment of all the people as their best vindication. But the bar has much to do with the formation of that opinion and a discussion before them may sometimes contain suggestions which bear good fruit.

Many persons whose good opinion is a high compliment regard the Federal judiciary with so much favor that they would deprecate a consideration of the criticisms already stated as likely to give an importance to them they do not deserve. I can not concur in this view. I believe that in large sections of this country there are many sincere and honest citizens who credit all that has been said against the Federal courts, and that it is of much importance that the reasons for the existence of these criticisms and their injustice be pointed out.

It is not unfair to those governors who are the chief accusers of the Federal judiciary to say that they knew they were not speaking as they did to unwilling ears. They were merely putting into language the hostile feeling of certain of their constituents toward the Federal courts, and but for such feeling the criticisms would hardly have been uttered. It will, therefore, in a large measure account for such criticisms if we account for the popular sentiment they were made to satisfy.

It will be my endeavor, therefore, first to show that much, if not all, of the present hostility to the Federal courts in certain parts of the country and among certain groups of the people can be traced to causes over which those courts can exercise no control, and is necessarily due to the character of the jurisdiction with which they are vested and not to injustice in its exercise; and second, that the criticisms which such hostility has engendered are in themselves without foundation.

The history of the Federal courts since their beginning is full of instances where the exercise of their jurisdiction has involved them in popular controversies and has brought down upon them the bitter assaults of those unfavorably affected by their decisions. Yet the event has justified their course and shown the injustice of the attacks.

The Federal Constitution was framed to create a national government with limited powers and to mark the line between its jurisdiction on the one hand and that of the States and the people on the other. By virtue of its eighth article the State courts and *a fortiori* the Federal courts were vested with the power and charged with the duty in judicial cases arising before them of ignoring State laws in conflict with the Federal Constitution. By necessary implication their obedience to the fundamental law also required them to ignore acts of Congress which were so plainly in violation of the Constitution that even the necessary and high respect due to the construction by Congress of its own powers could not give such acts the force of law.

The Federal judiciary at once became the arbiter in the first great political controversy of the United States, and one which is continually reappearing in various forms. The general language of the Constitution required construction to apply it to judicial cases arising in the organization and maintenance of the government. The two parties which had engaged in heated controversy over the adoption of the covenant at all continued it over its narrow or broad interpretation. The Supreme Court in the beginning was made up largely of men whose predilection was for a liberal construction and who believed thoroughly in the national idea. This was soon manifest in their decisions, which called down upon the court the anathemas of the strict constructionists, whose great effort it thereupon became to weaken the power of the judiciary. It was attempted to control their independence by making very wide the grounds for impeachment. The great Chief Justice was constantly threatened with this fate by partisans and the attacks upon his alleged usurpations were frequent and fierce. Jefferson's severe words concerning the Federal judiciary, now so often quoted by their latter-day critics, were written in 1820 and were provoked by the decision in Cohens *vs.* Virginia, reaffirming the power of the Supreme Court of the United States to reverse the decision of the Supreme Court of a State on the validity of a State law under the Federal Constitution. It is not surprising that he who had inspired the Kentucky resolutions of 1798 declaring the right of a State to decline compliance with a Federal law deemed by it to be in conflict with the fundamental compact, should regard the Federalist Supreme Court which itself asserted the right finally to decide such a question, as "a thief of jurisdiction."

Upon political questions, and such are those arising in the construction of a political charter, there always have been and always will be differences of opinion. There is frequently no absolute standard, even a century after, in deciding the abstract right of them. We must be content to abide the result reached by the verdict and acquiescence of the people whose interests were involved. Before this tribunal, the position of John Marshall and his associates on the Supreme Bench has been vindicated and the criticisms of Thomas Jefferson have been refuted.

Beginning then as arbiters in a political conflict and wielding similar powers until today, the Federal judiciary have never enjoyed immunity from hostile attack upon their conduct or their motives. The great controversy over the fugitive slave law needs no recounting here. In the eyes of the abolitionists the Federal courts and their marshals were instruments of hell in enforcing the law, and yet there could not be the slightest doubt that such a jurisdiction was plainly within the Constitution.

The change of feeling toward the Federal courts because of the change in their jurisdiction with respect to the negro race affords an apt illustration of how mere jurisdiction may affect the popular feeling toward a court. Before the war the Southern people had not looked with disfavor upon courts which did so much to preserve their property, while at the same time the abolitionists regarded them with aversion. After the war, when, for the protection of the negro in his electoral and civil rights, the election and civil rights bills were passed and their enforcement was given to the Federal courts, they became at the same time the objects of hatred and condemnation at the South and the great reliance of those who had been abolitionists at the North. Now that both parties have wisely decided to let the election problem work itself out and to await the local solution which the results of fraud and violence in elections will compel, the feeling of hostility at the South against the Federal judiciary has greatly abated.

This is but one of many historical instances showing how the Federal courts may be subjected to the most severe criticism without just grounds merely because of the character of their jurisdiction.

I come now to review the reasons why their mere jurisdiction has created a deep impression in many parts of the country that the evils due to corporations are fostered by them.

The last two generations have witnessed a marvelous material development. It has been effected by the organization and enforced cooperation of simple elements that for a long time previous had been separately used. The organization of powerful machines or of delicate devices, by which the producing power of one man was increased fifty or one hundred fold, was, however, not the only step in this great progress. The aim of all material civilization in its hard contest with nature was the reduction of the cost of production, because thereby each man's day's work netted him more of the comforts of life. Within the limits of efficient administration the larger the amount to be produced at one time and under one management, the less the expense per unit. Therefore, the aggregation of capital, the other essential element with labor in producing anything, became an obvious means of securing economy in the manufacture of everything. Corporations had long been known as convenient commercial instruments for securing and wielding efficiently such aggregations of capital. Charters were at first conferred by special act upon particular individuals and with varying powers, but so great became the advantage of incorporation, with the facility afforded for managing great enterprises and the limitation of the liability of investors, that it was deemed wise in this country, in order to prevent favoritism, to create corporations by general laws and thus to afford to all who wished it the opportunity of assuming a corporate character in accordance therewith. The result was a great increase in the number of the corporations and the assumption of the corporate form by seven-eighths of the active capital of the country. The great saving in the cost of production brought about by mechanical inventions and the organization of capital worked incalculable benefit to the public, but the necessary price of it under our system of free right of contract and inviolable rights of private property was a division of the profit between those who were to consume the product and those whose minds conceived and whose hands executed the work of production. The total wealth of the whole country was thus enormously increased, but of the increase more was necessarily accumulated in some hands than others. In the general prosperity caused by the revolution in methods of production, captains of industry amassed fabulous fortunes, and the aggregations of capital under corporate management became so great as to stagger the imagination. In the mad rush for money which previous successes had stimulated, it is not to be wondered at that some of the accumulated wealth was corruptly used to secure undue business advantages from legislative and executive sources and that many of the political agencies of the people became tainted. The impersonal character of corporations afforded a freedom from that restraint in the use of money for political corruption which is often present when the would-be briber is an individual. Men of good repute, with complacence and intentional ignorance, acquiesced in the use of corporate funds to buy legislators and councilmen in the corporate interest, when they would not wish or dare to adopt such methods in their individual business. The enormous increase in corporate wealth furnished the means of corruption, and the prospect of ill-gotten gains attracted the dishonest trickster into politics and debauched the weak, while the honest and courageous were often driven into private life. The genie of corruption in politics which the corporations called up has lived to plague them, and although many great companies have secured all they wish from legislative bodies, they are regarded by the political blackmailers as fair game and the corruption fund is still maintained to prevent oppression. The people not unjustly have charged these public evils to the management of corporations.

Another evil has been the injustice done to the real owners of corporate property by the reckless and dishonest management of its nominal owners. The great liberality of the general laws for the formation of corporations and the entire failure to exercise any stringent visitorial powers over them have enabled the active promoters and managers of large enterprises carried on at a distance from the homes of the real owners, to increase the corporate indebtedness and capital stock so far beyond any fair valuation of their property as to put the entire control of it in the hands of the holders of worthless stock who have nothing at stake in the corporate success.

The real owners, the bondholders, are at the mercy of this irresponsible management till insolvency comes. The reckless business methods which such an irresponsibility and lack of supervision invite create an unhealthy and feverish competition in every market, wholly unrestrained by the natural caution which the real owner of a business must feel. The concern is kept going with no hope of legitimate profit, but simply to pay large salaries or to favor unduly some other enterprise in which the managers have a real interest.

Another reason for popular distrust of corporate methods is the use by corporations of great amounts of capital to monopolize and control particular industries. It is my sincere belief that no such control or monopoly can be maintained permanently unless it is buttressed by positive legislation giving an undue advantage over the public and competitors. Of course, by close business methods and by improving all the economical advantages which the manufacture of a commodity on an enormous scale affords, the cost of production may be so reduced as to discourage competition on a smaller scale, but unless the fear of it performs the same useful office for the benefit of the public by continuing the lowest profitable prices, actual competition will certainly appear. Whatever the fate such trusts may ultimately have, it has often happened that in their formation and early history the plan adopted has been the forced buying out of every competitor or his ruin by underselling him at heavy loss, so as to put the public and the market for a time at least at the mercy of one greedy corporate concern. Such methods and such a result naturally fill the people with anxious fears and a hostile feeling toward aggregations of corporate wealth.

In spite of these well-known evils nothing can be clearer to a calm, intelligent thinker than that under conditions of modern society, corporations are indispensable both to the further material progress of this country and to the maintenance of that we have enjoyed. The evils must be remedied, but not by destroying one of the greatest instruments for good that social man has devised. Nevertheless, so strong has the hostility to corporations become, especially in certain of the southern and western States where the agricultural community is large, life is hard and wealth is rare, that any plan which can be contrived to diminish the property of corporations or to cripple their efficiency seems to meet with favor. The feeling is especially directed against the railway corporations, although without their aid and presence these very communities would be helpless and poor indeed.

The last decade in Europe has been prolific of doctrines and theories for the amelioration of the human race by the abolition of private property and private capital by the vesting of all the means of production in the government, for the benefit of all the people, and by the distribution of the product according to fixed standards of merit. While socialism, as such, has not obtained much of a foothold in this country, even in those sections already referred to, schemes which are necessarily socialistic in their nature are accepted planks in the platform of a large political party. The underlying principle of such schemes is that it is the duty of the government to equalize the inequalities which the rights of free contract and private property have brought about, and by enormous outlay, derived as far as possible from the rich, to afford occupation and sustenance to the poor. However disguised such plans of social and governmental reform are, they find their support in the willingness of their advocates to transfer without any compensation from one who has acquired, a large part of his acquisition to those who have been less prudent, energetic and fortunate. This, of course, involves confiscation and the destruction of the principle of private property.

Under the Fourteenth Amendment the question whether legislation and State action deprive any person of his property without due process of law has become a Federal one, and by the Act of 1875 it is cognizable by the Circuit Courts of the United States.

The prejudices above adverted to have led to much legislation hostile to corporations both resident and nonresident. It takes the forms of discriminating taxation, of the regulation of rates to be charged by those companies engaged in *quasi* public business and sometimes of the direct deprivation of vested rights. In all such cases resort is at once had to the inferior Federal courts by the corporations injuriously affected, to test the validity of the State's action, and it not infrequently happens that it becomes the duty of such courts to declare void the legislation involved and to enjoin State officers from seizing or injuring the property of corporations under its provisions. Such a decision in a corporation-hating community at once tends to mark the Federal courts as friends and protectors of corporations.

The repeated efforts of different State legislatures to impose restrictions upon interstate commerce to secure some apparent advantage to their own constituents, evidence the profound wisdom of the framers of the Constitution in vesting complete control thereof in the national government, but the tribunals whose jurisdiction is constantly invoked judicially to declare void all such legislation do not for the time commend themselves to the favor either of those who urged its passage or of those who were to profit by its operation, and the fact that the complainant in such litigation is frequently a railroad or transportation company only confirms the view of the undue favor of these courts to such litigants.

The jurisdiction of the Federal judiciary does not end with the enforcement of national laws in the interest of the whole country against the temporary interest of a part. They are also required to administer justice between the citizens of different States. It goes without saying that this judicial power was given to prevent the possibility of injustice from local prejudice and not because in every case it was supposed to exist. The entire jurisdiction rests on the exceptional instances, for in a great majority of cases the same results would certainly be reached in the courts of the State as in the Federal courts. But in those courts or States where there is real danger from prejudice against a stranger, the same cause which is likely to obstruct justice for the foreign suitor creates a local feeling of resentment against the tribunal established to defeat its effect.

The capital invested in great enterprises in the South and West is owned in the East or abroad, and the corporations which use it are therefore frequently organized in a different State from that in which the investment is made. Such companies all carry their litigation into the Federal courts on the ground of diverse citizenship with the opposing party, and, in view of the deep-seated prejudice entertained against them by the local population, it is not surprising that they do. That in most, if not in all, cases the feeling that prompts this avoidance of the State courts does great injustice to the State judiciary is undoubtedly true. In jury trials, however, the fear of injustice from local prejudice is certainly sometimes justified. In these same States where the narrow provincial spirit is strong and local prejudices exist, there is deep fear of the abuse of judicial power and the legislation of the State is directed to minimizing the influence and control of the judge over the action and deliberation of the jury. The extent to which this is carried was clearly set forth in an interesting address delivered before this Association by Mr. Justice Brown some years ago. The slightest circumstance, although furnishing but a scintilla of evidence to support the contention of either party, requires the submission of the case to the jury. The office of a judge is reduced to that of a mere moderator of the trial. He is only permitted to lay down a few general principles of law in advance of the argument, while the application of them to the facts of the case and conflicting evidence is really committed to the zeal of contending counsel. The tendency of such procedure is to leave to the unrestrained impulses of the jury the settlement of all the issues of the case. Though the injustice likely to result to corporations from this procedure is manifest, the people of a locality where local prejudice exists have come to think that they have a vested right to the chances of success which it gives them in a suit against such opponents. When, therefore, in controversies with corporations of other States, they are carried before a court in which the jury are not their friends and neighbors and in which the power is given to the judge to direct a verdict when the evidence for either party is so slight that a contrary verdict must be set aside, to comment on the evidence, to apply the law thereto, and to make plain, if need be, what the legal sophistries of counsel and their inaccurate statements of the evidence may have obscured, they feel that they are in a tribunal which they should avoid and which the corporation should naturally seek. The constant struggle of most corporations to avoid State tribunals in the sections of the country referred to, and to secure a Federal forum, even though it is followed by only limited success in the result of the litigation, is chiefly the cause for the popular impression in those States that the Federal courts are the friends of corporations and protectors of their abuses.

Those abuses, however, really find their chief cause in political corruption, which it is wholly beyond the power of the Federal courts to prevent or eradicate. Too frequently the popular impulse is to remedy or punish the evil by giving judgment against the great corporations in every case, no matter what the particular issues or facts are, on the ground that the corporation has probably increased its capital or attained its success by corrupt methods. It is hardly necessary to point out that this mode of punishment by forfeiture and chance distribution can not be countenanced in a court of justice, however meritorious the cause of complaint upon which it is founded.

Corporate corruption can not be directly punished in the Federal courts, because the bribery of which many corporations are guilty is most difficult of legal proof, and crimes of this character are usually committed against the State, so that Federal courts have no cognizance of them. It has been wisely settled by the adjudication of all courts, State and Federal, that the evils resulting from vesting in courts the power to set aside otherwise lawful acts of the legislature for alleged corruption in their passage, would exceed even the wrong done by such legislation, because of the uncertainty it would give to the binding effect of all laws and the overwhelming influence such power to inquire into legislative motives would give the judicial branch of the government in respect of all legislative action.

The abuses which too liberal charters and insufficient visitorial power permit, are either for the State legislatures or for the State executive and courts, by *quo warranto*, to correct and remedy. State laws which should forbid the issue of stock or the issue of bonds by any corporation until after an examination by a State board of supervision into the affairs of the company and a certificate that the assets justify it, would do much in this direction. The Federal courts can do nothing to prevent such abuses, and their action is not usually invoked until the evil is done and only a bankrupt estate is left to administer.

The combinations known as trusts are now before the State courts, and I have no doubt from their decisions that legislation which experience will suggest, both by way of supervision over corporations and by criminal laws, will suppress much of their evil methods. It is settled and rightly settled, I submit, that the national government can do nothing in this direction, except where such trusts are for the purpose of directly controlling interstate commerce.

The main public evil of corporate growth, the corruption of politics, must be reformed by the people and not by the courts. Courts are but conservators; they can not effect great social or political changes. Corporations there must be if we would progress; accumulation of wealth there will be if private property continues the keystone of our society; the temptation to use money to corrupt legislatures and other political agencies will remain potent as long as undue privilege for corporations can be thus secured. The only real remedy is in the purification of the politics of the country and the selection of incorruptible public servants. Dark as the prospect sometimes seems for such a change, we must not and need not despair. Public opinion is sound, the great heart of the American people is honest, and slowly but surely the light is breaking in on them. The adoption of civil service reform in Federal, State and municipal government is as certain to come as the nation is to live, and with its complete establishment, the end of those indispensable assistants of successful political corruption, the machine and its boss, will cease to be. The mad rush for wealth, the fevered condition of business and the opportunity for making sudden fortunes have taken the attention of the more intelligent people from politics and made them blind or callous to political abuses. With their greater ability to see and appreciate the dangers of the republic, their share of the blame for present conditions is greater. But there are many signs of a quickened public conscience and of a willingness on the part of the intelligent and the pure to interest themselves in politics for their country's good.

The present successful use of corrupt methods by corporations is directly due to the neglect of the people to exercise the eternal watchfulness which is the price of pure government; but those whose interest it is to secure popular support and who are willing to secure it by appeals to prejudice do not tell the people unpleasant truths and are glad to find a scapegoat for the people's sins in the Federal judiciary. It well rounds a rhetorical period to point to the Federal judiciary as an irresponsible and irremovable body, wholly out of touch with the people and conniving at corporate abuses.

To an impartial observer it must seem remarkable that judges should conceive a love for soulless corporations and unduly favor them. Living as most of these judges do on their salaries and deriving no profit from corporate investments, they would seem to find little in their lives to blind them to the injustice of any claim or defense which a wealthy corporation may make.

If it were conceded that greed of power is an incentive so strong that Federal judges have yielded to it and have extended their jurisdiction over corporations beyond the lines marked by the Constitution and the laws, this is far from establishing that justice has not been meted out to corporate suitors with impartial hand. The fact is that when we come to examine in detail the charges against the Federal courts, the burden of them is that they have assumed jurisdiction over corporate litigation without constitutional and legal right, and not that, in the hearing on the merits, corporations have been unduly favored. The latter is always assumed as a granted premise when the former is deemed to be established.

Having pointed out some of the reasons why the jurisdiction of the Federal courts in respect to corporations, be it exercised never so impartially, must under existing conditions arouse deep prejudice against them, and call forth severe assaults upon their conduct and motives, I come now to examine more in detail the charges which have been made by those who attempt specifications.

The first is that the Supreme Court in holding, in the Dartmouth College case, the legislative charter of a corporation to be a contract, the repeal of which was the impairment of its obligation and was inhibited by the Federal constitution, committed a fundamental error, induced thereto by greed of jurisdiction, and thus furnished to corporations the means of maintaining and enjoying corruptly purchased privileges. I do not propose to discuss this much-criticised case, because it was decided in 1820, and has now nothing but an historical interest; for no charter has been granted for years which does not contain a clause permitting its repeal or amendment, and a court could hardly give a wider scope to such a reservation clause in favor of the State's power than that which the Supreme Court of the United States gave in the Greenwood Freight Company case. With reference to the accusation that it was greed of jurisdiction which induced the court to hold that the revocation of a grant by a State was the impairment of a contract and so within the Federal constitution, it should be said that the people of the United States, instead of condemning this assumption of jurisdiction, have by subsequent amendment expressly extended the Federal judicial power to the cognizance of State aggression upon all vested rights whether resting in grant, contract or otherwise.

And this suggests the charge against the Supreme Court that it improperly seized additional corporate jurisdiction in its holding that the Fourteenth Amendment forbidding a State to deprive any person of life, liberty or property without due process of law protects the property of corporations as well as that of natural persons. It is difficult to see how any other result could have been reached. For, even if artificial persons are not referred to in the amendment, natural persons necessarily have vested rights in the property of corporations. It is said that the construction should have been limited so as to exclude corporations because the moving cause was only to give national protection to a newly freed race. In the light of the general language of the amendment, this would have been a narrow construction indeed, and one which nothing could have justified except the conviction, now firmly held and declared in some quarters, that Federal jurisdiction to preserve any rights, even those declared in Magna Charta, is an unmitigated evil, to be avoided by interpretation however strained.

And yet the Supreme Court is attacked with invective and epithet by the same critics for refusing to hold in the Sugar Trust case that the power to regulate interstate commerce includes within it the power to inhibit the purchase by one company of substantially all the plants for refining sugar in this country with the purpose of controlling its sugar markets. To extend the Federal regulation of interstate commerce to that of the purchase of the means of producing a commodity which, when produced, is to be the subject of commerce both State and interstate, requires a construction of the interstate commerce clause so broad that, if it had been accepted, it would have been difficult to fix a limit beyond which Congress might not go in the control of mercantile business and manufacturing in every community. It would have seemed to give some ground for the charge so often made, that, through Federal judicial decisions, rights of the States are being absorbed in the national government.

As I have already said, the burden of the specifications against the Federal judiciary, is not that they unduly favor corporations in the hearing of cases, but that they have improperly given corporations opportunities to avoid the State courts by resorting to the Federal courts. Hence the decisions of the Supreme Court, by which corporations organized in one State and suing or being sued in another are permitted to select the Federal courts as a forum, have been the subject of the severest animadversion, and the judges rendering the decisions are charged with having been consciously guilty of flagrant usurpation and with intentional violation of the law and the Constitution. When corporations first appeared in the Federal courts, it was held that a corporation was not a citizen within the meaning of the judiciary act or the Constitution, and that Federal jurisdiction asserted on the ground of diverse citizenship in a cause to which a corporation was a party, must depend on the citizenship of the stockholders or members of the corporation. As it had also been ruled that the words of the judiciary act giving circuit courts jurisdiction in every suit between a citizen of the State where it was brought, and the citizen of another State, only included suits where all the parties on one side were of different citizenship from that of all of those on the other, the result was that no corporation could resort to a Federal court unless all its stockholders were citizens of another State from that in which the suit was brought, and the ownership of one share by a resident of the same State with that of the opposing partly ousted the jurisdiction. And this the Supreme Court held until 1844. In that year the question arose again, and the court held that, for purposes of Federal jurisdiction, a corporation was a citizen of the State which created it, and soon thereafter laid down the doctrine, always followed since, that the members of a corporation are to be conclusively presumed to be citizens of the State of its creation. This conclusive presumption was a fiction, adopted, as Mr. Justice Bradley has explained, to avoid the difficulty and injustice caused by the frequent appearance in such cases of a single resident stockholder. It was in effect a changed construction of the judiciary act for reasons which had not forcibly presented themselves to the court when the question first arose. It was certainly true that when corporations, organized in other states than that where suit was brought, appeared in litigation, they represented members, a great majority of whom were either citizens of other States or aliens. If any local prejudice was likely to have effect against a non-resident natural person, it certainly would have effect against a corporation from another State, and the ownership of a few shares of its stock by a resident would not obviate it. The result reached by the decisions was quite within the constitutional grant of Federal judicial power, for that covers all controversies between citizens of different States, and it is immaterial whether in such controversies are also involved, on both sides, citizens of the same State. There was such a real difference for the practical purposes of a trial and the bearing of local prejudice upon it between a suit by or against a foreign corporate body with one or more resident stockholders, whose identity was lost in that of the corporate party litigant, and a suit by or against parties to the record who were natural persons, some of them residents and others non-residents, that the exception made in respect to corporations in the established construction of the judiciary act would seem sound and reasonable.

The holding that a foreign or non-resident corporation must be excluded from resort to a Federal forum because it had one or more resident stockholders would practically deprive the owners of nearly all foreign capital to be invested in the newer States of the Union of any opportunity to sue or defend in the Federal courts, because, in the nature of things, their capital must assume a corporate form, and in companies with thousands of shares of capital stock transferable without restriction, a share or two, at least, would be sure to find its way into the possession of a resident owner. And yet the reason for the constitutional provision applied more strongly to such corporate investments than to those of non-resident natural persons.

The ruling was directly in the interest of the new States who were thirsting for foreign capital, because it removed one of the hindrances to its coming. It was, therefore, exactly in accord with the intention of the Constitution. It gives but a contracted view of the purpose of the framers of that instrument in providing a tribunal between citizens of different States, which was equally related to both, to regard it solely from the standpoint of the non-resident and as intended only to secure a benefit for him. It is crediting them with a much more statesmanlike object to say, that while the provision was, of course, intended to avoid actual injustice from local prejudice, its more especial purpose was to allay the fears of such injustice in the minds of those whose material aid was necessary in developing the commercial intercourse between the States, and thus to induce such intercourse and the investment of capital owned by citizens of one State in another. In this light, it is only one of several provisions of the Constitution intended to prevent unnecessary and prejudiced restraints upon interstate commerce, and it confers more benefit upon those against whose prejudice it is intended as a shield than upon those whose interests are directly protected.

The decisions under discussion were made by the Supreme Court in the days of Chief Justice Taney, and with his concurrence, at a time when its members are now thought to have been inclined toward a narrower construction of the Constitution and Federal jurisdiction and powers than their predecessors.

Moreover, the people of the United States for fifty years have acquiesced in this holding. In the last half century, it has always been within the power of Congress by two lines of legislation to reverse it, and, although during that period the party of strict construction and State's rights was for years in control of Congress and the judiciary act was four times substantially amended, the decisions remain the law of the land. When it requires a constitutional amendment to correct or restrain an unwarranted assumption of power by a court, the machinery for securing it is so cumbersome that the failure by this means to restrain the court is not a conclusive argument in favor of the people's acquiescence in the court's assertion of jurisdiction. But where, as in the present case, the issue was merely one of construing a statute, the failure of Congress for half a century to amend or overrule the construction given is as strong an argument as can be adduced to justify the action of the court, and would in this case seem to be the best possible refutation of the severe charge that the judges, who made these decisions, were guilty of flagrant and intentional usurpation.

If it is true that citizens of one State organize corporations under the laws of another State to do business in the former State, and thereby carry controversies with their fellow-citizens into the Federal courts, this is an abuse which should be remedied by Congress, as other frauds upon the jurisdiction have been provided against.

The Federal courts have also been severely arraigned for undue amplification of their powers in the matter of receivers of railroad companies, due as it is charged to their leaning toward such corporations and a desire to protect them. This count of the general indictment against the Federal judiciary is more fully and elaborately treated in a memorial presented to Congress by the Legislature of South Carolina, than anywhere else. The occasion for the protest was the commitments for contempt by the Circuit

Court of the United States sitting in South Carolina of certain State officers. In one case, the contemnors were taxing officers, who, though they knew the property to be in the hands of the receiver of the Federal court, without any application to the court, seized it for taxes. In the other case, a constable without search warrant broke into the warehouse of a railroad in the hands of the court's receiver and seized a cask of liquor on the ground that it had been transported into the State contrary to the provisions of the State dispensary law. The cask had been imported before the dispensary law went into effect and had been held by the receiver because the whereabouts of the consignee could not be discovered. The circumstances in each of these cases rather indicate a desire on the part of the State authorities to seek a conflict with the Federal court than an aggressive and domineering spirit in the latter. When the State authorities in a decent and orderly way subsequently applied to the court for an order upon the receiver to pay the taxes, the objections of the receiver were heard and overruled and an order made upon him to pay.

The deep spirit of distrust of the Federal courts in which the memorial is written may be inferred from one of its concluding sentences, in which the Federal courts of equity are referred to as "having been degraded to their present position of being feared by the patriotic and avoided by the honest." We are permitted to conjecture that the memorialists were not wholly unbiased in discussing the decisions of the Federal courts and their integrity and standing, when we read the statement in the inaugural address of the present Governor of the State, who was one of the signers of the memorial, that he and the men to whom he was speaking in this year of grace, 1895, were "South Carolinians by birth and choice, Southerners on principle and Americans by force of circumstances."

The main purpose of the memorial was to show that the practice of Federal courts of equity in appointing receivers to operate railroads is a usurpation of authority wholly without warrant in the English High Court of Chancery, by the procedure in which the scope of equitable remedies in the Federal courts is usually governed. To establish this, the memorialists relied chiefly on the judgment of Lord Cairns in the Court of Chancery Appeals in the case of Gardner *vs.* The London, Chatham & Dover Company, in which the order of the Vice-Chancellor appointing a manager of the defendant railway on the application of a mortgagee of the railway tolls was reversed. The judgment was placed upon two grounds, first, that the mortgage gave no right of sale and liquidation, so that the order was really for a permanent management of a going business, while the practice in courts of equity justified the appointment of receivers only until a sale and liquidation; and, second, that by the charter of the company the franchises were personal and non-assignable, and could not be exercised by a receiver. The first reason has little or no application to the vast majority of cases in which railroad receivers have been appointed in this country, for generally the remedy sought has been a sale and liquidation, and the receiver has thus been appointed to serve only until the sale. The second ground of the judgment does not relate to the competency of a court of equity to manage a railroad or other going business through an agent, *pendente lite*, but only to the assignability of franchises, and it furnishes as little support as the first ground to the claims of the memorial. The power to mortgage conferred by statute on railway companies in this country usually contains express authority to mortgage both the railroad and the franchises to operate it. The necessary implications from this are the right to sell the franchises with the road at a foreclosure sale, and the power of the court in which fore-closure proceedings are had, to preserve the property with its assignable franchises, by temporary custody and operation of the road under such franchises pending the sale.

By reference to Lord Justice Baggallay's judgment, *In re* The Manchester & Milford Ry. Co., 14 Ch. D., 657, it appears that the result in Gardner's case was a surprise to the profession, and reversed the practice of appointing managers in such cases which had been in vogue in the chancery courts of England for ten years previous, and which had had the sanction of as great a chancery lawyer as Lord Hatherly. Moreover, no sooner was the decision announced in the Gardner case than Parliament passed an act expressly authorizing the appointment of railroad managers by the court of chancery, showing that, in the opinion of Parliament, jurisdiction to manage railroads, pending litigation over them, by officers of the court was a power that courts of equity should have, if they did not already have it.

The charge of usurpation in the appointment of receivers becomes still less maintainable when we consider the history of receiverships in this country. Gardner's case was decided in 1866. As much as ten years before this, the Supreme Court of the United States in Covington Drawbridge Co. *vs.* Shepherd, 21 How., 112, had referred to the practice in the English court of chancery to order a receiver to be appointed to manage railways and other corporate property, to take the proceeds of the franchises and to apply them to pay the creditors filing the bill, and had approved and adopted it in the case of a bridge company. Thereafter receivers were appointed for railways and it had become a settled practice not only in the Federal courts but in State courts when Gardner's case was decided. Even if that case can not be reconciled with the practice of appointing receivers under the conditions existing in this country, as I have attempted to show it can be, there would still seem to be no binding or jurisdictional obligation on courts of the United States to reverse their settled procedure of ten years' standing based on English precedent, to accord with a new and unexpected ruling in the English courts, and one the effect of which was immediately done away with by an act of Parliament restoring the old practice.

The appointment of receivers to operate railroads pending suits in foreclosure and creditors' bills, instead of being an abuse of authority by the Federal courts, was a most commendable use of an ordinary equitable means of preserving the *status quo* with respect to a new kind of property and in a pressing emergency. Generally no one but the parties are interested in preserving the subject matter of the suit as a going concern till it can be sold, but in the case of a railroad the public are even more interested than the parties in having this done. It is mentioned in the South Carolina memorial as a measure of the abuse of Federal jurisdiction in this regard that one-fifth of the railroad mileage in the United States is in the hands of Federal court receivers. Considering the severity of the times and the suicidal cutting of rates by railroad companies for the purpose of securing business, I do not know that this proportion unfairly indicates the number of embarrassed and bankrupt roads in this country, but it is hard to see why it is an argument against the appointment of receivers to operate them. The disastrous consequences to the whole country, were these great arteries of the nation to cease to flow, can hardly be overstated; and yet, unless in the course of liquidation, sale and reorganization, they could, when insolvent, be withdrawn from liability to seizure and dismemberment by ordinary executions in the various jurisdictions which they traverse, their operation would become impossible. The ordinary insolvent laws of each State, even if their procedure had been at all adapted to the running of railroads, as it was not, would have supplied in such case but a poor substitute for the present receivership. Most railroads are today interstate, and the advantage of an *ad interim* management under practically the same jurisdiction on both sides of State lines is apparent. In the absence of statutory provision for such an exigency, the flexible procedure of a court of equity is fitted to meet it, and although the remedy was adopted soon after the building of railroads more than forty years ago and has been applied with increasing frequency ever since, it has not been deemed necessary by Congress or State legislatures to provide any other means for bridging the undoubted difficulties presented by the insolvency of railroad companies.

One of the greatest objections urged to receiverships in the South Carolina memorial is that it removes the railroad property from local jurisdictions. But this objection would be incident to any imaginable temporary management of the railroad pending proceedings to sell and distribute the proceeds. The injury to the sovereignty of the State involved in the requirement that its taxing officers shall make application to the Federal court having custody of property for an order for the payment of the taxes due upon it, instead of violently taking it out of the court's possession, is one that must be charged to the Constitution of the United States, to the supremacy of the Federal jurisdiction where it conflicts with that of the State, herein declared, and to the circumstances by the force of which South Carolina is still in this country. The charge that in appointing receivers the Federal courts abolish the right of trial by jury in great stretches of country is untrue, for by the statute of 1887 suit may be brought against a receiver without leave of court, and this permits a suit at law with all its incidents. The fear entertained that the management by the Federal courts of property worth $13,000,000,000, without responsibility, would lead to malversation of funds and corruption does not seem to be justified by the history of Federal receiverships. The fact is, that no possible system of managing railroads could be better adapted to a summary investigation of the details of the management than that by a court of equity in which the court will always and at once entertain complaints by anyone in interest against its receiver and examine the facts upon which they rest. This may account, in part, for the very few instances of official corruption among Federal receivers.

On the other hand, if any other and better way can be devised for the temporary management of insolvent railroads pending their sale, it may be conceded that there are substantial reasons for relieving Federal courts of equity from the duty. The business has grown to such an extent that regular judicial labors are much interfered with by the consideration of mere questions of railroad management. Unpleasant public controversies often follow in the wake of receiverships, having a tendency to put the court in the attitude of a party. The more or less complete dependence of the court upon the receivers in matters of policy and the possibility that this confidence may be misplaced make the jurisdiction an irksome one. The immunity enjoyed by a receiver and a railroad in his charge from ordinary process *in rem* is very attractive to struggling railroad owners and friendly litigation is often begun merely to secure a receiver and tide over a stringency in the interest of all concerned. With no one in interest to oppose the appointment or to move its discharge after it is made, a receiver is secured and he is continued as long as all parties do not object and do not press the cause to final disposition. Courts usually have so much to attend to that they do not and can not investigate the weight or validity of reasons for delay in causes when not brought to their attention by complaint of some of the parties. Meantime the receivership is maintained and the irritation incident to the withdrawal of the railroad from local jurisdictions is continued. The work of managing the road is saddled upon the court pending the coming of a time when a reorganization may be agreed upon or a better price obtained. I sympathize heartily with every effort to impose a practical limitation upon the duration of receiverships. The use of the courts as a harbor of refuge from creditors during a financial storm may be abused, and doubtless has been. The temptation to this resort is greatly increased, if, as is too often the practice, the controlling officer of the company is continued in the management as receiver. The patronage incident to the jurisdiction is one of its evils. Recognizing this and wishing to avoid a disagreeable race for office, courts usually acquiesce in the appointment of a person recommended by the parties, who is not infrequently the president or manager of the company, and whose failure to oppose the receivership, it may be, has been secured by such a recommendation. Consent applications for receiverships would be much less common if it were provided by statute that, wherever a case is made on preliminary application for the immediate appointment of a receiver, the clerk or marshal should act as temporary receiver for thirty days, with a fixed *per diem* compensation, at which time a permanent receiver, not an officer of the court, should be selected by the court after full notice to all parties, and that no one connected with the previous management of the railroad or interested in its bonds or stock should be eligible, even with consent of the parties. It has sometimes seemed to me that by virtue of the power to pass a bankrupt law, and to regulate interstate commerce, a national bureau for the sale of the assets of insolvent interstate railroads and their *ad interim* operation might be established, something like that now provided for national banks, and that the executive head of such a bureau might be better able to speed the sale of the railroads and shorten the duration of their official management than courts. When, however, one attempts to formulate a system which shall have the flexibility of the present procedure and its adaptability for preserving the real *status quo* during the adjustment, one is obliged to admit that the court management *pendente lite* has advantages over any other, anomalous in some respects as it may seem. Probably this explains the failure of Congress or the State legislatures to provide any other system, and even the zealous South Carolina memorialists in their recommendation to Congress were unable to point out a better way than court receiverships with a few minor limitations. In any event, until some new way is devised for the temporary operation of railroads, pending insolvency or foreclosure and sale, courts must assume it, and it ill becomes anyone to criticise their action in doing so, and to charge it to their greed of power, when any other course would result in disastrous consequences to the parties in interest and the country at large.

On the whole, when the charges made against Federal courts of favoritism toward corporations, are stripped of their rhetoric and epithet, and the specific instances upon which the charges are founded are reviewed, it appears that the action of the courts complained of was not only reasonable but rested on precedents established decades ago and fully acquiesced in since, and that the real ground of the complaint is that the constitutional and statutory jurisdiction of the Federal courts is of such a character that it is frequently invoked by corporations to avoid some of the manifest in-justice which a justifiable hostility to the corrupt methods of many of them inclines legislatures and juries and others to inflict upon all of them.

We come finally to the relation of the Federal courts to organized labor. The capitalist and laborer share the profit of production. The more capital in active employment the more work there is to do, and the more work there is to do, the more laborers are needed. The greater the need of laborers, the better their pay per man. It is clearly in the interest of those who work that capital shall increase more rapidly than they do. Everything, therefore, having a legitimate tendency to increase the accumulation of wealth and its use for production, will give each workingman a larger share of the joint result of capital and labor, and it is in a large measure because this country has grown more rapidly in capital than in population, that wages have steadily increased. But while it is in the common interest of labor and capital to increase the fruits of production, yet in determining the share of each their interests are plainly opposed. Though the law of supply and demand will doubtless, in the end, be the most potent influence in fixing this division, yet during the gradual adjustment to the changing markets and the varying financial conditions, capital will surely have the advantage, unless labor takes united action. During the betterment of busi-ness conditions, organized labor, if acting with reasonable discretion, can secure much greater promptness in the advance of wages, than if it were left to the slower operation of natural laws, and, in the same way, as hard times come on, the too eager employer may be restrained from undue haste in reducing wages. The organization of capital into corporations, with the position of advantage which this gave in a dispute with single laborers over wages, made it absolutely necessary for labor to unite to maintain itself. For instance, how could workingmen, dependent on each day's wages for living, dare to take a stand which might leave them without employment if they had not by small assessments accumulated a common fund for their support during such emergency? In union they must sacrifice some inde-pendence of action, and there are bad results from the tyranny of the ma-jority in such cases, but the hardships which have followed impulsive resort to extreme measures have had a good effect to lessen these. Experience, too, will lead to classification among the members so that the cause of the skilled and worthy shall not be leveled down to that of the lazy and neglectful. Like corporations, labor organizations do great good and much evil. The more conservatively and intelligently conducted they are, the more benefit they confer on their members. The more completely they yield to the dominion of those among them who are intemperate of expression and violent and lawless in their methods, the more evil they do to themselves and society. Unfortunately, there are large organizations of the latter class, and, in the heat of a bitter contest with employers, rights of person and property are sometimes openly violated in avowed support of the cause of labor. The infractions of the law, actual and threatened, are palpable, and the interference of the courts by their usual processes to prevent irreparable injury to business and property becomes necessary. Such judicial action often results in discouraging the whole movement and brings down upon the courts the fierce denunciations of the defeated leaders and arouses the hostility of many who would not join in the open breaches of the law, and yet so sympathize with the cause as to blind them to the necessity of the suppression of such lawlessness.

The employees of railroad companies and others engaged in transportation of freight and passengers generally have well-organized unions, and the controversies arising over wages have been many. A vast majority of these have been settled without a resort to extreme measures, through the conservative influence of level-headed labor leaders and railroad managers, but in the last twenty years there have been some very extended railroad strikes, accompanied by the boycotts and open violence with which society has now become familiar. The fact that many railroads have been operated by Federal receivers, the non-residence of railway corporations in the States where the strikes occur, and the interstate commerce feature of the business, have brought some of these violations of property and private and public right within the cognizance of Federal courts. Because the participants in such contests have been spread more widely over the country than in similar contests with which State courts have had to deal, the action of the Federal courts in these cases has attracted more public attention and evoked more bitter condemnation by those who naturally sympathize with labor in every controversy with capital.

The efficacy of the processes of a court of equity to prevent much of the threatened injury from the public and private nuisances which it is often the purpose of the leaders of such strikes to cause, has led to the charge, which is perfectly true, that judicial action has been much more efficient to restrain labor excesses than corporate evils and greed. If it were possible by the quick blow of an injunction to strike down the conspiracy against public and private rights involved in the corruption of a legislature or a council, Federal and other courts would not be less prompt to use the remedy than they are to restrain unlawful injuries by labor unions. But I have had occasion to point out that the nature of corporate wrong is almost wholly beyond the reach of courts, especially those of the United States. The corporate miners and sappers of public virtue do not work in the open, but under cover; their purposes are generally accomplished before they are known to exist, and the traces of their evil paths are destroyed and placed beyond the possibility of legal proof. On the other hand, the chief wrongs committed by labor unions are the open, defiant trespass upon property rights and violations of public order, which the processes of courts are well adapted both to punish and prevent.

The operation of the interstate commerce law is an illustration of the greater difficulty courts have in suppressing corporate violations of law than those of trade unions. The discrimination between shippers by rebates and otherwise, which it is the main purpose of the law to prevent, is almost as difficult of detection and proof as bribery, for the reason that both participants are anxious to avoid its disclosure; but when the labor unions, as they sometimes do, seek to interfere with interstate commerce and to obstruct its flow, they are prone to carry out their purposes with such a blare of trumpets and such open defiance of law that the proof of their guilt is out of their own mouths. The rhetorical indictment against the Federal courts, that from that which was intended as a shield against corporate wrong, they have forged a weapon to attack the wage-earner, is in this way given a specious force which a candid observer will be blind to ignore. Thus are united in a common enmity against the Federal courts the populist and the trade unionist with all those whose political action is likely to be affected by such a combination. And yet their enmity has no other justification than the differing and unavoidable limitations upon the efficacy of judicial action in respect to corporate and labor evils.

As a matter of fact there is nothing in any Federal decision directed against the organization of labor to maintain wages and to secure terms of employment otherwise favorable. The courts, so far as they have expressed themselves on the subject, recognize the right of men for a lawful purpose to combine to leave their employment at the same time, and to use the inconvenience this may cause to their employer as a legitimate weapon in the frequently recurring controversy as to the amount of wages. It is only when the combination is for an unlawful purpose and an unlawful injury is thereby sought to be inflicted, that the combination has received the condemnation of the Federal as well as of State courts.

The action of the Federal courts all over the country in the recent American Railway Union strike in issuing injunctions to prevent further unlawful interference by the strikers with the carrying of the mails, and the flow of interstate commerce, followed by the commitment for contempt of the strike leaders who defied the injunction served on them, is what has called out the official protests of the Governors of Illinois and Colorado, and the phrase "government by injunction" has been invented to describe the alleged usurpation of power by the Federal tribunals in this crisis.

When the history of the great strike shall be written in years to come, the absurd expectations and purpose of its projectors and their marvelous success in deluding a myriad of followers into their active support will seem even more difficult of explanation than they do today. The mind that could conceive and so far execute the plan of taking the entire population of this country by the throat to compel them to effect the settlement of a local labor trouble in Chicago, was that of a genius, however misdirected The Governor of Illinois, who coined the phrase "government by injunction," says that the Federal courts have added legislative and executive functions to their ordinary judicial office, in that they have declared in their orders of injunction that to be unlawful which was lawful before, and have sought to enforce obedience to such orders by an army of marshals and soldiers. It is a little difficult to understand the working of a mind having the discipline of a legal training and the experience of judicial service, which can honestly and sincerely maintain (and I do not wish to impugn the sincerity of the Governor of Illinois) that the combination described in the bill in the Debs case and enjoined in the order of injunction was not unlawful. If it was not so, then there is no law in this country securing the right of private property, no law authorizing the Federal government to operate the mails, no law by which the regulation of interstate commerce is vested in the General Government. A public nuisance more complete in all its features than that which Debs and his colleagues were engaged in furthering can not be imagined. Such nuisances have been frequently enjoined by courts of equity on the bill of the Attorney-General. Was there any doubt that Debs proposed to continue his unlawful course unless restrained? Was there any doubt that the injury would be irreparable and could not be compensated for by verdict at law? Was it for the court to hesitate to issue its process because it had reason to believe that it would not be obeyed? The novelty involved in the application of such a remedy to such an injury was not that injuries of the same general character had not before been restrained by injunction, but only that never before in the history of the courts had injuries of this kind been so enormous and far-reaching in their effect. It was not that men had not before been ordered by process of court to desist from such injuries, but never before had so many men been engaged in inflicting them. Nor can it affect the power of Federal courts to remedy wrongs within their lawful cognizance that the wrong would have been prevented if the executive of another sovereignty than that under which they are constituted had acted promptly to suppress it. The Federal courts did not assume executive powers any more than they do so when they issue any process to the marshal, and the marshal as the subordinate of the President executes it. The extent of the actual and threatened injury and the possible resistance to lawful process required the marshal to call to his assistance much aid, but it is a latter-day doctrine that a court is usurping the executive function, in calling upon the executive to use additional force to avoid a possible defeat of its lawful process. The conservative course of the President and the Attorney-General in first applying to the courts for process and the subsequent firmness exhibited by those officers in executing that process by all the means available, will cause the country to hold them always in grateful remembrance. The duty of the courts to act on this initiative was so plain that while it does not entitle them to any especial commendation, it would seem that it should protect them from serious attack.

The real objection to the injunction is the certainty that disobedience will be promptly punished before a court without a jury. It is hardly necessary to defend the necessity for such means of enforcing orders of court. If the court must wait upon the slow course of a jury trial before it can compel a compliance with its order, then the efficacy of its process would be seriously impaired. Has any injustice been done to Debs in his trial by the court? Is there the slightest doubt in the mind of his fiercest supporter that he violated the injunction? Why, then, complain of his conviction before a tribunal authorized to try him? The argument seems to be that because many men are determined to violate the rights of the public and their fellow-citizens in spite of the lawful orders of the Federal court restraining them from so doing, they should, on account of their number and popular strength, have a right which no Anglo-Saxon has hitherto ever enjoyed, to interpose a jury trial between them and the enforcement of a court's order. If the criticisms under discussion are directed against the existence of courts, then their weight depends on different considerations from those which apply on the assumption that courts are to be maintained for the purpose of remedying wrongs. But they are professedly based on the Constitution of the United States, and that certainly contemplates courts, whose decrees shall be enforced, however much resisted, and which shall not be merely advisory councils whose efficacy depends on their powers of persuasion.

I am aware that there were many conservative, unprejudiced and patriotic citizens in this country, many of them members of the bar and of this Association, whose anxiety that the Chicago riots should be suppressed was as great as that of anyone, and yet who were of opinion that the action of the Federal courts in issuing the injunctions, which were issued on the application of the Attorney-General, was an unwise stretching of an equitable remedy to meet an emergency which should have been met in other ways. To all such persons, I commend the reading of Mr. Justice Brewer's opinion in the Debs case. It is a great judgment of a great court, and makes it as clear as midday that the process therein issued was justified by every precedent, and was the highest duty of the court. The exercise of that duty has, however, only increased the number of those who sincerely believed that the Federal courts are constituted to foster corporate evils and to destroy all effort by labor to maintain itself in its controversies with corporate capital.

I have reached the end of a much too-long discussion of the relation of the Federal judiciary to some of the important issues of the day. It will not be surprising if the storm of abuse heaped upon the Federal courts and the political strength of popular groups, whose plans of social reform have met obstruction in those tribunals, shall lead to serious efforts through legislation to cut down their jurisdiction and cripple their efficiency. If this comes, then the responsibility for its effects, whether good or bad, must be not only with those who urge the change, but also with those who do not strive to resist its coming.

The earliest assaults upon the Federal judiciary and their harmless character in the light of the event, reconcile one to much of the fiery invective and blood-curdling epithets hurled at men who, equally with their accusers, are American freemen, impressed with the absolute necessity for maintaining sacred the guaranties of life, liberty and property, and who are probably not more in love with corruption and greed, or more disposed to crush the humble and worthy, than the average of their fellow-citizens.

The saving grace of American humor, which delights in the contemplation of grotesque exaggeration, has often saved us from domestic turbulence, which the turgid exuberance of denunciatory language might otherwise have excited against lawfully-constituted authority; and it may be that the same useful trait will prevent the success of the present agitators against the Federal courts.

But whatever fate betide the Federal judiciary, I hope that it may always be said of them, as a whole, by the impartial observer of their conduct, that they have not lacked in the two essentials of judicial moral character, a sincere desire to reach right conclusions and firmness to enforce them.

15

Administration of Criminal Law

To the Graduating Classes of the Law School
of Yale University on June 26, 1905

Mr. President, Mr. Dean and Gentlemen of the Yale Law School: One of the most useful results of our recent territorial expansion for those who have had to do with uniting our new possessions with this country and adjusting certain of the Spanish codes which we found in force in Puerto Rico and the Philippines to the new American sovereignty, has been the comparative study made necessary of the two great systems of law—the Roman, or Civil Law, and the Anglo-Saxon, or Common Law. It must be admitted that those of us who have been educated in the principles of the common law and have not extended our study much into general jurisprudence, are apt to be narrow in our prejudices in favor of the common law and are prone to think that there is very little for us to learn from the civil law which can be usefully adopted by a government in which the liberty of the individual is held so sacred, and the power of the government towards the subject or the citizen is restrained by such careful regulations as in England, in America or any of the popular self-governments for which either of those countries is responsible.

But certainly when in actual practice the common law lawyer is brought to the study of the beautifully simple and exactly comprehensive language of the civil code governing the rights between individuals, he begins to feel the veneration that comes from consciously viewing the work of twenty centuries of jurists and lawgivers who have been struggling during all that period to simplify and make lucid the rules of law and to reduce it to the science that under the civil code it certainly has become. When he comes to an examination of the political or governmental theory of the civil law, he finds more reason for his pride in, and love of, the common law in this, that under the civil law the state seems a separate entity, different from the people who constitute it, different from the individual who comes into contact with it—an entity whose interest is to be more guarded and protected than that of any other in the community, and for the welfare of this entity it is the principle of the civil law that the interest of the individual must yield, while at the common law the theory is that the state is but an aggregation of the individual, a great partnership in which he has a voice. In the common law, the spirit manifested in the rule *caveat emptor*—that every man must look after himself—leaves blunt and harsh results (where actual and affirmative fraud is not committed) which the civil law would ameliorate by requiring one individual to treat the other with more equity, with more morality one may say, with more care that the other shall not, by his own neglect, lose his rights. There is more of paternalism in the civil law—more care for the subject by the government—less disposition to let individuals work out their rights between them. The common law stands for the utmost liberty of the individual, and as a price of this liberty it imposes upon the person enjoying it the burden of looking out for himself.

When we leave the subject of civil rights and come to the punishment of the individual for offenses against the state, we find in the civil law greater anxiety that the state should be protected against crime, than we do in the common law. The civil lawyer looks at the crime more from the standpoint of the government than from that of the individual and more from the importance to the community that crime shall be not only punished but prevented, while there runs all through the common law the anxiety that the prosecution of crime may not be used by the government to oppress the individual and that there shall be thrown about the individual safeguards so great as to give impression that at common law the liberty of the individual is on the whole of greater importance than the safety of the community from crime. Of course between the trend of the one system and the trend of the other is the golden mean of the legislator and government maker by which shall be secured the protection of society without the oppression of the individual.

When the common law lawyer faces the problem of reforming the criminal laws and procedure of a country that has heretofore been governed by the civil law, he feels certain that here at least is room for a wholesome change and the introduction into the patient of a very large dose of the principles which lie at the foundation of the prosecution of crime and are supposed to involve the protection of the rights of civil liberty in the individual.

The institution of the writ of *habeas corpus* which, though a civil process, and not a criminal action, is generally used to test the validity of some pretended criminal process, is attended with unmixed good. The principle that no man shall be confined save under due legal process is as well known to the civil as to the common law, but the difference between the two systems from a political and practical standpoint is well illustrated in respect to the enforcement of the principle. At the civil law the rule that no man shall be illegally confined is operative upon the conscience of the judges and the jailers, and if their consciences do not move them, the poor prisoner and his friends are without a remedy. At the common law the prisoner or his friends has the practical remedy of the writ, which being of high privilege he may obtain for the asking of any judge, who runs the risk of incurring the heaviest penalty himself if he refuse. This is but one of the many instances in which our Anglo-Saxon ancestors hammered out their civil liberty by securing from their would-be royal oppressors not general declarations of principles of freedom like a French constitution, but distinct and definite promises that certain rules, not of substantive, but of adjective law should obtain. To them, it was the securing of the means by which they could themselves secure their liberty that must be preserved, for with the machinery at hand, with the procedure available there was no difficulty in maintaining the ultimate object, civil rights and liberty. Run through the Magna Charta of 1215, the Petition of Right of 1625, and the Bill of Rights of 1688, the great charters of English liberty, and you find in them an insistence, not on general principles, but upon procedure. Take the most comprehensive—"No man shall be deprived of life, liberty or property without due process of law": this does not attempt to define the cases in which a man shall be entitled to life, liberty and property, but points to, and insists upon, the necessity for a legal procedure by which it shall be done.

Then the requirement that no man shall be convicted save by a jury of his peers. That again is mere procedure. So too that he shall be informed of the accusation against him, that he shall be confronted by the witnesses; that he shall not be compelled to testify in a criminal case against himself; that he shall not be convicted of treason save by evidence of two witnesses to the overt act; that he shall not be subject to unreasonable searches; that he shall not be put twice in jeopardy for the same offense—all these are but instances of judicial or other procedure by which general and ultimate rights could be maintained and protected. An Anglo-Saxon had but little use for declarations of abstract principles that rested for their preservation on the consciences of their rulers.

The means of securing civil rights and preserving the individual from the oppression of the government which I have mentioned above, have been embodied in the Federal and State constitutions, and as they served their purposes as well in ancient times when the battle for civil liberty was fought and won, the first impulse of the American lawyer is to apply them all as a panacea to the government and criminal procedure of our new possessions. But further investigation, with a deepening sense of responsibility for the government of a body of people whose welfare has been forced upon us as a sacred trust, leads to a much more conservative attitude in respect of the needed changes in the existing procedure. We can not escape a re-examination of the reasons for the constitutional limitations I have been discussing. We must cease to regard them as fetiches to be worshiped without reason and simply because they are. We must follow them to their source, trace their development and elaboration or modification due to contemporaneous needs, and determine whether their existence today is due rather to a veneration for the great use they served in the past than to any present utility. We have no right to force on the Puerto Ricans or the Filipinos institutions of our own which have proved of the highest benefit to us, unless we can see, on other than mere sentimental grounds connected with our own history, that such institutions will now prove beneficial to them in their present condition.

The great bulwark and protection of the individual at common law against the power of the government and the king, exerted through judges removable at will in criminal prosecutions for political offenses, was trial by jury. I have no time, if I could do so, to trace the growth of this venerable tribunal from a mere collection of individuals in the vicinage who were generally witnesses of the facts they were assembled to adjudge, to the present body of twelve persons selected from the community in which the crime is committed, but required to be impartial and so wholly without knowledge of the facts as witnesses.

Suffice it to say that as an effect of the trend toward civil liberty and popular rights in the French Revolution and the uprising of 1848, the trial by jury in criminal cases was adopted in France, in Belgium, in Germany, in Norway and Sweden, in Spain, in Italy and Russia except in trials for political offenses, and is now in use in these countries. This constitutes a tribute to its value as an institution in countries in which it did not have its beginning and growth, and perhaps would furnish a solid reason for our adopting it in Puerto Rico and the Philippines. It has been adopted in Puerto Rico. It has not been adopted in the Philippines. I do not think it too much to say, however, that it has proven to be a failure thus far in Puerto Rico.

The first question was in the Philippines, shall it be adopted in civil cases? No civil law country, I think, has adopted it for this purpose. Shall we do so? It would seem unwise. In the first place, it is by no means clear that in our own jurisprudence trial by jury in civil cases is an unmixed good. It is true that in the Federal Constitution the right of trial by jury in cases at common law involving more than twenty dollars is secured by fundamental mandate in all courts in the United States. But when we examine as a whole the civil litigation in our courts, we find the tendency is toward trial without a jury in all cases but suits for personal injury against corporations. In respect to jury trials in civil actions in Anglo-American law, we find one of these anomalies, entirely illogical, but easily explainable on historical grounds, that would disgust a civilian, but which only endears the system to one of Anglo-Saxon origin and education.

When an Anglo-Saxon wished to mend his structure of jurisprudence, he merely added a room where it was needed without any regard to the general symmetrical appearance of the building, and with the addition of many rooms for various reasons, other parts have become useless but remain to testify to the history of the growth of the structure. Much more than half the civil suits now brought are what would have been called actions in equity before the modern state codes of procedure had united common law actions and equitable action in one form called a civil action. Equity, as you know, was a system of remedial procedure which grew up side by side with the ordinary common law practice and was instituted in early days by the King, to whom appeals were made against the rigors and injustice of his own courts. He delegated the lord keeper of his great seal, then usually an ecclesiastic, the power to moderate the severity and inelasticity of the common law methods, and the ecclesiastic statesman, nothing loath to exercise power for the glory of his masters, Divine and temporal, introduced methods of remedial justice which he derived from the canon law and the ecclesiastical courts. With this beginning came the great body of equity jurisprudence which, as I say, is the basis for a large majority of civil suits brought today, certainly suits for personal injury against corporations are excluded. In suits in equity the judge hears and decides the issue of fact. The issues may be, and often are, very similar to those arising in suits at common law, the genuineness of a signature, the existence of fraudulent motive, the identity of an individual, damage to business by violation of patents, trade marks or contract rights, and all the variety of issues presented in civil litigation. Now the Federal constitution requires that such issues arising at common law shall be tried by a jury, but if in an equity suit the court may try them. Since the abolition of the distinction between law and equity in civil actions in our codes of procedure, it requires a lawyer to tell whether a suit brought is in equity or law. Certainly a constitutional mandate that requires a jury in less than half the civil issues, and only in those when in a certain form of action, distinguishable only by a lawyer, can hardly be said to rest on any very broad and sound principles. Of course in suits for personal injury against corporations, the plaintiff relies on the supposed sympathy of twelve laymen with the poor plaintiff against the rich corporation, both to find the facts in favor of the plaintiff and also to swell the damages to a large sum. But this hardly constitutes a reason for maintaining the jury in a system which is supposed to dispense justice to all, whether rich or poor—impartially. The abolition of the jury in civil cases would relieve the public of a great burden of expense, would facilitate the hearing of all civil suits, and would not, I think, with proper appeal deprive any litigant of all he is entitled to, an impartial hearing. Of course, it will never be done in courts of the United States and perhaps never in any of the states, although in some of them the tendency is strong in that direction. However this may be in view of present conditions, we are not called upon to introduce the jury in civil cases into the Philippines.

In the matter of the criminal procedure, the question is very different.

In a country where a part of the judges are aliens, it would add much to the satisfaction of the people if a part of the judicial tribunal were made up of a jury of natives, and if this were consistent with the safety of the community, those responsible for the new government would certainly introduce the jury system in the trial of crimes. The whole theory of the trial by jury is that out of the body of the community you may select, at haphazard, twelve men who will be so deeply impressed with the necessity of punishing crime on the one hand and of allowing innocent defendants to escape on the other hand, that they will decide truly and justly as between the community and the defendant. The system assumes a sense of responsibility in the ordinary citizen subject to jury duty for the good working of the government and for the interests of society at large, which will overcome the natural disposition to avoid inflicting punishment on another, and will enable the jury to find the verdict as the law and evidence shall require. Manifestly such a tribunal would have no place among an ignorant people, or indeed even among a people who are somewhat educated, if they have not inculcated in them a sense of responsibility for, and of sharing in, the government. Such people are likely to prove unworthy jurors and to be affected in all their verdicts by their emotions and by every other motive than that which should control them, to wit, the well-being of society. It is this sense of justice which is implanted naturally in the Anglo-Saxon breast, but which is absent in the Puerto Rican and the Filipino. Its absence disqualifies either from filling the measure of stiffness and conservativeness of character required to make a proper juryman.

Another difficulty involved in introducing the jury system into the Philippine Islands, and indeed into any civil law country, is the absence of a code of evidence without which the jury system is not likely greatly to promote just findings on issues presented. In the Anglo-American law, there is an extensive series of rules governing the admission of evidence, which now may almost be called a code of evidence, which had its origin, as Professor Thayer of Harvard so clearly shows, in the necessity for protecting the jury in its consideration of issues brought before it, from being led astray and misled by evidence of a kind likely to have greater power of persuasion than judges and men of affairs from wide experience thought it ought to have. Some of the rules of evidence seem arbitrary, but generally the rules of relevancy and competency are based upon the long experience in human affairs. It is judge-made law which has been worked out, as Professor Thayer shows, to meet the exigencies of a trial by laymen not experienced in hearing cases, who would not, with everything allowed to be presented to them, winnow the wheat from the chaff. The civil law has no such code. The question whether evidence is relevant to an issue and will assist in its decision, is largely a matter in the discretion of the judges, in hearings at the civil law. We can well remember the astonishment and almost horror that thrilled this country during the second trial of Dreyfus before the court martial, when witnesses were allowed to testify to all sorts of hearsay tending to show Dreyfus' guilt, and French generals were allowed to go before the court and testify with their hands on their hearts of their conviction that Dreyfus was guilty, without really having any personal knowledge on the subject at all. I am not prepared to say that the Dreyfus trial did not go beyond what is ordinarily permitted in a French court. I think it did. But I am certain that no such rules of evidence as obtain in our procedure are known to the civil law countries of Europe unless adopted within very recent years. It has been necessary for use in the Philippine Islands to introduce a code of evidence for the trial of crimes even without a jury, which is also applicable to the trial of civil cases. By order of President McKinley all the constitutional protections to the defendant in a criminal case were extended to defendants in criminal cases in the Philippines except the right of trial by jury.

I am not certain that in a new country this was entirely wise. When examined as an original proposition, the prohibition that the defendant in a criminal case shall not be compelled to testify seems in some aspects to be of doubtful utility. If the administration of criminal law is for the purpose of convicting those who are guilty of crime, then it seems natural to follow in such a process the methods that obtain in ordinary life. If anything has happened and it is important to discover who is the author of it, the first impulse of the human mind is to inquire of the person suspected whether he did it and to cross-examine him as to circumstances. Certainly this is the domestic rule by which your wife or your mother proceeds to find out who it is that broke the window, who it is that stole the jam from the pantry, or why it is that the sweeping has not been done by the person charged with that duty. She goes to the suspected culprit and asks the questions natural under such circumstances, to see whether her suspicion of guilt is well founded. Now the proposition that it is unjust to call upon the person suspected of a crime to tell of his connection with it is at first sight untenable. Why is it unjust? If he is not guilty, will he not have the strongest motive for saying so, and if he is guilty and seeks to escape liability, will he not use every effort to make his conduct consistent with his innocence? Why, then, does it expose the defendant to improper treatment if an officer of the law at once begins to interrogate him concerning his guilt? But the answer is, he has the right to consult counsel. He should not be hurried into statements which he may subsequently desire to retract. In other words, he should be given an opportunity, after he has committed the crime, to frame in his mind some method by which he can escape conviction and punishment. I am inclined to think that the expression: "No person shall be compelled to testify against himself," if traced back to its original source, had reference to a system of torture which did prevail in the time of the early English kings, and which was intended to denounce, not the mere calling of a defendant to testify and inviting him by questions so to do, but the actual compulsion of evidence by physical means. Now, as Bentham shows, the principle does not include compulsion; it is construed to mean that before the jury or tribunal trying the defendant, he may not be called upon to answer questions. Bentham's criticism of this rule is well known. He says it can be only supported by the fox-hunter's reason—that it is right that the criminal or the fox should have a little start, and this advantage in the beginning, in favor of the defendant and against the state, is the refusal of the law to allow the state to call the defendant to prove its case. It makes the conviction of the criminal a game which is played out under certain rules, and the interests of society are lost sight of. At common law, the defendant was not allowed to testify, even if he would, but that rule was found to work harshly against innocent men who, going on the stand, might explain the suspicious circumstances connecting them with the crime and show their innocence; so that the rule for years in this country, and very recently in England, is that the defendant may take the stand if he will, but if he fails to take the stand the counselor for the prosecution may not comment on his failure to do so. The result of the change has been, I think, to lead to more convictions than before, for a jury may be charged as explicitly as possible to disregard the fact that the defendant does not go on the stand, but it is impossible to eradicate from the minds of sensible men the impression that if one who is charged with the crime refuses to explain by his own evidence that he was not guilty, that the reason for his so doing is because he is afraid he can not so explain.

Another principle of the law of evidence embodied in the constitutional limitations is that the defendant must be confronted with the witnesses who testify against him. This seems to impose unnecessary hardship upon the government, because it certainly would not injure the defendant if depositions were taken and the defendant or his counsel were permitted to cross-examine. It is a case of undue tenderness toward the defendant. There is no such restriction upon the defendant when he is seeking to prove his innocence, for he may use depositions without number.

The limitation upon unreasonable searches is another constitutional restriction which has been used to save men from conviction. Indeed, uniting that with the one preventing the court or prosecutor from interrogating the defendant as to his guilt, makes it impossible in some classes of cases to convict persons well known to be guilty. It is the great shield which the powerful and unlawful trusts and violators of the interstate commerce laws have to prevent their successful prosecution. It prevents the use of process to obtain books and papers in which the defendant has violated the law or has recorded statements showing guilt. Our supreme courts generally, instead of restricting the operation of these constitutional limitations, have given them, whenever occasion arose, a wider scope than the letter of the limitation seemed to require, in the interest, it was said, of the liberty of the individual.

Then there is the general rule that the guilt of the defendant, in order to justify conviction, must be shown beyond a reasonable doubt. This is a fair and proper rule, and has usually been regarded as the other side of the rule that the defendant is presumed to be innocent. But the Supreme Court of the United States has recently carried it to such a point by construction as to treat the presumption of innocence, not as being only the mere counterpart of this rule, but even as substantive evidence and as the equivalent of a witness testifying affirmatively, and continuing to testify from the beginning to the end of the case in favor of the innocence of the defendant, a construction not sustained by Professor Thayer, and seemingly much enlarging the previous operation of the presumption of innocence, all out of tenderness to the defendant. These rules and others intended to make it as difficult as possible to convict a defendant were the result of the savage character of the common law crimes, when the defendant was not allowed counsel, and there were one hundred and sixty capital offenses at common law. The judges, of course, being men and having pity, sometimes seized the opportunity themselves to act as counsel for the defendant, and introduced the rules which we have alluded to and maintained them in the interest of mercy. They have been moderated a very little, although the reason for them has long passed away. Defendants are now allowed counsel, and if unable to pay counsel the state employs counsel to defend them.

Therefore I say that if a jurist from Mars were to come down to earth and be charged with the duty of framing a criminal code which should reach the golden mean between preserving the interests of society by punishing and preventing crime on the one hand and saving the individual charged with crime from liability of unjust conviction on the other, I think it doubtful whether he would adopt the constitutional restrictions which I have been discussing. The general law of evidence, especially that which excludes hearsay, can well be defended on grounds of general policy, for though hearsay at times might convict in proper cases where its exclusion acquits, cross-examination is such a searcher of the truth that the wisdom of ever admitting hearsay evidence as the basis for the conviction of crime may well be doubted.

In adopting a system such as we have been considering for the punishment of crime for a new country, the first and most apt question which can be asked is, "How have these so-called guarantees of liberty of the defendant worked on the whole?" While in England, in which all these restrictions are still observed, crime is punished with as much severity and uniformity as the public weal demands,—and this although they have the trial by jury, although the defendant can not be compelled to testify, and although all the other rules of evidence to which I have referred have full application,—how is it in this country? I grieve for my country to say that the administration of the criminal law in all the States of the Union (there may be one or two exceptions) is a disgrace to our civilization. We are now reaching an age when we can not plead youth, sparse civilization, newness of country, as a cause for laxity in the enforcement of law.

What makes the difference between the administration of the criminal law in England and in this country? In the first place, while the jury has always been a sacred and untouched part of the tribunal constituted to try crimes in England, the judges upon the court have always taken and maintained their part at common law in the trial of every defendant, and that part has been, first, the retention of complete control over the method by which counsel try the case, restraining them to the points at issue and preventing them from diverting the minds of the jury to inconsequential and irrelevant circumstances and considerations; and, second, the power to aid the jury by advising them how to consider the evidence and expressing an opinion upon the evidence, leaving, however, to the jury the ultimate decision. In this way the sophistical rhetoric and sentimental appeals of counsel are made to lose their misleading effect, and the jurors are brought to a sense of their responsibility in deciding the actual issues of fact as to the guilt or innocence of the defendant upon the evidence before them.

Another reason why English justice still maintains its reputation for certainty of punishment is the fact that there are no appeals allowed from the trial in the first court unless the judge presiding in the court shall deem certain questions of law of sufficient importance and doubt to reserve them to a court of crown cases reserved. When, therefore, after a long or short trial the defendant is convicted, the conviction is final in ninety-nine cases out of a hundred.

A possible third reason is to be found in the ability of the English court to secure the best character of men in either a common or a special jury—men charged with the earnest responsibility for the enforcement of the law.

How is it in our own country? We find that these constitutional limitations adopted centuries ago in tenderness to the defendant and which have to some extent outlived their usefulness because the reasons for their adoption have ceased to be, have been elaborated in their scope and operation not only by the court but also by the legislatures, because thought to be in the interest of liberty. And this has made them greater obstacles in the conviction of the guilty. The institution of trial by jury has come to be regarded as a fetich to such an extent that state legislatures have exalted the power of the jury and diminished the power of the court in the tribunal made up of both for the hearing of criminal cases.

Although the judiciary of nearly all the states is now elective, legislatures have seemed to resent any intervention by the judge in the trial of the cause beyond a very colorless and abstract statement of the law to be applied to the case. It is manifestly impossible for a judge to instruct a jury in the law well and possess it of the law as applied to the facts without discussing the facts in detail, and without commenting on them. But so jealous have legislatures become of the influence of the court upon the jury that it is now in most states made an error of law for the court to express his opinion upon the facts, although he leaves the ultimate decision of course to the jury. It frequently is the case that under the statute the judge is required to write his charge and discuss the abstract principles applicable in the case, and that then the counsel are permitted to discuss the law of the case in view of the judge's charge and apply the facts. The opportunity which this gives the counsel to pervert the law, and the wide scope which the system in restricting the judge gives to the jury of following its own sweet will, of course doubles the opportunity for miscarriages of justice. The function of the judge is limited to that of the moderator in a religious assembly. The law throws the reins on the back of the jury, and the verdict becomes rather the vote of a town meeting than the sharp, clear decision of the tribunal of justice. The counsel for the defense, relying on the diminished power of the court, creates by dramatic art and by harping on the importance of unimportant details, a false atmosphere in the courtroom which the judge is powerless to dispel, and under the hypnotic influence of which, the counsel is able to lead the jurors to vote as jurors for a verdict which, after all the excitement of the trial has passed away, they are unable to support as men.

Another cause already alluded to is the difficulty of securing jurors properly sensible of the duty which they are summoned to perform. In the extreme tenderness the state legislatures exhibit toward persons accused as criminals and especially as murderers, they allow peremptory challenges to the defendant far in excess of those allowed to the state. In my own state of Ohio for a long time, the law was that the state was allowed two peremptory challenges and the defendant twenty-three in capital cases. This very great discrepancy between the two sides of the case allowed the defendant's counsel to eliminate from all panels every man of force and character and standing in the community, and to assemble a collection in the jury box of nondescripts of no character, weak and amenable to every breeze of emotion, however maudlin or irrelevant to the issue.

I do not think that the members of the Bar can escape the responsibility for the demoralizing tendency of the legislatures to wrest from the judges in the criminal procedure the conserving power which they ought to retain and which they had at common law, and to exalt the jury's power beyond anything which is wise or prudent, and to extend to the defendant the opportunity to reject all good men from the jury and to select the weak, the unintelligent and the irresponsible. The perversions of justice in my own city of Cincinnati and state of Ohio in 1884 led to the appointment of a committee of the Bar to visit the legislature to see whether it was not possible to rid our criminal code of procedure of those features which placed the prosecution at great disadvantage in the trial of capital cases. The indignation of the public had led to a mob and to the burning of our courthouse, and it was thought that the time had come for some more active members of the community to organize and see if reform could not be effected. I had the honor of being one of those who waited upon the judiciary committee of the Ohio legislature and preferred the request, that the twenty-three challenges allowed to the defendant be reduced to twelve, and that the state be allowed a similar number; but we found that there were upon that committee lawyers a substantial part of whose practice consisted in acting as counsel for the defendants in important criminal trials. When I protested that twenty-three challenges was an outrageous number, the chairman of the committee leaned back with the remark, "Many a time have I seen when I would have given all my fee to have had twenty-four challenges for the defendant." I cite this instance because I believe that the unjust disposition to curtail the power of judges, to exalt the power of the jury, to subject them to influences that ought not to control them, and to give opportunity to the defendant's counsel to manipulate the selection of juries by the use of peremptory challenges, is due more or less to the intervention of some members of the bar whose practice is more or less beneficially affected, as they conceive, by these obstacles to the course of justice.

The third reason for the distinction between the enforcement of law in England and in this country is to be found in the right of appeal which is given in every criminal case, and in many cases the appeal is to two courts. The code of evidence with its complicated rules, the technical statutory limitations supposed to be in favor of the defendant, are all used as a trap to catch the trial court in some error, however technical, upon which in appellate proceedings a reversal of the judgment of the court below may be asked. The rule which obtains throughout this country is that any error, however small, which it is impossible to show affirmatively did not prejudice the defendant, must lead to reversal of the judgment. The same disposition on the part of the courts to think that every provision of every rule of law in favor of the defendant is one to be strictly enforced, and even widened in its effect in the interest of the liberty of the citizen, has led courts of appeal to a degree of refinement in upholding technicalities in favor of defendants, and in reversing convictions, that renders one who has had practical knowledge of the trial of criminal cases most impatient.

In a case carried on error to the Supreme Court of the United States, the point was raised for the first time in the Supreme Court that the record did not show an arraignment of the defendant and a plea of not guilty, and on this ground the court, three judges dissenting, reversed the case. There was not a well-founded doubt in that case that the defendant was arraigned and pleaded not guilty. The perusal of the record raised this as a presumption of fact and the judgment was reversed, although there was not a pretense that the defendant had suffered any injury by reason of the alleged defect of the character in question. When a court of highest authority in this country thus interposes a bare technicality between a defendant and his just conviction, it is not too much to charge some of the laxity in our administration of the criminal law to a proneness on the part of courts of last resort to find error and to reverse judgments of conviction.

And now, what has been the result in this country? Criminal statistics are exceedingly difficult to obtain. The number of homicides one can note from the daily newspapers, the number of lynchings and the number of executions, but the number of indictments, trials, convictions, acquittals or mistrials it is hard to find. Since 1885 in the United States there have been 131,951 murders and homicides, and there have been 2286 executions. In 1885 the number of murders was 1808. In 1904 it had increased to 8482. The number of executions in 1885 was 108. In 1904 it was 116. This startling increase in the number of murders and homicides as compared with the number of executions tells the story. As murder is on the increase, so are all offenses of the felony class, and there can be no doubt that they will continue to increase unless the criminal laws are enforced with more certainty, more uniformity, more severity than they now are.

Certainly the result of the American criminal procedure as distinguished from the English criminal procedure does not encourage us to think that it would be wise to introduce into the Philippine Islands a system of jury trial which now prevails in most of the States, especially under the restrictions of the power of the court which we find as we go west in this country. The cure for this growing cancer in the body politic is more practical and more available than most public evils because it may be found in statutory amendments. If laws could be passed either abolishing the right of criminal appeal and leaving to the pardoning power, as it is in England, the correction of judicial wrong, or instead of that, if appeals must be allowed, then if a provision of law could be enacted by which no judgment of the court below should be reversed except for an error which the court, after reading the entire evidence, can affirmatively say would have led to a different verdict, ninety-nine reversals out of one hundred under the present system would be avoided.

Second, if the power of the court by statute to advise the jury, to comment and express its opinion to the jury upon facts in every criminal case, could be restored, and if the state and the defendant were both deprived of peremptory challenges in the selection of a jury, 25 percent of those trials which are now miscarriages of justice would result in the conviction of the guilty defendant, and that which has become a mere game in which the defendant's counsel play with loaded dice, would resume its office of a serious judicial investigation into the guilt or innocence of the defendant. I presume it is useless to expect that courts will turn from their present tendency to amplify technicalities in behalf of defendants until legislatures shall initiate the change by the broad limitation already suggested upon the power of the court to reverse the judgment of the court below. Our country is disgusted by the number of lynchings that occur both in the North and in the South, and excuses are sought for the horrid and fiendish cruelties perpetrated by mobs in such cases in some other cause than the delays of justice. Instances are cited of where the mob has executed men whom they had every reason to believe were about to be justly punished under the law, to show that an improvement in the criminal procedure would not prevent lynchings. But every man of affairs who has studied the subject at all knows that if men who commit crime were promptly arrested and convicted, there would be no mob for the purpose of lynching. A mob, after it has organized, loses all conscience and can not be controlled, but it is the delays of justice that lead to its organization. Nothing but a radical improvement in our administration of criminal law will prevent the growth in the number of lynchings in the United States that bring the blush of shame to every lover of his country.

Commentators

DONALD F. ANDERSON wrote the first full-length study of Taft's presidency, *A Conservative's Conception of the Presidency.*

DAVID H. BURTON, in addition to *William Howard Taft in the Public Service,* is the author of *Taft, Holmes and the 1920s Court.*

A. E. CAMPBELL's *America Comes of Age: The Era of Theodore Roosevelt* offers fresh judgments of a much written about period.

FRANK X. GERRITY has written institutional history as well as pieces on American domestic and diplomatic affairs.

FRANCIS GRAHAM LEE is an authority on the Supreme Court. His books include *Neither Conservative nor Liberal,* which deals with civil rights and the Burger Court.

WILSON CAREY McWILLIAMS's writings give special attention to presidential elections since 1980, including *Beyond the Politics of Disappointment? American Elections, 1980–1998.*

DAVID POTASH's recent work has centered on the roles of Henry Cabot Lodge, William Howard Taft, and Nicholas Murray Butler in the return of conservative Republicanism.